Henry M. Grey

In Moorish Captivity

An Account of the Tourmaline Expedition to Sus, 1897-1898

Henry M. Grey

In Moorish Captivity
An Account of the Tourmaline Expedition to Sus, 1897-1898

ISBN/EAN: 9783337186838

Printed in Europe, USA, Canada, Australia, Japan

Cover: Foto ©Andreas Hilbeck / pixelio.de

More available books at **www.hansebooks.com**

IN MOORISH CAPTIVITY

Photo by Fryone, Gibraltar.

Mr. HENRY M. GREY.

[Frontispiece.

IN MOORISH CAPTIVITY

An Account of the 'Tourmaline' Expedition
to Sus, 1897-98

BY

HENRY M. GREY

A MEMBER OF THE EXPEDITION

LONDON
EDWARD ARNOLD
37 BEDFORD STREET, STRAND, W.C.
1899

[All rights reserved]

CONTENTS

PROLOGUE 1

CHAPTER I.

AN ILL-OMENED START.

A rainy night — Found drowned — We clear for Sakiet-el-Hamra — Crowded quarters — Novel stowage — Rough weather — A long night and slow progress . . 9

CHAPTER II.

ACROSS THE BAY.

Sea-sickness — Sabbah tells of 'some emotions' — Beyerle points the 'moral' — A traveller on the cheap — His opinion of the yacht — Life among the Moors — Moralizings thereon — We slacken speed — Cape St. Vincent — Arrival at Lanzarote — A Carlist alarm . . . 18

CHAPTER III.

ISLAND NIGHT'S ENTERTAINMENT.

Arrecife — Our reception ashore — Description of the town — Our Christmas dinner — Beyerle and I seek dissipation, and find a club — Beyerle's little joke — Loyal toasts — A distinguished visit and a breakdown — A magic-lantern show — A medical discussion and its sudden ending — A Spaniard's dignity — We bribe the officials and give a concert — I receive an official and professional visit — Parting counsel — Adios! 29

CHAPTER IV.

DANGEROUS DELAY.

In sight of land—Chasing a derelict—A false report—Primitive mail-boats—Concerning dog-fish—New Year's Day—We make a balloon and lose it—A trip northwards—Ifni and its saint-house—Concerning Moorish saints—Sidi Warzuk—Back again to Arksis . . . 43

CHAPTER V.

ARKSIS.

A pessimist—Preparations for landing—The Major goes ashore—An unsatisfactory pow-wow—An ingenious proposal—Moorish diplomacy—Landing of the tents and stores—Description of the cove—Port Hillsborough—European relics—Curtis's expedition—His death in the Sudan—Difficult landing—Dress and appearance of the natives—Their 'wealth and taste for luxury'—Our camping-ground 52

CHAPTER VI.

THE INDABA.

A rough-and-ready meal—The *Ait Arbain*—Reading the treaty—The prospects of trade—How to get rifles on credit—The Major returns to the yacht—He leaves three 'sportsmen' ashore—Laziness as a fine art—Native offerings—Theft in the camp, and how it was dealt with—A novel pillow 63

CHAPTER VII.

THE COUNCIL OF THE 'FORTY.'

A quiet discussion—Dispensing and surgery—Sidi Hashem's matrimonial troubles—A terrible threat—'Mr. Garden'—An unpleasant discovery—The mineral wealth of Morocco—An earthly paradise—Sworn friends—Bad weather still cuts our communication with the yacht—'Important news'—Tea-making and tea-drinking—An impudent forgery—A dignitary of the desert . . 73

CONTENTS

CHAPTER VIII.

DAMP DAYS.

An execution—The etiquette of eating—Sidi Hashem and his 'magnificent barb'—How a Susi sleeps—A bedraggled camp—Our commissariat department—Grinding corn—We go mussel-fishing—The wreck of our launch—A false alarm, and its moral—The Moslems at prayer . 85

CHAPTER IX.

TREACHERY AT WORK.

The *Tourmaline* disappears—We discuss our prospects of getting home—British prestige in Morocco—A boar-hunt without the boar—Wreckage—An impudent request—The weekly market—The yacht sighted again—Welcome and unwelcome guests—A native barber at work—Thieves again—Muley Abdallah gives us bad news—Treachery in the camp 94

CHAPTER X.

NAVAL MANŒUVRES.

A reconnoitre from the *Tourmaline*—The arrival of the *Hassani*—A disappointment—The *Hassani* goes in pursuit—Novel method of communicating at sea—An attempt is made to board the *Tourmaline*—The chiefs agitate for rifles—More naval manœuvres—A pitiable spectacle—The Susi open fire on the *Hassani's* boats—A warm quarter of an hour—Sabbah loses his appetite but finds his tongue 102

CHAPTER XI.

EL ARABI TO THE RESCUE.

A signaller's narrow escape—Our situation becomes grave—The chiefs wish us to retreat inland—Discussions thereon—I receive a letter from the Major—We resort to stratagem—More rifles landed—A night vigil, and a quarrel—Muley Abdallah tells his story—Sabbah disguises himself and leaves camp—His return—A rotten boat 114

CHAPTER XII.

THE ATTACK ON THE CAMP.

El Arabi gets his instructions, and leaves camp—An ominous quiet—We dispense hospitality—El Arabi gets on board the yacht—Fatal dallying—A hot skirmish—'Mr. Garden' proves his loyalty—Our flight, pursuit, and escape—A painful ride—Peace and war—A peculiarity of Sus—We are told the result of the fight—Capture of El F'kir Embarak's grandson—The old chief's house . 129

CHAPTER XIII.

IN THE HOUSE OF THE WOLF.

We are lodged in Mulud's house—We make the acquaintance of his son and 'Morocco kangaroos'—Close prisoners—'Twixt hopes and fears—News of El Arabi—Flight of Muley Hamed—We suspect treachery—An unpleasant pantomimic performance—We are searched and robbed—A trying ordeal—We are handed over to the Moors—A midnight march—Sidi Hassan . . 141

CHAPTER XIV.

EL ARABI COMES ASHORE AGAIN.

How El Arabi got on board the yacht—How his news was received—Mr. Henfrey's plan of campaign—The relief-party selected—Betrayal and capture—El Arabi appeals for mercy—The march inland—A halt on the way—A heated discussion—De Reya's cheerfulness under adverse circumstances—An act of kindness—A bad prospect—An unpalatable meal—The march resumed . . 151

CHAPTER XV.

BEFORE THE KAID.

We learn our destination—The march resumed—Mohammedanism and Truth—We meet El Arabi again—Our fate in the balance—Kaid el Bashir settles it—Concerning Kaids generally—A Sultan's tax-gathering—Raiding in Sus—Kaid Dakhman uld Bairuk—Arksis again—An ambitious suitor—Kaid Said el Giluli—An unsatisfactory interview—News of the *Tourmaline*—Captain Siebert prophesies—A novel substitute for tobacco—We are searched and thrown into chains—An unpleasant companion—Cheerfulness in adversity . . 161

CHAPTER XVI.

THE BEGINNING OF THE RAID.

Breaking camp—A Moorish war-song—The raid commences—The search for grain—Camel-riding—Arrival at Tlata—We try to see the Kaid, and are punished accordingly—We are put on show—A pleasant visitor—A captive's welcome—Muley Abdallah is brought in—Moorish philosophy — How Muley Abdallah and El F'kir Embarak were captured 181

CHAPTER XVII.

THE CAMP AT TLATA.

Close confinement—Kaid Bel F'kuk's generosity—*Kuss-kuss*—Fresh captives are brought in—How a Susi changes his clothes—Our camp at night-time—El F'kir Embarak confesses—Forty hours without water—We are transferred from our tent to a mud hovel—We make a new friend—The fast of Ramadan—Reflections on Mohammedanism — The Moor as a marksman — A soldier's regrets—The force of example 193

CHAPTER XVIII.

GILULI'S VOW, AND HOW HE KEPT IT.

We make an unpleasant discovery — Chains 'made in England'—We resort to judicious bribery—An English-speaking Moor—Courier or spy?—I write to Consul Johnston—Al-al appointed interpreter—An epicurean meal—'The Spaniard'—The filling of the chain—Death of Kaid Giluli's cook—The Kaid makes a vow—The Moor and his horse—Fire and slaughter—A sickening sight—Mulud's house burned 205

CONTENTS

CHAPTER XIX.

ON THE ROAD NORTHWARD.

The order to march is given—Death of a prisoner—Sbooya stratagem — Magnificent country — We leave Sbooya land—Giluli's terms to the Imsti—The Sultan's 'paper-chase'—Al-al leaves us to our own resources—A Job's comforter—The Kaid's generosity (?)—A touching incident—De Reya has a fall—Arrival at El Arba—We have a washing-day, and a treat generally—We learn our destination—A venerable patriarch—The three-card trick—Camp beggars 217

CHAPTER XX.

STILL NORTHWARD.

The laziness of the Moors—The camel in Morocco—Romantic scenery—The women come out to curse us—Khamis Ait Bubka—The vagaries of a saint—A wrestle and its good results—Beyerle falls ill—Giluli's kind message—An imaginative correspondent—I meditate on Kaids in general—Arrival of a courier—The Kaid's plans upset—Al-al has a fit—Concerning *kìf*—The lullaby of the ocean 233

CHAPTER XXI.

TISNIT.

An early start—A fairy picture—Fragmentary humanity—A jeering crowd—Welcome home to the raiders—*Lab el barud*—We arrive at Tisnit—How their houses are built—Description of the town—A vile den—Embarak, the faithful—Concerning *mona*—Kaid Hassan's mission—A saddening sight—Treatment of prisoners in Morocco—Lord Salisbury's opinions and his acts—Recruiting the chain-gang—Al-al prophesies—Unsubstantial diet . 244

CHAPTER XXII.

GOOD-BYE TO GILULI.

I give a lesson on the uses of instruments—A penitent gaoler — Preparations for leaving Tisnit — Kaid Bel F'kuk's last act of kindness—A Moslem gem—Harangue

from camel-back—Our new escort—Arrival at Massa—
A 'square' meal—A woman in the party—Description
of Massa — Highway robbery — The treelessness of
Morocco—Dar el Kaid Hadj Hamed Ksim—Fording
the river—We sight Agadir and the Atlas . . 261

CHAPTER XXIII.

ACROSS THE BORDER.

The 'irritability of Africa'—Collapse of the mules—We
arrive at Agadir—Its history and present appearance—
Our last look at Sus — Reflections thereon — The
Governor of Agadir—An impromptu entertainment—
Taga-zoost—Disappearance of my diary—I recover it
by stratagem — Our supposed swimming powers — A
companionable Kaid—The music of the Moors—Scandalous robbery—The Sultan's letters wetted—Misti has
a narrow escape—Arrival at Eda Gilul—Last has an
attack of fever—No more chains . . . 274

CHAPTER XXIV.

AN UNWELCOME INVITATION.

To the Sultan or Mogador?—An incident without a parallel
— The Khalifa congratulates us— Halt!—Sabbah is
exultant—Letters from the Sultan—We are invited to
stay at Giluli's *kasbah*—Improved lodgings—A spider
and his flies—A musical evening . . . 286

CHAPTER XXV.

LIFE IN THE KASBAH.

Letter received from Consul Johnston—A parcel of good
things—Moorish superstition—We manufacture *djinns*—
The end of Ramadan—A gorging orgie—Ba-Hamed's
policy—Description of the *kasbah*—Its internal economy
—The prison and its occupants—Arab the slave-boy—
Moorish etiquette in eating—Market-day at Eda Gilul
—A courier arrives from the Sultan—A deluge of rain
—A change of quarters 293

CHAPTER XXVI.

LIFE IN THE KASBAH—*continued.*

A well-used pack of cards—An overheard conversation—News of the *Tourmaline*—A 'Bashador Inglìz' at the Sultan's camp—Fate of the Moslem prisoners—A murder trial—The 'leather glove'—I make a sketch of the *kasbah*—A quarrel with our guards—We resort to strategy to obtain tobacco—Pigs, *djinns*, and devils—The Khalifa makes a bargain with Sabbah—A Moorish idea of England 305

CHAPTER XXVII.

NEWS AT LAST.

We discuss the possibilities of escape—But resolve to wait—Good news for Giluli—Arrival of Ben Omar—Obila is confidential—The major-domo's news—We prepare for our departure—A strange request—How the news came—An irritating delay—Arab is moved to tears—Sabbah indulges in a little light banter—A sample of the Khalifa's 'justice'—Departure from the *kasbah* . . 315

CHAPTER XXVIII.

DELIVERED UP.

A last look at the *kasbah*—On the road to Mogador—A halt at Eda Igirt—The journey resumed—I kill a snake—Hydrophobia unknown in Morocco—The legendary founder of Mogador—A tedious wait—Arrival at Mogador—Our reception—Popular indignation in the town—A civilized Governor—European visitors—Departure from Mogador—We embark on board the *Hassani*—Arrival at Tangier—Beyerle is set free—Arrest of the British subjects—Concerning the British Consulate at Tangier—Conclusion . . . 327

APPENDIX 340

LIST OF ILLUSTRATIONS

	PAGE
PORTRAIT OF MR. HENRY M. GREY	*Frontispiece*
OUR CAMP AT ARKSIS	*To face page* 60
THE 'HASSANI' CHASING THE 'TOURMALINE'	,, ,, 104
'WE WERE RUNNING FOR OUR LIVES'	,, ,, 134
IN CHAINS	,, ,, 178
PRISONERS ON THE MARCH	,, ,, 226
A BLACKSMITH AT WORK	,, ,, 254
KAID GILULI'S KASBAH	,, ,, 298

IN MOORISH CAPTIVITY.

PROLOGUE.

SOME time in the year 1896 there appeared in London an individual of a Jewish cast of countenance, dressed in a frock-coat and fez, calling himself Dr. Abd-el-Kerim Bey. His real name was Geyling, and Austria was the country which could claim the proud distinction of having given him birth. In the course of a by no means uneventful career, he had been many things to many men in many countries; but, according to his own account, he had most recently occupied the post of private physician to H.M. the Sultan of Morocco, with which potentate he was still on terms of friendship. Indeed, the worthy doctor would have one believe that his Sherifian Majesty was under considerable obligations to his late physician for important medical services rendered, obligations of which his Majesty was duly sensible. Under these happy circumstances the doctor had been loath to relinquish his lucrative post, but royalty—especially Mohammedan royalty—is notoriously fickle; and, as the doctor had been in negotiation with certain tribes in Sus with a view to opening up direct trade with Europe, and thus avoiding the heavy dues levied by the Sultan, he had left the Court and come to Europe, intending to raise money to develop and work the concessions he had secured.

While thus prospecting, he came into contact with Major A. Gybbon Spilsbury, an officer in the R.E. militia, to whom he unfolded his scheme. The Major lent a sympathetic ear to the Austrian adventurer's tale, and, having a somewhat extensive acquaintance with company-promoters in the city, succeeded in inducing the Globe Venture Syndicate, Ltd., to provide the necessary capital.

In the spring of the following year a preliminary expedition was sent out to Morocco, with the object of endeavouring to secure the co-operation of the Moorish Government. Residents in Tangier to-day say that such an imposing caravan never before set out from the town. Neither Geyling nor Spilsbury was likely to travel 'on the cheap' when touring at other people's expense, but to say that they 'travelled like an Ambassador' would be to give but a faint idea of the escort, animals, and baggage that they thought necessary to take with them. The journey overland to Morocco city lasted a month, the trip including Wazzan, Fez, and other places *en route*. Arrived at the southern capital, neither the Sultan nor the Grand Vizier would grant an audience to Geyling, but the Major was more fortunate. When, however, he came to unfold his projects in regard to trade with Sus, His Excellency would neither give his sanction to the Major's proposed visit to that country, nor guarantee his personal safety if he went.

Having failed in his endeavour to secure the support of the Moorish Government to the Sus development scheme, the Major turned his steps towards Mogador.

Here the interesting discovery was made that Abd-el-Kerim's 'treaties' were, to put it mildly, worthless. A quarrel ensued, and the Austrian went back to London vowing all sorts of vengeance against the Major, while the latter remained behind in Mogador with Sabbah, a Syrian Jew, as his interpreter. He soon made the acquaintance of one Pepe Ratto, a merchant of Mogador, with an extensive knowledge of languages and people. By this gentleman Spilsbury was brought into contact with two men, Embarak o-Hamed and Mohammed el Tamanari, who posed, or were represented, as delegates of the principal chiefs of Sus. The terms of a new treaty were discussed, and, to quote Spilsbury's own words: 'The draft treaty, as settled between us, was then sent by courier to Sidi Hussein ben Hashem, the paramount chief of Sus; and when returned with his approval, was signed at the British Vice-Consulate and duly certified.'

By this time the Sultan had got a hint of what was going on, and took prompt measures to checkmate the enterprise. Emissaries were sent down to Sus to bribe the chiefs into allegiance, and complaints were made to the British Minister at Tangier, who reported the matter to the Foreign Office in London. Spilsbury was communicated with, and an undertaking was given by him 'that he would not cross the Atlas.' But the situation was becoming very awkward for the Susi chiefs, who were spied upon and dogged wherever they went. Had they attempted to return overland, they would never have reached their own country alive. Spilsbury thereupon hit upon the idea of taking steamer to Las Palmas, and smuggling the natives on board. In this he was successful. On arrival at Las

Palmas, the British Consul informed the Major that he had received cable instructions from Lord Salisbury to persuade him not to go to Sus, as it was unsafe, and that if he went there it would be at his own risk. In reply, the Major pointed to the treaties between England and Morocco, which provide that British subjects 'shall have a free and undoubted right to travel, and to reside in the territories and dominions of his Sherifian Majesty, subject to the same precautions of police which are practised towards the subjects or citizens of the most favoured nations,' and determined that *coûte que coûte* he would see this curious country, which both the Sultan of Morocco and the British Government seemed so desperately anxious to keep from the prying gaze of all Christians.

If there is one inducement to explore an unknown region which is stronger than all others, it is the fact that someone has said, ' Thou shalt not go.' The toy the child wants most is the one its nurse says it must not have. And so it is with children of a larger growth. The hoary monarch of the frozen pole entrenches himself behind his icy ramparts, and silently forbids the foot of man to invade his snow-robed solitude; and straightway the hardy and rebellious children of men take up the defiant challenge at the risk and peril of their lives, yet with scarce a hope of greater reward than that men shall praise them for their courage and daring. Colonel Fred Burnaby, in his 'Ride to Khiva,' tells us that his resolution to undertake the perilous journey was born of a newspaper paragraph, stating that the Russian Government had forbidden all other Europeans to go there. In the pure spirit of defiance and contradiction he determined on the instant to go there, and he went. And so it was with Sus. The British Government forbade Major Spilsbury to go there, and straightway there was no place on earth that had so strong an attraction for him.

Chartering a thirty-six ton schooner, he embarked with Sabbah and the two Susi, and, after beating about for many days in a heavy sea, ultimately succeeded in making a sheltered cove called Arksis, which was pointed out by the natives as the most favourable landing-place. There the two chiefs were put ashore. What followed only Spilsbury and his interpreter can tell, and I therefore quote the former's own account, though subsequent observation showed that the Major had somewhat exaggerated the actual state of things.

'Our arrival being anticipated' (doubtless notified by courier from Ratto), 'the following day some 4,000 of the tribes, with their long guns, came down to the coast to welcome us, anxious to commence trading. So you see I was very glad to have run the risk, for, notwithstanding all the warnings, and although I was the first European in modern times to land there as a European, and without disguise, I was received with open arms. The horse, a magnificent barb, which was brought for me to ride, was bedecked with trappings of green velvet and gold such as might have been seen at the Court of the Mogul Emperors of India. I mention this by the way, simply to show that the people we have to deal with are wealthy, have a taste for luxury, and enjoy a certain degree of civilization—a state of affairs entirely different, and far superior, to what obtains in the territory of the British South Africa Company, or that of the Royal Niger Company. . . . Of course I had to explain that this visit was merely preliminary, and that I must return home and come out again with a steamer and a proper cargo; and so, after many farewells and protestations of friendship, I sailed back to Las Palmas and thence by steamer to England.'

On his return home he seems to have had no difficulty in convincing the syndicate that he had secured a 'splendid trading monopoly' which was going to bring in huge profits to the shareholders. Kerim Bey had done his little best to discredit his late companion to their employers in the meantime, but the syndicate directors had come to the conclusion that Codlin was the friend, not Short, and went on busily with preparations for the despatch of a fully equipped expedition with the first cargo. The attitude of the British Government, however, somewhat interfered with their plans. Official notice was given by the Foreign Office that her Majesty's Government regarded any attempt to open up trade with the Sus tribes contrary to the Sultan's wishes as illegal, and anyone going to Sus for the purpose would not be supported or protected. Now, it so happened that Sir Edward Thornton, G.C.B., was chairman of the Globe Venture Syndicate, and as an ex-Ambassador, Privy Councillor, etc., it was not his policy to run counter to the wishes of the Foreign Office. As the first consignment of goods to Sus was intended to consist chiefly of rifles and ammunition—goods absolutely forbidden entry through the ports of his Majesty of Morocco—it behoved the Foreign Office pensionnaires in the Globe Venture Syndicate to be extra cautious. A way out of the difficulty was found by the formation of the Mauritania Syndicate, which was to furnish the funds for the expedition, the Globe participating in the profits in certain eventualities, but being able to pose as innocent parties in the event of things going wrong. To this syndicate the present writer subscribed. Spilsbury was not a member, but he showed the confidence he had in his own scheme by investing his money in a steam-yacht which was to take out the cargo and the members of his expedition to Sus.

The steam-yacht *Tourmaline* was a neat little craft of 100 tons net register, capable of steaming thirteen knots an hour in a quiet sea. By November, 1897, all was ready for the start. Under the command of Captain George Graham, an ex-P. and O. officer, she left Cowes for the Thames, there to be fitted up with a three-pounder quick-firing Maxim-Nordenfeldt, and take in the stores for the voyage. On arrival in London, the crew—'a crowd of Cowes bummers and river Itchen lurchers,' as the skipper described them —left in a body, having no fancy for African exploration. A fresh crew was signed on, Sabbah the interpreter signing as purser, and in addition to the Major there were Mr. Arthur Watling, a director of the Globe Venture Syndicate and member of the Mauritania; Mr. A. C. Beyerle, an ex-Lieutenant in the German cavalry; and the present chronicler. We numbered nineteen all told, but of that number there were probably not more than three that knew that, while we were embarking on what would probably turn out to be a perilous enterprise, we were engaged in a venture that was illegal from its inception. The crew signed ordinary ship's articles, ignorant even of their destination beyond 'the Canary Islands and a port in Africa,' but that did not save two of them from being subsequently sentenced to three weeks' imprisonment for illegally importing arms. Nor did the present writer's belief in the absolute independence of the Sus tribes save him from a four months' sentence for the same 'offence.' But what befell, and how some of us traversed a country hardly seen, much less trodden, by any living Europeans, is told in the following pages.

CHAPTER I.

AN ILL-OMENED START.

A rainy night—Found drowned—We clear for Sakiet-el-Hamra —Crowded quarters—Novel stowage—Rough weather—A long night and slow progress.

It was a very wild night. The wind was sweeping across the low dreary marshes of the Schelde in sudden gusts which swayed the yacht at her moorings, and heavy showers of rain from the dark driving clouds seemed almost to quench the feeble lights that flickered in the streets by the well-nigh deserted quayside.

I had expected a friend to dinner, but we had finished our meal without a sign of him, or any message to excuse his absence. It was easy to imagine that a comfortable chair at home had more attractions than a drive to the Quai du Sud through the pitiless rain, and a search along the riverside crowded with bales and packing-cases, and cumbered with railway lines to stumble over and ship's cables to trip up the unwary; and I was making excuses for my friend on this score over my coffee and cognac, when a piercing scream rang out above the whistling of the wind and the creaking of cordage. Simultaneously we looked at one another, and Beyerle and I donned our mackintoshes and went out to investigate.

A little knot of people was gathering on the quayside, and, scrambling over the deck of the *Bendearg* and up its ladder to the shore, we were just in time to see a limp, dripping, and bedraggled form brought from the river and laid upon a pallet of packing-cases. A hasty examination showed the bundle to be a woman —all that was left of her—of about sixty years of age. Poor creature! She had come down to the docks to pay a visit to someone on board the big sailing ship, on which she herself had once been stewardess, or something of the sort, and, her foot catching in a rope, she had fallen headlong into the swollen river. Some man who heard her shout had just time to run down the ladder, grasp her by her clothing as she floated by in the rushing tide, and haul her to land. No effort was made to restore her to consciousness, and the doctor, who was quickly on the spot, pronounced life extinct. She had died from the shock. I was unpleasantly struck with the apparent callousness of the men who had lent a hand to rescue her from the river's greedy clutches; but I found out afterwards that a reward is paid by the authorities to anyone recovering a *dead* body from the river. For saving a life there is no fee.

To me a dead body is never beautiful, but there was something so horrible in the sight of this ill-clad, dripping corpse that the memory of it haunted me for days, and I could not shake off the idea that this was an ill omen for the success of our voyage.

'Come along,' said Beyerle, 'let's go and have a brandy and soda.'

And we turned and went.

The next day, December 14, the last box of ammunition was put on board and lashed down on deck, and the last package of stores stowed away in the already crowded-up saloon. In the sleeping-berths amidships, rifles, taken out of their packing-cases, were stacked from floor to ceiling, 4,300 in all. The cartridges, of which we took half a million, were stowed aft to trim the vessel. Altogether there was little prospect of that comfort which is usually associated with a yachting trip.

Steam was up, and while Beyerle and I were paying a visit of inspection to our neighbour the *Bendearg*, under the guidance of her chief mate, three long shrill blasts from the yacht warned us that she was impatient to be off. 'Good-bye,' said the mate, a good-looking hearty young Scotchman; 'I wouldna mind going with ye, but ye're about a foot and a haf too deep in the watter all the same;' and a hasty glance showed that the cabin ports were almost entirely under water.

The Customs officer was just getting his last items of information, and drinking his final glass of Scotch whisky, as we entered the little saloon on deck.

'And where are you bound to?' he asked the Major in French.

'Sakiet-el-Hamra, viâ the Canaries,' was the Major's bland reply, in the tones of one saying 'New York, calling at Southampton.'

'Ah oui, je le connais bien,' said this intelligent officer as he made an entry in his note-book; and it was impossible not to admire the graceful ease and readiness with which the man lied. With a formal salute and a 'Bon voyage' he bowed himself out, and five minutes later the captain had rung the telegraph 'half-speed ahead,' and the *Tourmaline* was gliding down the river past the maze of shipping and the town, on the top of a strong ebb-tide.

The crew were all wanted to put things shipshape, trim the cargo, and clear the decks of ropes and other lumber, so I took the wheel until we had got clear of the city, and entered the first of those long marsh-girt reaches which wind in snake-like curves between Antwerp and the sea, when I relinquished my post to the pilot. The rain came on again during the afternoon, and when the lights of Flushing hove in sight, between five and six o'clock, a stiff breeze was blowing, which augured anything but well for our run down Channel.

Orders were given to drop anchor, as the cargo and stores in the lower saloon were not in such a state as to justify our putting to sea. Rolls of calico were stacked up in piles, reaching from floor to ceiling. Tins of biscuits, bags of rice and coffee, were heaped up indiscriminately, and through all this heterogeneous mass of cargo a gangway had to be left clear to admit of passage to the chain locker and forward cabin, where Mr. Watling had taken up his quarters.

Watson, the chief steward, therefore set to work to shore up the calico, and so arrange it that there was room on top to lay a mattress, on which to sleep at night. They were rough-and-ready sleeping-quarters, and a bang on the head was likely to half stun him if, on getting up in the morning, he failed to recollect that the ceiling was only two feet above him. On the other hand, there was the consolation that he ran small risk of being rolled out of his bunk in heavy weather.

The Major occupied 'the owner's cabin,' a comfortable little den abaft the engine-room, to get to which he had to pick his way down a steep flight of narrow stairs, and climb over a barricade of ammunition-boxes at the foot. In rough weather no small amount of dexterity was required to get into this retreat, but once inside, the cabin was cosy enough. Two berths were fitted up on the port side, and a settee ran along one end, while a pedestal-table and mirror were fixed on the other. On the starboard side a door communicated with a bath-room, and only the electric light was wanting to satisfy the requirements of the most fastidious.

Captain Graham managed to stow both himself and his belongings into the little chart-room on deck, which was also floored with one layer of cartridge-boxes. Fortunately, the Captain was below the common height of man, otherwise the shortness of the improvised bunk on the settee would have compelled him to practise sleeping in the shape of a streak of forked lightning. That was not the only advantage his short stature gave him, as he was saved many a crack on the skull, which fell to the lot of his taller passengers, through coming in contact with the iron stanchions on which the steam-launch rested.

Beyerle and I roughed it in the dining-saloon, and grimly speculated on our chances of salvation in the event of an extra heavy sea washing the whole deck-house away. An old log-book of the yacht had been found in the chart-room, and it was with no little interest that we examined its pages to find out what weather the little craft had already encountered, but we could find nothing more dangerous than summer cruises in the North Sea. However, the boat, though by no means in her first youth, had been built by honest Scotchmen of Moulmein teak and Clydeside iron, and had no affinity with the 'pack of rotten plates puttied up with tar,' which is Rudyard Kipling's way of describing many modern 'tramp' steamers. All the same, there were not wanting people who thought us mad to cross the Bay of Biscay in the depth of winter in such a craft, and all efforts to insure the vessel, even against total loss only, had failed, though the underwriters, both in England and on the Continent, had been tempted and coaxed by numerous brokers.

While we were in Antwerp, a telegram had been received from Ratto urging a speedy departure, as the natives were impatient to begin trading operations as soon as possible, and many circumstances had arisen to delay our start from London. The sight of a yacht loading up with arms and ammunition, and fitted with a quick-firing gun, would have aroused the curiosity of a London or New York reporter, but the Antwerp pressmen are not so curious, and we had no visitors inquiring if we were going to run the blockade in Cuba, the age of the Captain, what his favourite recreation was, and a hundred other impertinent trifles such as go to make the modern 'interview.' Nevertheless, our departure from Antwerp had not passed unobserved, nor our proceedings there unnoticed, as will be seen hereafter. Not that there was any secrecy on our part, as everything had been done openly in the light of day; but Belgium is not the country to stop the exportation of arms and throttle the trade of its own manufacturers for such sentimental reasons as seem to sway the actions of the British Government.

We had also received information that the Moorish steamer *Hassani* had been down the Sus coast looking for us, and it seemed not improbable that there might be some fighting before we reached our destination. Sabbah, too, in one of his bursts of confidence, had let out the fact that Aflalo, the Sultan's agent in London, had had more than one interview with our discreet interpreter, and on one occasion had even been down to the West India Docks when the *Tourmaline* was lying there, to try and get some information concerning her movements. Our purser would have us believe that he had been a perfect model of discretion, and had completely succeeded in throwing his questioner off the scent ; but I, who had had some opportunities of observing Sabbah's powers of keeping confidential information to himself, entertained no doubt whatever but that the Sultan in Marrakesh knew all that was needful of the expedition before the yacht had left her moorings in the Schelde.

With all the Major's anxiety to put to sea, however, the Captain insisted on remaining all night at anchor in the river off Flushing, and putting the last finishing touches to the stowage of the cargo and the lashings of the deck hamper. The five tons of Manchester goods had been put on deck, as the bales were too big and too unwieldy for stowage below, and as these had been the last things taken on board, no little time was consumed in opening the bales and stowing the rolls of cloth in drawers and lockers below, wherever room could be found for them. A dozen bales or so had to remain on deck for lack of other space, and these were stowed as far aft as possible, and it was not until six o'clock on the following morning that the yacht hove anchor and stood out to sea.

The wind was blowing fresh from the south-west, and, in spite of his impatience to get away, the Major very soon ceased to regret the delay which the Captain's prudence had caused. While land was still in sight, the wind freshened considerably, and gave us fair warning of what might be expected when we got well outside.

After breakfast, I took a turn at the wheel to see how the yacht behaved herself in 'weather,' and a spell as far as the Wielingen lightship was sufficient to prove that an easier boat to steer would be difficult to find, whilst the way she lifted her nose to the head-seas, and shook the water from her sides like a dog that's swum ashore, was enough to arouse the admiration of the rawest landsman.

As the gale increased, however, the handicap of being overladen began to tell on her, and resigning herself to the inevitable, she dipped her bows into the advancing waves, which she could now no longer override, and began to show us that she was by no means a novice at the gentle art of rolling. Before mid-day the Chief Engineer allowed his fears to get the better of him, and asked the Captain to put back to Flushing. He had been accustomed to the omnibuses of the ocean, and had probably staggered through many a worse gale, in many an under-manned and overrated 'tramp,' but a yacht was a thing he did not understand.

'Turn back now?' said Captain Graham, with the accent on the *now*—'no fear. Why, man, you must remember this is December; we're bound to get a gale somewhere between here and Finisterre at this time of the year, and as we're in it now, we'd better stick to it and get it over.'

And with this specimen of shell-back philosophy Mr. Banks was fain to be content; but he went down below with anything but a happy glow upon his face.

We crept down under the lee of the coast as far as Dunkirk, as many a time and oft I have seen the skippers of the Ostend-Dover packets do, and then made a dash across for the English side of the Channel. The gale got worse as night approached, but there was no shelter nearer than Margate, and the Captain still held on. At 10 p.m. we made out the South Foreland light, and, with head turned down Channel, the little yacht stuck gamely to her work.

For us in the deck saloon, there was little sleep that night. The vessel staggered like a drunken man, and rolled to such an extent that Beyerle on one side, and I on the other, had to hang on to the table in the middle, to prevent our being lurched on to the floor. All night long big green seas came tumbling over the bows on to the deck, and broke with a thud against the strong teak deck-house. About two bells in the middle watch, one wave, bigger than the rest, landed on the top where coils of rope were piled, and as these were washed off on to the deck below, I made sure from the noise that something serious had happened. Above the confused trampings of the sailors in their big sea-boots, I heard the mingled orders and imprecations shouted from the bridge, but presently all was quiet again, except for the shrieking of the gale through the cordage, and the dull, heavy thud of the seas as they pounded the little craft, and swept through the scuppers astern with a hissing, seething swish. Sea and sky were intermingled, and only at rare intervals a light would show up out of the gloom like some dim star, but whether on land or sea it was hard to tell. The hours dragged on, and it seemed as if day was never going to break again. But the longest night comes to an end at last, and when the first gray glimmer of dawn climbed up in the eastern gloom the lights of Folkestone bore right abeam. In nine long hours we had steamed but nine short miles!

CHAPTER II.

ACROSS THE BAY.

Sea-sickness—Sabbah tells of 'some emotions'—Beyerle points the 'moral'—A traveller on the cheap—His opinion of the yacht—Life among the Moors—Moralizings thereon—We slacken speed—Cape St. Vincent—Arrival at Lanzarote—A Carlist alarm.

THE recollection I have of the next few days is not a happy one to dwell upon. Sea-sickness is not a pleasant thing at any time; but when one has no bed to take refuge in, but only a settee two feet wide, and without lee-boards to keep you from rolling off, and no deck to take a walk on, unless you wish to be drenched through in five minutes by the rain from above and the sea breaking overboard, and are unable to open the windows of the saloon without serious risk of being drowned in spray, then the discomforts of *mal-de-mer* are considerably increased.

It is curious that human nature should find consolation in the misfortunes of others when we ourselves are afflicted, but so it is; and I derived some gleam of satisfaction from the knowledge that not only were my fellow-passengers all under the weather, but that even the first and second mates had not escaped. Excepting the Captain, the cook, and one A.B., I think the whole ship's company was more or less affected while we were in the Channel and in the Bay; and it was with the liveliest satisfaction to all on board that at sunrise on the 20th we sighted the coast of Spain. The passage across the Bay had occupied forty-eight hours, the yacht averaging seven and a half knots an hour. Frequently she had to be slowed down to half-speed, as it would have been impossible to drive her through the heavy seas; so that, on the whole, it was not a bad performance.

With the sight of land, everybody's spirits seemed to rise like the barometer. The morning broke fine, and the sea smoothed itself out, and for the first time since we had left Flushing we were able to dispense with the fiddles on the breakfast-table. Keeping fairly close in shore, we came abreast of Finisterre just before luncheon, and ran up our number, S. H. N. L., and the answering pennant from the signal-station told us that Lloyd's vigilant official had read the sign. In an hour or two our friends at home would know that we had passed the dreaded Bay in safety.

The sunshine and calm also brought up from below a round-shouldered, stooping form enveloped in a heavy Inverness coat. His pallid face, the complexion the hue of pale pea-soup, peered out from underneath the peak of a cycling-cap, and a close inspection showed that it was what was left of Sabbah. Since leaving Antwerp our purser had scarcely been visible to anyone on board except the second steward, who had to listen a dozen times a day to his piteous appeals for food and relief.

'Tom, Tom, give me a little bit cocoa!' or 'Tom, Tom, get me a bottle of stout; I'm dying!' would wail through the sailors' mess-room from the invalid's cabin; but sailors are never very sympathetic towards sea-sick people, especially those who take it 'lying down.'

Bottled stout and cocoa would not strike most people as remedies for sea-sickness, but Sabbah had liberal views on that subject. He was wont to recount his experiences on a former occasion, when he was advised that a lump of fat pork on the end of a piece of string swallowed and hauled up again was a sovereign remedy for *mal-de-mer*—in fact, *the* one and only radical preventive and cure which all sailors adopted. He tried it! He swallowed the pork *and* about ten inches of string, but all efforts to get it back again were fruitless. There was nothing for it but to cut the string as close to his mouth as possible, and—take pills.

Beyerle said, when he told us this amazing yarn:

'I expect the reason it didn't do you any good was because you are a Jew. Jews have no business to eat pork.'

'I ain't a Jew,' he retorted in the dulcet accents of Houndsditch. 'Jewce religion no good for me; I can't beer it. I got to earn my job, and I must work Saturday in London; and if I do that, I not a proper Jew, so I give it up.'

And, indeed, he seemed to have a wonderful faculty of accommodating himself to any religion or any nationality, the only consideration being, as he frankly admitted, what best suited his interests for the time being. Born in Syria, the son of a Rabbi who had acquired French protection during his residence in Algiers, he had on several occasions claimed and received assistance from French Vice-Consuls in Turkey, Egypt, and the United States, whilst in

Morocco he liked to pose as a protégé of the British Government; and once, when he found himself stranded in Marseilles, and knowing only a smattering of French, he had resorted to his father's co-religionists, and been presented with the fare to take him to Paris. On another occasion he had 'stowed away' on board ship, as he had not the wherewithal to pay his fare; in fact, as he subsequently admitted to me, he had never paid his own fare from one country to another in any single instance.

These and similar discreditable stories of incidents in his past career he would tell with the most amazing candour, and with an utter absence of shame, chuckling only at the success of his duplicity and deceit. And certainly he could on occasion assume an expression of such hopeless misery as would almost have melted the heart of a stone.

On this occasion he confided his views on things in general, and the *Tourmaline* in particular, to the Major as soon as he saw him.

'This boat no good, Major—rotten boat. I wish I'd never come to sea in her. Sea no good for me. I shan't go to sea no more.'

The Major only smiled indulgently, as he was wont to do even at this curious individual's most impudent familiarities, and said:

'What's the matter, Sabbah? Have you been seasick?'

'Sick? Yahs, I should think I have; I've been in bed all the time.'

'Oh, I'm sorry for that,' replied the Major. 'Have you tried swallowing a piece of pork on the end of a string?'

But Sabbah did not reply. He seemed suddenly to have remembered something he had forgotten, and went aft hastily and gazed for some time over the bulwarks.

The conversation at dinner that evening turned on Morocco, and the Major had naturally an interested audience in relating stories of the Moors, and the terrible conditions of life that obtain under the autocratic and tyrannical rule of the descendant of the Prophet. On certain occasions every year all the Kaids and Bashas—*i.e.*, governors of provinces and towns—are expected to send 'presents' to the Sultan. These officials are paid no salary, but are supposed to collect the taxes from the people in their district, and remit the proceeds to the Sultan, after deducting a certain amount—or, rather, a very uncertain amount—for their own private benefit. Should the amount tendered for his Majesty's acceptance be considered by the Grand Vizier to be inadequate—for that official has to have a picking out of it also—the unfortunate Kaid or Basha receives an invitation to present himself at the Court and talk the matter over. Maybe the sum of £5,000 has been sent, when £10,000 was expected, and the Sultan may send him to prison until the other £5,000 is forthcoming. The Kaid may perhaps promise the money with too great an alacrity, and thereby arouse the Sultan's suspicions.

'Ah, thou vile slave! then thou hast this money in the secret hiding-places of thy *kasbah*. What shall be done to thee that thus darest to steal what belongs to thy Lord the Sultan? By my beard, unless thou sendest now and payest me £10,000 thou shalt rot in prison, and thy place shall know thee no more.'

The screw thus applied, the money is generally forthcoming, and the Kaid returns to his district and his tax-gathering with renewed zest. Punishment without the option of a fine is rare in Morocco, but cases are recorded of the most barbarous tortures being inflicted upon wretched officials who were unable to satisfy a Sultan's rapacity. Slitting the fingers, filling up the wounds with salt, and binding the fist tight with hide, was at one time a favourite device. If the wounds healed the man was lucky, but more frequently they mortified, and the hand had to be cut off.

In spite of the risks attendant upon the holding of such positions in Morocco, the struggle to secure them is very keen, on account of the vast opportunities afforded to the occupants of enriching themselves. Bribery is resorted to on a large and wholesale scale, and it is stated that last year (1898) the Governor of a large and fertile district, having been deposed, offered 200,000 dollars to the Grand Vizier to be reinstated, but he was outbid by two rival aspirants to the post, who offered 400,000 dollars between them for the privilege of government by a dual control. Probably this money would have to be borrowed in the first instance from coast Jews at ruinous rates of interest, on the uncertain security of future tax-levies; but the ultimate sufferer would be the wretched tribesman, who would be squeezed to the uttermost farthing. Under such conditions as these, and with such powerful inducements to extortion and tyranny, how could any other result be looked for but the ruin of the most fertile and thriving province for years to follow?

It is not, however, the unfortunate tribesmen who

are the only sufferers from this intolerable system of government; but Europeans in the coast towns who have commercial transactions with country Moors are unable frequently to recover their debts from these native creditors. Under this system of licensed pillage and robbery there is no inducement to a man to cultivate more land than is necessary to furnish him and his family with the barest requisites of life, knowing that any surplus will be claimed by the Kaid in the name of the Sultan.

Robbery by Government is one thing, but robbery by the individual is quite another, and is visited in Morocco with the greatest severity. Until quite recent times the punishment inflicted for theft was the cutting off of the hand, the stump of the arm being thrust into boiling pitch to prevent bleeding to death. Indeed, so frequently was this practised at one time that the brother-in-law of the late British Minister to Morocco set apart a room for the reception of these victims in order that they might receive the attention of an English doctor. For a second offence the remaining hand was similarly sacrificed, and on conviction a third time the criminal's eyes were put out, as he was then thought fit for nothing on earth, not even good enough for dung upon the soil.

The influence of European civilization has, however, done something of late years towards mitigating these and similar horrors in Northern Morocco, and we seldom hear now in the coast towns of mutilation, of women being bastinadoed to death, and of the rolling of persons in casks studded with spikes, after the manner of the Carthaginians; but atrocities of the most fiendish character are still committed by the authorities in many places in the interior.

And so it will continue until the light of civilization shall have illumined all the dark places of this dark land, or, more happily, the day shall have dawned when the rule of the Moslem shall be no more. They know that this is their destiny, for one of their old *fikths* (learned men, seers) has written that the Frank shall one day batter at the gates of Fez, and some of the more enlightened Moors would gladly welcome the day. But in the meantime most of them cling with incomprehensible tenacity to their old ways and their old customs. They strive with might and main to keep the hated Christian from their shores, and in this direction receive unaccountable encouragement from the British Government and its officials. So recently as last year the present British Vice-Consul in Tangier gave utterance to the astounding statement that Englishmen were not wanted in the town; but the fanatical hatred of the Mohammedan, the chill discouragement of the British Government, and the officious interference of any number of Vice-Consuls, are alike powerless to stop the hands of the clock of Fate, or keep alive a nation that is as surely dying of its own inherent rottenness as a man that is stricken with a mortal sickness. Nevertheless, the Foreign Office continues to slam the door in the face of the man who dreams of commercial enterprise in Morocco, and the gates of Fez are solemnly closed on every Friday of the year to exclude the invading Frank. Mrs. Partington with her mop has found distinguished imitators.

In discussions such as these we would often beguile the time, almost always concluding with speculating upon the issue of our expedition.

'Suppose you find the *Hassani* off the coast when

you get there; what will you do?' I asked the Major one day.

'I have a perfect right to trade with the natives if I like,' he replied, 'and if any ship tries to stop me by force, I shall fire on her. I expect the *Hassani* will come down; but she carries no guns, and would be no match for us. One of our shots through her engine-room would send her to the bottom pretty quickly. But I don't suppose she will interfere with us; it would be rank piracy if she did.' And we adjourned to the Major's cabin below to have a look at the three-pounder shots which were to defend us against the possible attacks of 'pirates.'

With the continuance of fine weather we made rapid progress southward, but some uneasiness was caused by the announcement of the Chief Engineer that we had not enough coal to carry us to Lanzarote. This was reported on the 21st, and was decidedly disquieting, as the Major was strongly averse to putting into either Lisbon, Cadiz, or Madeira if it could possibly be avoided. The Captain therefore ordered a thorough examination to be made, the result of which was that the next day Banks replied that there was enough to last us to the Canaries if the speed were reduced. This was accordingly done, and with that order all hope of passing Christmas Day ashore at Arrecife was dispelled.

At four o'clock we passed Cape St. Vincent close enough to take some snapshots of that historic headland, and the lighthouse on the top of the cliff, which in days gone by had been a monastery. Here, in days of yore, this refuge from the world doubtless gave comfort to thousands of poor souls who sought a haven within its walls, and now from out its topmost tower is thrown the beam of light which in calm seas cheers the mariner on his outward or returning way, and in stormy nights warns him of his peril, and guides him into safety.

Just off the Cape we were overtaken by two or three tramps, whose officers looked long and hard through their glasses at that little yacht lying low in the water, and their wonderment must have been increased when they observed that we did not round the Cape and make for the Straits of Gibraltar, but turned our back on Europe and steered south-westward for the open sea.

The weather continued fine, and nothing happened to mar the even tenor of our way. The sighting of a Mediterranean-bound liner from the Plate some five miles off was an incident, and the gambolling of numerous shoals of porpoises was a mild excitement.

On Christmas Eve our course was set to make the north-east point of Lanzarote, which we expected to sight at sunrise on the following day; but a strong current carried us miles to the eastward, and it was not until 10 a.m. that we saw the faint outlines of the mountains through the haze. At three o'clock we arrived off Point Naos, the harbour for Arrecife. In response to our signals the pilot came off, and we anchored outside the reefs in front of the town, about a mile further down the coast. Shortly afterwards the port doctor and other officials, resplendent in the glory of uniform, gold lace, and swords, came off and gave us *pratique*. Our agent informed us that telegrams had been received from Madrid at all the islands in the group, instructing the authorities to watch us closely, as it was suspected that we were associated with some

Carlist movement. What precise object they imagined we had in view it would be difficult to say, but the officials soon satisfied themselves that we had no intention of making an armed landing and seizing the island, or of bombarding Arrecife. Their fears being thus allayed, their behaviour thereafter was courteous and hospitable in the extreme.

CHAPTER III.

ISLAND NIGHT'S ENTERTAINMENT.

Arrecife—Our reception ashore—Description of the town—Our Christmas dinner—Beyerle and I seek dissipation and find a club—Beyerle's little joke—Loyal toasts—A distinguished visit and a breakdown—A magic-lantern show—A medical discussion and its sudden ending—A Spaniard's dignity—We bribe the officials and give a concert—I receive an official and professional visit—Parting counsel—Adios!

LANZAROTE is the most easterly and the most northerly of the Canary Islands, and, like the rest of the group, of volcanic origin. One volcano, about twelve miles distant inland from Arrecife, is still hot at the crater, and constitutes the 'lion' of the place, the sight which all the good inhabitants are desirous of conducting strangers to see. At a distance all the mountain slopes look barren and uncultivated, but as one approaches nearer one can see that the rich red soil is fertile in the extreme, and one learns without surprise that immense quantities of onions and tomatoes are produced for exportation. Grain also is grown to supply the needs of the island, and vines are cultivated, but the wine is of indifferent quality. There are no textile industries, nearly all their manufactured goods being imported from England, their timber from Scandinavia, while their fans, which adorn (?) their walls, and aid the coquetry of their maidens, bear a distinctly Teutonic imprint.

Of course, we were anxious to go ashore as soon as possible, and in the afternoon a party of us landed, including the Major and the Captain. We immediately directed our steps to the telegraph-office to wire home our Christmas greetings. The reception from the townspeople was embarrassing in the extreme, especially from the younger members thereof, who awaited our landing on the quay as if we had been distinguished visitors, and escorted us through the streets wherever we went. If we went into a *fonda*, or hotel, to taste the wine of the country, our bodyguard waited below, or thronged the entrance to the hostelry, what time we dispensed largesse from the upper floor in the copper coin of the realm.

The houses are built in the Hispano-Moorish style of architecture, with flat roofs, the windows mostly opening on to the *patio*, while those that overlook the street are protected with green jalousies, through the little flap-shutters of which many a pair of dark eyes peeps coquettishly out upon the passer-by below. The streets are very uneven, and very badly paved with rough lava blocks, with here and there a *trottoir* of cement in the principal thoroughfares. Of any system of drainage there is none visible, household refuse being thrown into the street in the primitive manner of their forefathers of long ago.

There is no public supply of water, the storage of that useful fluid being left to individual effort. A well is, therefore, to be found in the *patio* of nearly all the larger houses, and when the rainy season comes in December and January, there is every possible contrivance to make the most of it. The rain that pours down upon the flat roofs is carried off by troughs and pipes, which empty themselves into the well below, to be drawn up by buckets when required. And these two months of rain are what they call their winter season.

Eatables and liquid refreshments are subject to *octroi* on entering the town, and the mule-drawn carts conveying them are only allowed to go along certain streets that are marked 'Transito de Consumo.' The object of this regulation is presumably to make the collection of the tax an easier operation, and if any cart so laden be found proceeding through any other streets, the owners are fined.

Horses are to be seen in the island, but are kept principally for pleasure, while the humble donkey is, of course, much in evidence. Camels are there also, brought over, probably, from the Spanish settlement of Rio de Oro in Africa, and are used for the heavier kind of burdens.

I took snapshots of a group of these ungainly beasts, that were grunting and growling on the quayside, by way of protest against being loaded—as is their playful habit—and afterwards Sabbah and I mounted one of them, one on each side, and gave the owner half a dollar to take us for a short ride. Little thought I then that before many weeks should have passed I should have had enough camel-riding to satisfy me for the rest of my natural life, and free of cost to myself except considerable bodily pain and weariness of spirit.

Young women are seldom met with in the street, taking their views of the outside world chiefly from the terraces of their houses, and through their shuttered windows. Like their sisters in Spain, they wear the graceful black lace *toca*, or *mantilla*, and are probably as anxious to be serenaded by the *caballeros* of the little island when the sun has gone to his rest, and the moon comes up from the sea, as any *bella niña* in Sevilla or Cadiz.

At home in England people were perhaps trudging through the snow or fog, or maybe keeping indoors all day before a roaring fire, and here were we revelling in the balmy sunshine of the Fortunate Isles, and sitting down to our Christmas dinner with the windows of the saloon open to catch the evening breeze. Englishmen carry their customs with them, and our steward was able to put upon the table that evening turkey and sausages, plum-pudding, and mince-pie. And what matter if both turkey and sausages had seen the inside of the preserving-tin much more recently than Leadenhall Market so long as a good old English custom was faithfully observed? And if anything else were wanting to make glad the heart of man, was there not on board some excellent 'fizz' and some fine old tawny port?

The next day it was deemed fitting that the party for shore should land in such state as befitted distinguished visitors, and the engineers were busy early in getting ready the steam-launch, the engine of which had got out of order and had not been repaired while we were at Antwerp. Neither of the engineers seemed to be making much progress with the work, until Watling, who knew something of launch engines from his up-Thames experiences, took his coat off and buckled to. The coal-lighters were alongside by this time, and the yacht was practically in the possession of a crowd of grimy coal-heavers, so that it was a great relief when Watling announced that steam was up, and all was in order for a start.

A crowd of townspeople was in waiting to receive us on the *plaza*, as before, and great interest was manifested in the launch, many of these people having probably never seen such a thing in their simple lives before. In Arrecife the great event of the week is the arrival of the mail-steamer from the neighbouring islands, and a native who has been as far as Spain is regarded as a travelled man of the world, and looked up to and envied accordingly.

There were some matters of business to be settled by the Major with the agent, but we all met later at the *fonda* in the Calle Real for lunch. It did not boast a *table-d'hôte* such as the Cecil or Savoy, but one has a peculiar zest for a meal ashore after some days at sea, and though one perhaps may not acquire a taste for donkey-sausage at once, eggs are much the same the wide world over; and presently, with the aid of a bottle of wine and some good cheese, we were looking out upon the world with that contentment of mind which is born of a satisfied stomach.

We returned to the yacht in the afternoon, but Beyerle and I were minded to pay an evening visit to the town, and see the dissipations of the place. So far, we had seen nothing more demoralizing than a thing on the quay square, or *plaza*, that looked like a bandstand, but which proved on investigation to be a drinking kiosk. Accordingly, after dinner we lowered the dinghy, and got the captain's permission to take one of the sailors with us to row the boat and mind it while we were ashore. We chose de Reya. I volunteered to act as pilot and steersman, but not without serious misgivings of piling up the craft on the reefs, which showed their teeth at low-water. And indeed it was no sinecure. The tide was dead-low, and the current swirled very trickily through the narrow channel between the reefs which formed the entrance to the 'port.' But the water was so clear and shallow that even in the moonlight the bottom could be seen. Very cautiously we made our way to the steps which led up to the *plaza*, and it was with decided feelings of relief that we made fast the dinghy.

At the aforesaid kiosk we made inquiries as to the entertainments of the place, and learnt that the only dissipation was the Casino on the Marina, of which all the young bloods of the town were members. And indeed, while we sat drinking our lager beer—made in Wales—we were addressed by a couple of young Arrecifians with that polite familiarity which the insular Britisher finds so hard to acquire, and which comes so naturally to his Continental neighbours, and invited to partake of the hospitality of the club.

The ceremony of introduction was quickly got through, and we were soon on the best of terms with them all, from the President downwards. Beyerle was minded for a joke, and introduced me as the ship's doctor. Thereupon the local apothecary was very anxious to make my personal acquaintance, and told me in flowery Spanish of the honour he felt to be conferred upon him on being presented to a *maestro* from London. The best champagne—made in Lanzarote—was called for by the President, and we were made honorary members of the club. Some pretty orations of a highly complimentary character followed. The President welcomed us as strangers and Englishmen—the Hispano-American War had not then been dreamt of—and wished us success in our enterprise. They in Lanzarote knew the dangers of Sus, and the treacherous character of the Moors in general, as some of the islanders had been employed in former years at the English settlement at Cape Juby, but he hoped that we should be able to establish another similar trading-station, and would make Arrecife our depôt in the Canaries. Visions of his native town transformed into a busy and thriving port perhaps flitted through his jovial, enthusiastic mind, and then he drifted off into the realms of foreign politics. The British, he said, were encountering serious difficulties with the Afridis in India, just as Spain with the *reconcentrados* in Cuba, but he was confident that both nations would eventually surmount them, and he concluded with proposing the toast of '*La Reina Victoria y el Rey Alfonso XIII.*' '*Viva Victoria y viva Alfonso XIII.!*' rang through the room, and we could do no less than respond with the toast of prosperity to the Casino of Arrecife and the health of its worthy President.

Many of our newly-made friends expressed a desire to go on board the yacht, so we very readily extended an invitation to the President and a party of friends, whom he should select, and the launch should call for them at the *plaza* the following afternoon. The yacht had meanwhile left her anchorage in front of the town, and taken up a more sheltered berth at Port Naos, as there were signs of a coming blow. She was therefore about a mile from the town, and the following afternoon the launch was prepared, and steam got up. There was a canal for lighters and small craft which connected Port Naos with the little harbour of Arrecife, and obviated the necessity of the longer journey by sea outside the reefs, but here and there it was spanned by bridges where the road crossed it. This was the route taken by the launch, but on the return journey, with her full complement of distinguished townsmen, the steam gave out in consequence of the funnel having to be constantly unshipped when passing under the low archways, and we had to ignominiously resort to the oars to get back to the *Tourmaline*. What had been intended for an impressive trip had been a melancholy fiasco.

Once on board, however, we were in a measure compensated by the manifest delight which the inspection of the yacht afforded our friends. The little Maxim-Nordenfeldt quick-firer aft especially took their fancy, and doubtless provoked an involuntary comparison with the ancient cannon that surmounted the old fort which once guarded the approach to the bay, and which probably dated from the latter days of the Middle Ages. The Major, who spoke Spanish fluently, entertained the party with small-talk, and whiskies and soda in the saloon, until some of them, who perhaps had never been on board a ship in their lives, began to feel the qualms of sea-sickness, although there was scarcely a motion to be felt, and a move for the shore was suggested.

Before they left, however, we promised to give them a magic-lantern show at the Casino the same evening, and accordingly after dinner a shore-party was made up, consisting of Watling, Beyerle, Henfrey, Sabbah, Watson, and myself. Sabbah was to act as showman, and on our arrival we were welcomed by the Vice-President, in the absence of the President himself, who had not yet arrived. The walls of one of the large rooms were whitewashed, and formed an excellent substitute for a sheet. The lights were turned out, and before an easily interested audience the show began. The scenes were not of a very remarkable character, being chiefly representative of London streets and buildings. St. Paul's and the Thames Embankment left them unmoved, but a representation of a hansom-cab aroused great interest, and an encore was called for. The finale was a coloured portrait of the Queen, and the little hall rang with *vivas* to testify their admiration of her Majesty, and their appreciation of the entertainment. By preconcerted arrangement we of the *Tourmaline* sang the National Anthem, and then called upon the audience for its Spanish equivalent; *but alas, there wasn't one who knew it!*

An adjournment was then made to the bar, the worthy President, who had by this time arrived, again occupying the position of master of the ceremonies. He was evidently in a mood for festivities, and speeches, and under his hospitable wing we were soon a merry party. A prophet is not without honour but in his own country—apparently also Canary cigars. For, instead of being regaled with 'Teneriffe twisters' where most we should expect to find them, the President produced some of the finest brands of Havana.

While thus enjoying ourselves, Sabbah brought me a message that the 'Medico del Municipalidad,' who was in another room, wanted to be introduced to me. I immediately rose and left the room, not without some qualms of conscience as I recalled Beyerle's reckless joke, and wondered what results it might lead to. I was presented to a grave and dignified Galen, who, after a polite exchange of greetings, expressed a desire to have a private chat with me.

I wondered what was coming, and began to feel decidedly uncomfortable when I found that he wanted to compare notes on professional matters with a supposed *confrère* from London. Open confession may be good for the soul, but I felt I had gone too far to draw back now, and determined, with a blush of shame, to brazen the imposture out to the bitter, and perhaps humiliating, end. My imperfect acquaintance with the Spanish language here stood me in good stead, as I could pretend not to understand his meaning when I felt that I was floundering hopelessly in the deep waters of medical science; but when I rashly referred to quinine as the treatment for thrush, and saw the look of intense astonishment that crossed his face, I saw no way out of my difficulty but to loftily declare that the use of honey and borax in such cases was an antiquated superstition long since discarded by the faculty in London.

My position was becoming desperate, and the hot perspiration of shame stood out in beads upon my face; but if I could only save the situation till this painful interview was over, I might breathe freely again. But there was more to follow. My worthy friend expressed his great regret that he had not been one of the party that visited the yacht that afternoon, and said that nothing would have given him greater pleasure than to look over the vessel — and the medicine-chest. Inwardly, but none the less fervently, I cursed Beyerle as the cause of all my misery, but endeavoured to put on my sweetest smile as I said I hoped he would do me the honour of paying a visit the following morning at eleven o'clock.

I mentioned that time, as I thought that was the hour when he would be the most likely to be busy, but he assured me he would come without fail.

Matters were really getting serious, and when the President burst into the room, and began to abuse the worthy doctor for taking me away from the company, I felt I could have kissed him in gratitude for my relief. But the President was not to be easily mollified by the doctor's explanations, and I was very much afraid a 'row' was imminent. He allowed himself, however, to be coaxed back to the convivial circle he had left in search of me, and by way of restoring him to his wonted good-humour, and showing our appreciation of him, we lifted him up in his chair, and carried him from room to room despite his protests, singing the while, 'For he's a jolly good fellow,' like a Queen's-prize winner at Bisley.

Our amiable intentions, however, were quite misunderstood, and when the poor President once more found his feet he was exceeding wroth, and swore lustily in anything but refined or choice Castilian. Such proceedings do not accord with a Spaniard's idea of dignity, and the poor fellow felt as much offended and insulted as if we had carried his effigy round the public square. We explained to him that it was a great honour in our country, reserved only for those for whom we entertained the highest regard.

'*En cada tierra su uso*' (Other countries, other customs), said Sabbah.

'*A otro perro con eso hueso*' (Throw that bone to another dog), he snarled; but he was reassured by his friends, who saw that we meant only well.

Our kind-hearted host had passed the stage of jovial intoxication, and was rapidly becoming quarrelsomely drunk. We therefore considered it a favourable moment for suggesting that it was time we were thinking of getting back to our ship, but he wouldn't hear of that; so we took him on another tack. We told him we had been so hospitably received that we couldn't think of abusing his generosity any further, and suggested an adjournment to the kiosk on the *plaza*, where we might all have a parting bottle or two at our expense. The suggestion was adopted, and the proceedings developed into an al-fresco concert, some of our party contributing English songs, while our friends responded with both song and guitar.

In this quiet little town, 11 p.m. was the time for the lights to be extinguished in the public square, but when the man came round to blow out the paraffin lamps, we all felt that it would be a pity to part so early, and that a concert in the dark was scarcely *en règle*, so we bribed the man with a few cigarettes to go for a walk, to which temptation he very obligingly succumbed. To give further tone to the proceedings, someone went to invite the Colonel commanding the 'garrison' hard by. That gallant officer had retired to bed, but he slipped on his clothes and very soon joined us. We felt that only the presence of the Mayor was wanting to make our patronage-list complete; but before any further invitations could be sent the lamplighter had returned from his walk, and the concert had come to an end.

A considerable bodyguard escorted us back to Port Naos, and it was long after midnight when we hailed the yacht to send a boat. The doctor stayed to the last, and on bidding me good-night assured me that he would not fail to keep his appointment for the morning.

Still hoping against hope that at the last minute some unexpected patient would keep him in town, I remained on board the yacht next morning. Eleven o'clock came, and brought no signs of him. But half an hour later I espied a figure on the shore making signals to the yacht, so I sent a boat ashore, and a few minutes afterwards my worthy friend came up the gangway ladder arrayed in his very Sunday best, resplendent in white waistcoat and gold watch-chain, accompanied by his son, a boy of nine, also immaculately attired.

I welcomed them effusively, and conducted them to the deck saloon, and endeavoured to divert his mind with refreshments and general conversation. But he was not to be baulked, and in sheer desperation I pulled out a drawer in the locker and displayed a variety of commonplace drugs, pills, and lotions—the property of the late owner of the yacht—and apologized for my inability to show him the principal medicine-chest, as that was in the Major's private cabin, and he had locked the door and gone to town with the key in his pocket.

The ordeal was over, and the conversation drifted on to the Moors and the land of Sus. The general opinion in Arrecife seemed to be that the Susi had plenty of money, but that they, like the Moors, were treacherous in the extreme. Spaniards generally hold the Moors in universal abhorrence, and give them a wide berth, as far as possible. The doctor observed, from the small-arms we showed him, that we were not altogether unprepared for emergencies, and his parting advice was, pointing to a knife I carried in my belt :

'*Este el principal ; no se parta con este.* They will

be very friendly with you, and then put a bullet into you.'

The same afternoon the mail-steamer from the islands arrived, bringing letters for us from England; and having taken all requisite coal and fresh stores aboard, we prepared to leave the same evening. All the town turned out on to the quayside to bid us farewell and see us off, and though they wished us a safe return, I am sure most of them never expected to see any of us again.

At eight o'clock we weighed anchor, and it was with feelings of genuine regret that we watched the town lights fade from sight, and steered for the African shore. Those hospitable islanders had given us a kindly and open-hearted reception, and if any of them should ever happen to see these lines, I hope they will forgive me for the harmless deception I practised upon them, and be assured that I hold them in very kindly remembrance. Adios!

CHAPTER IV.

DANGEROUS DELAY.

In sight of land—Chasing a derelict—A false report—Primitive mail-boats—Concerning dog-fish—New Year's Day—We make a balloon and lose it—A trip northwards—Ifni and its saint-house—Concerning Moorish saints—Sidi Warzuk—Back again to Arksis.

A LONG unbroken line of red-brown cliffs rising perpendicularly from the water or from a narrow strip of sandy, yellow beach, against which the great Atlantic rollers broke in clouds of spray with one unceasing roar, like the rumble of a distant train; and behind, the rugged outline of the mountain ranges, lifting their towering peaks to kiss the azure sky—such was the African coast as we approached it on the afternoon of December 29. We had sighted land at sunrise, but the distance one can see in the clear atmosphere of these latitudes is almost incredible. Our destination was Arksis, which is situated in 29° 10' N.

On his former visit the Major had omitted to make a record of the *exact* latitude of the place, but knew its proximate whereabouts, and had noted a peculiar white-faced cliff, which, in contrast to the prevailing dun colour of the coast-line, formed an easily distinguishable landmark. We failed to hit the mark at the first attempt, and therefore took a short cruise up and down the coast, keeping a sharp look-out for any signs of the natives. From our mast-head fluttered a green flag, which was the agreed-upon signal by which the natives were to recognise us, but there was not a sign of life anywhere along the coast, and, as the sun was getting low, the Captain decided to drop anchor for the night. Good ground was found in about ten fathoms of water with a sandy bottom.

It wanted still half an hour to sunset, so Beyerle and I decided to get out the dinghy and spin for mackerel, which at certain seasons of the year abound in those waters. In his eagerness, however, Beyerle, who was at the bow-end, forgot to fix the painter, and when we let the boat down into the water and unshackled the hooks, she began to drift gracefully but rapidly towards the shore. Beyerle threw the blame on to me, and I threw the blame on to him; but we both soon agreed that a better plan than abusing one another was to lower the jolly-boat, and go in pursuit of the derelict. By the time we had got the other boat out and caught up the dinghy, she had drifted about half a mile, and we had a hard pull back against the tide. Meanwhile the sun had gone down, and darkness was rapidly falling, but a light hung over the stern of the yacht guided us back. After that we gave up mackerel-spinning, and went in for fishing for 'snappers' over the side of the yacht.

Before darkness had fairly set in, the Major sent up a rocket as a signal to the tribes ashore, and ordered a sharp look-out to be kept for any answering signals. We had hardly sat down to dinner, when Mr. Last, the second officer, reported two beacons on the hills, and we all turned out of the saloon in haste, to find that what he had taken for beacon-fires were only rising stars. It was quite an easy mistake to make, but we all had a good laugh at poor Last. Someone said it was his anxiety to be First that had led him into error, but the Major looked severe, and solemn silence fell upon the company.

The next day, in the forenoon, we observed three natives on the beach, and shortly afterwards others came down from the top of the cliffs and joined them. The Major had by this time discovered his former landing-place, and recognised the peculiar white cliff, which was distinguishable from sea at a considerable distance. By lunch-time about a dozen men were visible on the shore, one of whom was energetically waving a green flag in response to ours. Then a white flag was displayed, and we replied by hoisting the 'C' signal-flag, which was the nearest approach to the flag of peace that the ship could boast.

There was no possibility of landing, as the surf was too heavy. Any attempt to do so in the boats we had would simply have resulted in a spill, but we were doubtful whether the natives ashore would understand that fact or not. Accordingly, we busied ourselves in constructing a small raft to send through the breakers with a message. All the designing talent of the saloon was called into requisition, and the result of our labours was a triangular-shaped raft, made of old biscuit-boxes, with a small mast in the middle, to which a little flag was attached, in order that it might be more easily seen while in the water. Finally a message was written in Arabic by Sabbah, telling them that we had come to keep our promise, and would come ashore as soon as the surf would allow. This was enclosed in an empty soda-water bottle, the neck of which was passed through a hole in the deck of the raft and securely lashed. By the time our raft was finished, it was too near sundown to launch it, as the darkness would hide it from view before it could reach the shore, but all was made ready for the morning.

After our shipbuilding exertions we amused ourselves with fishing from the yacht. Dog-fish about a foot long swarmed all about the ship, and the way they struggled when on the hook made one think that some big prize was about to be landed until we became accustomed to the deception. They are not good eating, the flavour being strong and oily; but their skins, which resemble the colour and texture of the shark's, though of course much finer, make excellent polishing-cloth for such purposes as emery is used for. Several of them on being cut up contained young ones, of which I kept some specimens preserved in spirits. One or two 'snappers' completed the haul, so there was scarcely enough variety to stock a fish-shop.

In the morning a heavy swell from the westward was still rolling in, the waves breaking a long distance from shore, and all hope of landing that day had to be abandoned. Where there was no beach, the waves would dash themselves against the cliffs, and clouds of spray would rise at times to the height of 150 feet. I felt as if I would very much like to have a dip in the sea, but the ominous sight of a dark fin on the surface of the water, now and then, warned one of the proximity of sharks, so I refrained.

After breakfast, there being plenty of natives visible on the shore, I went in the dinghy with Henfrey and a couple of sailors to post our letter. The sea was breaking about half a mile from shore, but we went as close in as was prudent, and committed our little craft to the waves, firing several rifle-shots at the same time as a signal to the shore. A strong current was running down the coast from the north-east, and instead of the breakers carrying the raft straight on shore, as we had hoped, we watched her drift rapidly towards the southwest, where she would probably be dashed to fragments against the cliffs.

The next day—New Year's Day—the weather was still the same—fine and bright, but with the eternal great Atlantic rollers, the aftermath of some Western ocean storm, sweeping remorselessly along like the hordes of some invading army. The Major decided to make a larger raft, and one was accordingly constructed out of the lid of one of the rifle packing-cases. A mast was rigged up, with stays from each corner, and a soda-water bottle lashed as before. This time the message told the natives that the surf was still too bad to allow us to land, but they were not to be disappointed if we went away for a little while, as we should come back again. Our idea was to make another exploration along the coast northward to see if there was any more favourable landing-place.

This, our second raft, was launched in the afternoon, Beyerle accompanying the first mate. Three rifle-shots were fired when the little craft was sent adrift, and the natives evidently could see what we were doing, and understood the signal, as shots were sent in reply. Unfortunately, the wind was blowing off the land, and when the raft got amongst the breakers it capsized at once, its mast and little green flag lying helplessly on the water. We put this second attempt down as a failure too, as it was very doubtful if the message would drift ashore close to where our friends were, even if they could follow its progress from their point of vantage on the head of the cliff.

Our ingenuities were therefore further requisitioned, and a balloon was the expedient next resolved upon. The materials for making such an article were, however, somewhat primitive. Of silk we had none on board, except a few pocket-handkerchiefs, and paper was voted too flimsy. A roll of calico—thin, cheap stuff—was considered to be the most suitable material at our disposal, and all the next morning—Sunday, by the way—the Major, Watling, Beyerle, and I were occupied in cutting out and stitching together the requisite number of pear-shaped pieces. When completed, it was oiled to make it more air-tight, and the next thing to be considered was the lamp. It was necessary that it should be fairly light, or the balloon would never reach the shore, and the Major had a brilliant idea. Out of an old circular tobacco-tin he constructed a very efficient lamp to burn paraffin, and it was hoped that the hot air thus generated would be sufficient to float our message over the half-mile or so of sea that intervened between us and the land.

As a stand-by in case of failure, the Captain and Mr. Henfrey busied themselves with making a large paper kite; but to ensure success in either case a westerly wind was necessary. Alas, for all our trouble! The balloon was hung up on one of the ropes to dry, but Mr. Henfrey, who was taking the second dog-watch, forgot to order it to be taken in when he came down to dinner, and when we came to look for it in the morning, we found it had been blown overboard. The kite was also useless, as a heavy breeze was blowing from the south-east, and though the swell seemed to have gone down somewhat, there was no chance whatever of getting ashore that day. Everyone was gloomy and low-spirited, and it was even hinted that we might have to go back and wait till the good season in May or June.

'I've been in a good many parts of the world in sail and steam,' said Mr. Henfrey; 'but I never saw anything like this damned coast in all my life, except at Cape Cross, and there they have proper surf-boats.'

'Never mind, Mr. Henfrey,' I said. 'Let's get the dinghy out and have a spin for mackerel;' and anything being better than idly staring at the shore, he readily assented.

But our ill-luck still pursued us. Not a bite did we get, nor even the sight of a fish, except a brute of a shark that swam lazily round our boat as though he were loafing about on the off-chance of our being upset by one of the big waves that came rolling along, now lifting us up on the crest, now hiding the yacht and all the coast from view.

The next morning brought some slight improvement in the swell, but the wind was still blowing from the south-east, rendering the kite useless. If only it would blow pretty hard for about twenty-four hours we thought there would be a prospect of it flattening out the sea; but there was nothing for it but to wait and possess our souls in patience. If it had not been that the day we arrived off the coast the sea had been smooth, with no swell to speak of, we should all, I think, have come to the conclusion that we might have to wait weeks before landing. In fact, most of us, I believe, had come to that conclusion, but the Major alone, like Brer Rabbit, 'lay low, and kept on saying nothing.'

By way of a diversion, if nothing else, the Major

ordered steam up, and we went slowly along the coast northwards, keeping a sharp look-out for any break, either in the shore or in the surf, which would provide us with an opportunity to land. All those streams that were marked in the chart appeared to us only as dried-up watercourses, although we supposed the rainy season to be at its height. And, indeed, it rained very heavily that day—not persistently, but in sudden downpours, with bright intervals—and the clouds lay low, shrouding the mountain-tops in mist.

About ten miles' steaming brought us to Ifni, a town at the mouth of the Wad of the same name, and built up the side of a hill 300 feet above the level of the sea, easily recognisable by the little white saint-house on the beach. Throughout Morocco there is a great similarity between all these saint-houses—the tombs of some venerated followers of the Prophet—built generally of *tabbia*, or mud, in the form of a square, with turreted walls, the roof surmounted by a dome, and the whole generally whitewashed.

What constitutes a saint in Morocco is difficult accurately to state, but judging by the number of their tombs that one meets with all over the country, the qualifications for canonization cannot be very stringent. The infidel traveller is apt to form the conclusion that the greater rogue and blackguard a man is in Morocco, the better chance he stands of being venerated after death and obtaining a tomb at the public expense. As in all Mohammedan countries, idiots are considered as 'afflicted of Allah,' and therefore regarded as more or less sacred, and vagaries are tolerated from them that would land any less favoured of Allah in the nearest prison.

Quite recently there was a man in Saffi whose

particular craze was to perform acts of the grossest indecency. Frequently he would appear in the streets in a state of absolute nudity. Unfortunately, his indecencies were not always of this passive character, but his relations with the opposite sex were not interfered with, even when of the most flagrant description, because he was a saint. When one considers that any woman to whom this vicious lunatic had devoted special attention was thereafter regarded as 'favoured,' and partaking somewhat of his reflected glory and sanctity, one can easily understand that a state of things was created that was highly detrimental to the welfare of public morals.

But this is digressing. No more favourable landing-place was discovered, except perhaps at Ifni itself, but the Wad marked the northern extremity of the territory mentioned in the treaty between the Major and the tribes, and it was uncertain whether the tribe that dwelt there was friendly with the Sbooyas, who occupied the sea-coast in the Arksis district. On our way back to our old anchorage, the Major pointed out to us, about five miles from Arksis, another saint-house—the tomb of Sidi Warzuk, who gave his name also to the district—which the two natives whom the Major had brought from Mogador on his previous trip had used as a landmark to guide them home. And so off Arksis we dropped the hook again, and fell to staring at the hills we longed to climb, the outline of which we now knew by heart, and waited with what patience and good temper we could command for more favourable weather.

CHAPTER V.

ARKSIS.

A pessimist—Preparations for landing—The Major goes ashore—An unsatisfactory pow-wow—An ingenious proposal—Moorish diplomacy—Landing of the tents and stores—Description of the cove—Port Hillsborough—European relics—Curtis's expedition—His death in the Sudan—Difficult landing—Dress and appearance of the natives—Their 'wealth and taste for luxury'—Our camping-ground.

AT last! On the morning of January 5, after having been off the coast a week, we woke to find that the swell had almost disappeared, the sea only breaking when close to the beach. Where the cliffs dipped sheer into the sea there was no surf visible, the waves licking the rocks gently, instead of foaming at the mouth.

'This looks better, Mr. Henfrey,' I remarked, as I went up on the bridge to sharpen my appetite for breakfast with the morning breeze.

'Yes,' he admitted—reluctantly, I thought. 'If the wind keeps in this quarter, and blows as hard as this for another twenty-four hours, I think we might get the boat out to-morrow and see what it's like.'

This sounded very conditional, but Mr. Henfrey's worst enemy would not accuse him of being an optimist.

At breakfast the Captain thought we might try and effect a landing that morning, and ordered steam to be got up. The Major was evidently of the same opinion, as he came up attired in his khaki riding-suit instead of his yachting toggery. Watling, Beyerle and I followed his example, and the final details of the proposed expedition inland were speedily settled. The Major anticipated that Sidi Hussein ben Hashem would be at Arksis to meet us, as a large concourse of people was visible on the cliff-head, but in any case a journey to his *kasbah* at Ilirgh, some two or three days' journey inland, was looked upon as an essential part of our programme.

Horses, said the Major, would be provided by the tribesmen, but we had each brought a European saddle, as the Moorish saddles, with their high pommels and short stirrups, are anything but comfortable to one who is not used to them. These were all brought out and overhauled, the salt-laden atmosphere having tarnished the brightness of the steel work somewhat. The only members of the crew selected to accompany the party were Sabbah, who was to act as interpreter, and Tom, the second steward, to act as cook and general orderly. Each was supplied with a Marlin rifle and cartridges, a revolver, and a knife, made out of the bayonet of a Mannlicher, which was fitted with a metal sheath, and, when sharpened, made a very formidable weapon at close quarters. Thus armed, our little party would have been able to give a pretty good account of ourselves in the event of treachery or attack.

After breakfast, the yacht moved inshore about half a mile, and the gig was launched, the Major taking with him only Henfrey and Sabbah, with two sailors to row. A stiff breeze was blowing off the land, and it was some twenty minutes before we saw the boat rise on the bosom of a roller and shoot into the mouth of the cove. A few moments later, the Major, in his buff uniform, and Henfrey, in his six feet odd of stature, were easily visible, surrounded by excited natives on the cliff. Sabbah had taken a sample Mannlicher to show the natives, and presently five shots rang out. The thought flashed through my mind that something might be awry, knowing the unsavoury reputation the natives had for treachery, but there was no mistaking the report of a magazine rifle, and the natives had only flint-locks. Moreover, a glance at the cliff-head through the glasses showed the Major squatting down with his legs crossed, after the manner of the Moors, in the centre of a group of long-robed Susi. He had only been showing the capabilities of the magazine rifle.

We on the yacht were in a great state of suspense to learn the result of this pow-wow. Before the boat landed, there had been considerable waving of green flag from a venerable *shiekh* in white, and from this, and the fact that within the last few months urgent appeals had been sent to us, through Ratto, to come and trade as soon as possible, we drew a hopeful augury. The tribe, however, was evidently on the alert for any surprise, for on the highest peak of the cliff two men were posted, whose gaze was steadily fixed towards the north, whence come the *Hassani*, Sultan's troops, and other unwelcome visitors.

Henfrey returned to the yacht about one o'clock with an order to send ashore after lunch as much tent gear as could be put into the boat, but we were not cheered by his report. He said he hadn't heard, or

he couldn't understand, all that had been said ashore;
but the tribe had no money, and wanted the rifles for
nothing, as far as he could make out.

'I thought as much,' said Watling. 'These sea-
coast tribes never have any money. I felt sure there
was something wrong when Ratto told us they wanted
that $1,500.'

'What $1,500?' said I.

'Why, Ratto said they wanted $1,500 to bribe
some of the chiefs who were opposed to the treaty.
It doesn't look healthy.'

'Well, never mind,' I said. 'We know there's
plenty of money in the country, and if these beggars
don't want to pay for the guns, there are plenty of
tribes in the interior ready enough to trade.'

But to get at them was the difficulty. Still, as the
Major had ordered the tents, etc., to be sent ashore, I
presumed he had made arrangements to go up country.

The Captain and Beyerle went ashore this time,
and all returned to the yacht about five o'clock. The
Major looked rather glum as he came over the side,
and asked Watling to go down with him to his cabin
and have a chat about matters. He confirmed
Henfrey's statement that the Sbooya tribe had no
money, and said they wanted to have 2,000 rifles now.
According to the terms of the treaty, 10 per cent.
duty *ad valorem* was to be paid on all goods landed at
Arksis, and the chiefs suggested that the Major should
pay himself for the rifles out of the duties to be levied
on future consignments coming into the port. The
tribes in the interior, they said, had money, and
would buy the rifles readily enough; but if the
Sbooyas were to allow us to trade with the interior
before they themselves had new rifles, the interior

tribes would come down and seize their port, and the Sbooyas, with their flint-locks, would be unable to defend themselves, or the territory which they had sold to the Christian, against their better-armed neighbours.

It was a subtle and ingenious argument, worthy of people who, perhaps, above all the nations of the earth, are more greatly endowed by nature with the diplomatic instinct—the bad old diplomacy, I mean, which, according to the *Neue Freie Presse*, has no affinity with honesty or truth. It is recorded that when the late Sir William Kirby-Green, returning from a successful mission to the Court with a draft treaty approved by the Sultan, was seized with the apoplectic stroke which caused his death, the Grand Vizier asked the English principal Secretary of Legation, who wished the treaty confirmed in his name, whom he represented? The Secretary answered, 'Sir William.' Then said the Grand Vizier, 'The matter is finished. We have no treaties with dead men.'

But to return. The Major told them that the rifles had been bought with money that belonged to people in England, and he could not, therefore, make presents of them. He suggested letting them have 500 to go on with, but the chiefs replied that their tribe numbered 2,000 fighting men, and 500 would not be sufficient. If some got rifles and others didn't, there would be jealousy and trouble generally. The Major then tried to compromise with 1,000, hoping to balance matters by charging a higher price to the purchasing tribes; but the chiefs would not listen, and finally the *indaba* was postponed until the morrow, when more chiefs would be assembled. It also gave us an opportunity of 'sleeping on it,' but for my part I didn't think hopefully of the prospect.

The next morning I was up shortly after sunrise, intending to get Beyerle out of bed, and the dinghy off the davits, to go and grope for the anchor and thirty fathoms of chain which had parted during the breeze the day before. The sea was beautifully smooth, and the weather delightfully fine, but the engineer had not finished making the grappling-hooks, so we had to abandon our proposed enterprise.

After breakfast, the Major ordered the remainder of the tent gear, the Berthon boat, and a quantity of stores to be put into the launch. Beyerle, Henfrey and I accompanied him ashore. As we were not without hope that we might yet come to some arrangement with the tribe to allow us to travel inland, all the saddles were also put aboard the pinnace, and two sporting-gun cases, one belonging to Beyerle and the other to the Major. The Major also handed us a dozen sporting cartridges between us.

A mariner sailing casually down the coast of Sus might pass Arksis a score of times without discovering that there was a harbour for even as much as a rowboat. This is to be accounted for by the peculiar formation of the coast at this spot. At the southern extremity of a gently-sloping beach, from the other end of which a reef of rocks, almost submerged at high-water, runs at right angles into the sea, the land rises almost perpendicular from the water to the height of 170 feet. A close scrutiny reveals a break in the cliffs, and through this narrow opening the sea has rushed in for who knows how many cycles of years, and washed out for herself a snug little landlocked cove. A more perfect ideal of the smugglers' cove of romance could not well be imagined, for the bay, as soon as the entrance is gained, trends sharply to the right, and is thus almost entirely screened by the friendly cliff, which frowns menacingly out to sea. To complete the list of its virtues, the upper or southern end of the cove terminates in a narrow, sandy beach, which is completely invisible from the sea. In addition to the surf, which beats almost continuously upon this coast, the drawback to Arksis as a port is that the cove is too small for any ocean-going vessel to enter, and the submerged rocks which abound in it render it necessary that the greatest care should be exercised in the handling of even much smaller craft.

On the best maps—and here, be it remarked, the map-makers of this part of the world are often grievously at fault—its situation is marked in lat. 29° 10′ N.; and in some of the older charts it is named Port Hillsborough. This name was conferred upon it by a Captain Glasse, who ransomed some Europeans detained by the Berbers in slavery in 1760. But of a 'borough,' or even human habitation of any kind, not a sign is visible at Arksis to-day. To the south a mile or two are to be seen the ruins of a building of some description, only four rude stone walls being left standing, but this may be a relic of the last European expedition under the leadership of the late Mr. James Curtis, who visited Arksis for the last time early in 1883. I am inclined to the belief that it is of European origin, as stones were the material used in its construction, whereas all the native buildings throughout Sus are of *tabbia*—a mixture of rubble that is held together by the addition of water and an inferior kind of lime that is found throughout Morocco and Sus. No definite information, however, was obtainable from the natives, although they well remembered 'Curti,' and spoke of him in kindly terms.

Poor Curtis! His trading venture with the Sbooyas was a dead failure. He was swindled right and left by these scoundrelly thieves, and shortly afterwards went to Egypt to try and reach Khartum, where Gordon was upholding the British flag against the Mahdi, and wearily waiting for the relief that was sent to him two days 'too late.' Curtis spoke Arabic, or, at least, Moghrebin, fairly well, and travelled, as he had done in Sus, in the garb of a Moslem; but his disguise was not sufficient to deceive the Mohammedans themselves, and he vanished, like many another brave man before and after him, in the devouring maw of the insatiable Sudan.

One relic of his stay at Arksis is certainly visible to-day. From the head of the cove the red rock rises sharply upwards, but up its steep slopes a narrow zigzag pathway was cut under his directions by the natives to facilitate the climb, and the carriage of goods, from the beach to the plateau above. But where the booted Christian would painfully climb with faltering steps, the native Berber from the hills, and the Arab from the desert, run up and down these sharp rocks and stones in bare or slippered feet with the agility and surefootedness of the mountain-goat. Their lean, brown, sinewy legs are scored with white lines where the sharp thorns of the cactus scrub have scratched their hardened skins.

We did not consider it safe to beach the launch, for fear of damaging the screw, so the Berthon canvas boat was brought into requisition, and one by one we landed, being finally carried ashore on the backs of the natives, who tucked their clothes under their arms and waded into the water. The tents, instruments, etc., were brought ashore in a similar manner, and deposited on the beach.

The excitement of the natives on our landing was amusing to witness. The more dignified of them squatted on their haunches on the ridge of the cliff, and cuddled their long guns after the manner of Moors. But the rest came scrambling down the rocks chattering and gesticulating like a lot of monkeys, and formed round each of us an eager and curious group. Our weapons were, of course, the object of the greatest interest, the revolvers especially evoking wonder and covetousness in a marked degree. Our watches also created considerable astonishment, but as they were not things wherewith you could slay your neighbour or your enemy, they soon fell back on fingering our revolvers, and admiring the points and edges of our knives.

They were not by any means prepossessing in appearance, being unwashed in body and *farouche* in expression. The wives of many of the Susi tribesmen are negresses—slave or freed—and the large admixture of negro blood is evidenced in their thick lips and dark skin. In stature they are of medium height, and, though thin and slender, are exceedingly strong and wiry. Their physical endurance is remarkable, and nothing is thought of a man covering on foot forty or fifty miles a day for several days together, with perhaps only one meal in every twenty-four hours. They have also that exquisite grace of pose and carriage which is characteristic of the Berber race; and, indeed, I think it is no exaggeration to say that one has to go back to ancient statuary to match the

OUR CAMP AT ARKSIS.

beauty of their bodies and the elegance of their attitudes.

Their clothing consists of a pair of cotton drawers tight at the knee and tied in at the waist, such as are common throughout Morocco; a *keshaba*, or sleeveless shirt—also made of cotton—and a hooded *sulham*, or cloak, made of calico, bleached or unbleached, and sometimes dyed blue, of rough woollen material woven in the country by their womenkind, and even sometimes blue Melton cloth imported from England. The *haik* is seldom worn, but the *jelaba* is frequently worn in cold weather. The *sulhams* of these people were mostly made of coarse unbleached calico, and dirty in the extreme, which gave their wearers the appearance of certain domestic insects when seen at a distance scrambling up the cliffside. Taken altogether they were a cut-throat-looking crowd, and externally, at any rate, showed no signs of that 'wealth and taste for luxury' which the Major had described in such glowing and picturesque terms to his financial backers in London.

When all our goods and baggage had been landed in safety on the beach, the Major took a survey and measurements of the cove, the natives meanwhile carrying the tents, etc., to the plateau on the top, where under our direction the three smaller ones were pitched, and the baggage, etc., stored. We learned that all our messages had come ashore, the bottle in one instance only having been smashed against the rocks.

On reaching the summit, a great plateau was spread before us, stretching inland to the depth of a mile or so, where it was bounded by a range of hills rising some 1,500 feet above the level of the sea, and up and down the coast as far as the eye could reach. The position commanded a magnificent view of the sea, the aforesaid hills, and little else. Not a tree was to be seen, the ground being covered with short, scrubby cactus growth, so firm and hardy as to bear the weight of a man. There was scarcely a foot space between one plant and another, and, while we cursed as we tripped at nearly every other step, we little thought that two of us would owe the saving of our lives to those same wretched roots before many days had passed.

CHAPTER VI.

THE INDABA.

A rough-and-ready meal—The *Ait Arbain*—Reading the treaty—The prospects of trade—How to get rifles on credit—The Major returns to the yacht—He leaves three 'sportsmen' ashore—Laziness as a fine art—Native offerings—Theft in the camp, and how it was dealt with—A novel pillow.

BUSINESS was on the *tapis*, but before we could deal we must needs dine, as is the way of Englishmen. A rough-and-ready meal was made of tinned meats, captains' biscuits, and water, a liquid quite ruddy with the clay that the recent rains had washed into the streams and wells. To cut the meat we used our pocket-knives, to break the biscuits we used the butt-end of our revolvers, and to drink the water we shut our eyes and forgot everything but the pleasure of having something cold and wet trickling down our dried-up throats. The day was cloudless and the heat intense, and the water almost 'sizzled,' like a splash on a hot oven, as it passed down our sun-baked throats.

Throughout Sus the sovereignty of the Sultan is recognised only in spiritual matters. He is the acknowledged head of the Church, but in temporal matters each tribe is a republic, governed by its *Ait*

Arbain, or Council of Forty, elected from among its members. This was the council that was then summoned, and mats were spread out in front of the tent for a solemn conference.

In the middle of the tent sat the Major; next to him was Sabbah, to interpret, while the rest of us squatted round on provision-boxes, saddles, or anything else available. At the door sat Muley Abdallah, a sheríf who had acted as agent or intermediary between Ratto and the tribes, and Sidi Hassan, an *adul*, or notary, who was armed with a reed pen and an ink-well, made of one barrel of an old pair of field-glasses, the bottom being tin where the glass had been, and the screw top still preserved. Behind these were grouped Sidi Mohammed el Tamanari, and Embarak o-Hamed, the two chiefs who had signed the treaty with the Major in Mogador, and some fifteen or twenty of the Sbooya *Ait Arbain*. Since his return to Sus, Embarak o-Hamed had been dubbed by his tribe El F'kir* Embarak, but whether on account of the success of his mission, or his increasing weakness of intellect, I never discovered, though I inclined to the latter belief.

After the reading of the treaty by the notary—which was interrupted by the ejaculation of '*aiwa smad*'† at every difficult word he came to, and which sounded to us like a reflection on his own sanity—the Major asked for the names of the tribes that were agreeable to join in carrying out its provisions, and a list of fifteen was handed in. The chiefs expressed their pleasure at seeing us in their country, and stated that the protection of our lives and property would be their unsleeping care. They added, however, that the

* Saint. † You know.

Sultan's troops had recently been down to that part of the country, but the Susi had beaten them back. They would be sure to return, and we must protect them against their attacks. Muley Abdallah referred to the treaty, which contained a provision to this effect, and the Major replied that it was precisely with that object in view that we had brought the rifles. He was, however, disappointed that, of the forty-seven tribes in Sus, only fifteen were there represented, and he urged that the treaty would be valueless unless the adherence of all the others, or, at any rate, the most powerful of them, was secured. They replied that letters had been sent to them all, and more chiefs were expected daily. The Major said he was specially anxious to get the co-operation and adherence of Sidi Dakhman Bairuk, of Wad Nun, and Sidi Hussein ben Hashem. The former had so far not taken any active part in these negotiations, and Sidi ben Hashem had only treated through agents. The chiefs replied that they didn't care for Dakhman, as he was friendly with the Sultan, but Hussein ben Hashem would be down on the coast in three or four days.

The Major again impressed upon them the desirability of getting the co-operation of as many tribes as possible, so as to avoid jealousy and inter-tribal wars, and pointed out that the more trade they succeeded in diverting through Arksis, the better for them all, as there would be the more Customs duty to divide amongst the signatory tribes. They assented, and said that there was no reason why we should not tap the trade of Timbuctoo, the great Sahra, and the Western Sudan. The country in the interior was extremely rich, and produced ivory, gold, gum, wool, skins, leather, olive-oil, honey, almonds, ostrich feathers, etc. A letter was then produced by them purporting to be signed by fourteen tribes, which set forth that, if the Christian came, any arrangement that the Sbooyas should make with him would be agreeable to them, as they were very desirous of opening up a port in their own country, instead of being obliged to use the Sultan's. They reiterated, however, that the whole project was attended with danger, as Kaid Said el Giluli, one of the most powerful chiefs in the neighbourhood of Mogador, had been sent by the Sultan a short while before to fight the Sbooyas, but the latter had beaten him off, with the loss of 300 or 400 men, and about 60 horses. Consequent upon this reverse, Giluli had retired across the Sus border, but he would be sure to return as soon as he had collected reinforcements.

'Well,' said the Major, 'so far as to trade generally. Now, as to the rifles, I am prepared to carry out the arrangement made yesterday as soon as the tribes who have the money to pay for them come down here and buy them. For every rifle thus sold I will let you have one on the terms of deferred payment agreed upon yesterday, up to the number of 2,000.'

But this was hardly to their liking.

'Sidi Hussein,' said their spokesman, 'has much money; his gold and silver pieces are as the stars of heaven for multitude; and he will come and see the Christian, and buy his guns and his cloth before many suns have set, but our enemies—Allah burn their fathers—are at hand, and unless we have the Christian's rifles to fight with, they will come upon us and eat us up. Give us therefore our rifles before the sun goes down, and we shall then fear nothing, neither the Sultan nor his armies.'

The suggestion was excellent from their point of view, but left much to be desired from a commercial standpoint. We had really no guarantee that the statements they made would be verified by after-events, or that the attitude of Sidi ben Hashem and the other tribes towards us had been correctly represented; and to arm the Sbooyas—an eminently warlike rather than commercial tribe—with 2,000 magazine rifles would be simply putting a strong temptation before them to go off and try their newly-acquired weapons upon the first enemy they could find.

They were, however, very insistent, and urged upon the Major the danger of some unfriendly tribe making a raid upon them, and seizing their port. But if they had the new rifles they would have no fear, and would make trade easy for us with friendly tribes, and get us 40 or 50 dollars for each rifle.

The Major then suggested that they should provide an escort for us, and we would march inland to Ilirgh to see Sidi ben Hashem himself; but this also they resolutely refused to do until the whole tribe was fully equipped, in case of attack whilst we were away.

It was very disheartening, and no alternative seemed left to us but to comply with their wishes, unless we were to throw up the whole deal, and return home with our cargo undischarged. The Major therefore agreed to land as many as we could that night, and go on from day to day until Sidi ben Hashem came; and the pow-wow broke up. But his intention was to spin out the process of discharging as long as possible, to allow developments to occur, and as it was then nearly four o'clock, orders were given for the launch to go back to the steamer, and bring only fifty rifles, a quantity of cartridges, and a number of bales of cloth.

A stroll on the head of the cliff was tempting after the close and oppressive air of the tent, and there we bent our steps.

'What do you think of that for an *indaba*?' the Major asked me.

I ventured to suggest that it might have been more satisfactory.

'Well, we have burnt our boats now,' he added with a smile.

I endeavoured to show a satisfaction I was far from feeling by remarking that that was often the way to victory, and the Major said he didn't believe in hesitating when decision was imperative. Considerable disappointment was expressed by the natives when the launch returned with only fifty rifles, but the Major endeavoured to pacify them by telling them that the boat couldn't carry very many, and the cartridges were heavy. The crowd on the plateau numbered some 2,000 men by this time, and many of them came running down to the beach in the cove in the hope that they would be the lucky recipients; but the rifles, ammunition and cloth were all given to the principal chiefs for them to dispose of as they thought fit. The goods were, therefore, carried up the cliff, and deposited in one of the smaller tents that we had pitched.

'Are *you* going to stay ashore?' said Watling, turning to the Major.

'No,' he replied; 'why should I stay ashore when I have got a comfortable bed on board the yacht? Grey and Beyerle and Sabbah are going to stop.'

And as it seemed to both Beyerle and me that it was desirable *someone* should look after the instruments, and other property of value that had been landed by the Major's orders, and he himself, contrary to our expectations, was returning to the *Tourmaline*, we stayed. If the question resolved itself into the comparative comfort of our beds afloat or ashore, we had no doubt that it would have been decided in favour of a camp-bed, but we little knew then the risks we ran, or dreamt of such things as afterwards befell us. In any case, it was not that we preferred to stay ashore to get some shooting, as Major Spilsbury afterwards reported. People don't, as a rule, go partridge-shooting at night-time; and, anyhow, there is not much sport to be had with only a dozen cartridges between two men. If there was any shooting to be done at all, it was more likely to be *at* us as targets, than *by* us as sportsmen. Moreover, the Major himself was expected to come ashore again first thing the next morning.

Returning to our camp, we found our tents—a soldiers' bell-tent and two Moorish ones—were occupied by natives. In one of them an old man, suffering from ophthalmia, was calling upon Allah to relieve him of his sufferings, but was too lazy even to brush away the flies that came to torment him, contenting himself with merely exclaiming 'Balak, balaka, wa!' when a fly settled on his sore lids. Seeing me, he appealed for medicine, evidently sharing the belief common among the Moors, that all Christians understand the healing art. And certainly they make the best of patients, having the sublime and perfect faith which, if not enabling them to remove mountains, certainly assists them to remove their pains. I hadn't the heart to tell him I could do nothing for him, so I got out some lanoline—which at least was harmless—and applied a little to his inflamed lids. He didn't trouble to thank me, but gratitude is not a strong point with these people. If one were to save the life of a Moor, the rescued man would in all probability turn round and ask his benefactor for the means of maintaining the life he had interfered to preserve!

But there were other things to think about just then. The largest tent of all, which we intended for our use, was not yet pitched, and as the sun was on the point of sinking below the horizon, it behoved us to make haste, if we wished to finish before the short tropical twilight had faded into darkness. With the help of the natives it was soon rigged up, and it was then time to see about getting supper ready, and make sure that all our personal belongings, the instruments, provisions, etc., were safely housed.

Meanwhile presents of honey in goatskins, fowls, etc., were brought, which we accepted with that matter-of-fact air that seems to be the proper thing to assume under such circumstances in Morocco. Sabbah, who knew the customs of the country, went farther, and upbraided the chiefs for their meanness. Where was our meat? Why, not even a sheep or a goat had they slaughtered for us! For people of our distinction, who had travelled so far to see them, a bullock at least should have been offered, and so on. And, indeed, his exhortations and abuse had such an effect upon them that a bullock was brought and presented to us with all due solemnity; after which they borrowed my knife wherewith to kill it.

Their method of killing is different from ours in that they cut the animal's throat, and let it bleed to death. In like manner also, they do not wring the necks of fowls, but cut their heads off. Nor would they touch the meat of animals or fowls killed by Christians. A Jew will only eat the flesh of animals killed in prescribed form by one of his religion; the Moor has no religious ceremony in connection with the slaughter of animals, but unless they have been killed by a Mohammedan or a Jew, he will not eat the meat. The Christian cares not who killed the beasts, being only interested in who shall eat them.

A large fire of brushwood was made in front of our tent, and the bullock having by this time been cut up and dressed, we gave most of it to the tribesmen, ourselves preferring to make a meal of canned tongue, or *bœuf à la daube*, to meat from which the blood had scarcely ceased to run. What was left we laid on the ground outside the tent, and looked forward to succulent steaks on the morrow.

We had scarcely finished our supper, when there was a great row outside in the camp, everybody talking and shouting at once. Rushing out to ascertain the cause of this disturbance, we found that one of the tribesmen had been detected stealing the bullock's head. He was immediately haled before the *Ait Arbain*, or Council of Forty, which throughout Sus is the governing body of the tribe. Our first impulse was to intercede for the culprit, as he had worked hard for us during the day, carrying goods up the cliff, and pitching tents, etc., but we were advised to let the law take its course, otherwise we should be subject constantly to theft. And, after all, we were somewhat curious to see how justice was administered by these wild, unruly people. It was short and sharp. Proof of the crime having been given, the offender was fined 6 dollars, or three-fourths of the value of the whole bullock, and, as he had nothing like this sum in his possession, his gun and two *cumias* (curved and pointed dagger-knives worn throughout Morocco and Sus) were taken from him as security, and lodged in our tent.

It was a strange sight, this camp of ours among the wilds of Sus. We had expected that with nightfall most of the men would have gone to their homes, but to these hardy mountaineers, wrapped in their *sulhams*, with the hoods drawn over and enveloping their heads, a night passed under the wide canopy of heaven was as comfortable as under the shelter of a roof. Before turning in, Beyerle and I took a turn round. The watch-fires still gleamed brightly, revealing round each a circle of sleeping natives, while the clear, full moon shone like a silver lamp in the cloudless, starry sky above. And as we turned towards our own tent-door, there, in the shadow, lay a man fast asleep, his long gun cuddled in his arms, and his head *resting on our side of beef!* Our visions of juicy steak on the morrow suddenly lost their charm.

CHAPTER VII.

THE COUNCIL OF THE 'FORTY.'

A quiet discussion—Dispensing and surgery—Sidi Hashem's matrimonial troubles—A terrible threat—'Mr. Garden'—An unpleasant discovery—The mineral wealth of Morocco—An earthly paradise—Sworn friends—Bad weather still cuts our communication with the yacht—'Important news'—Tea-making and tea-drinking—An impudent forgery—A dignitary of the desert.

I WAS awakened very early the next morning by the crowing of the cocks, which, tied by their legs so as to prevent their escape, had shared the shelter of our tent; but I dozed off again, to be thoroughly roused by a great clamour outside. Hastily dressing, I inquired from Sabbah the meaning of all that disturbance, and what they were quarrelling about. Looking out of the tent door, I saw a crowd of natives that had formed themselves into excited groups, and were shouting and gesticulating at one another at the top of their voices. I expected every moment to see the knives flash out of their sheaths and blood drawn, but Sabbah quickly disabused my mind of that idea.

'They not quarrelling,' he said—'only talking among themselves.'

If that was the row they made when they were just having a little friendly conversation, I wondered what sort of a pandemonium they would make when they were angry.

'What are they talking about—politics?' I asked.

Like the Irish, they have their burning question of Home Rule, and their discussions suggested the proceedings of an Irish Parliament—everyone talking and nobody listening—and politics seemed the most likely topic of discussion, if it was not a blood-feud. In matters of religion, of course, they were all agreed, and next to religion, I suppose, politics are the most calculated to rouse the angry passions of a multitude.

'They're talking about the rifles; they want them now,' said Sabbah; but a glance at the sea didn't give much hope of their getting any more rifles that day at least. A very strong wind had sprung up in the night, and the waves were breaking a couple of hundred yards from shore in the good old style of a week before.

We had scarcely got breakfast over before a regular procession of lame, halt, sick and blind came to our tent begging for medicines. All sorts of ailments, real and imaginary, were exhibited or described. The *malades imaginaires* were easily disposed of with a bread-pill or a mild dose of salts; but such ailments as cataract, deafness, broken limbs, and bullet wounds of several years' standing, were beyond my simple remedies.

Their fortitude in bearing physical pain was admirable, and their simple faith was beautiful to witness. Quite calmly one man bared his arm, and showing the spot where a bullet was embedded, requested me to cut out the ball with the scissors I was then holding in my hand. On my declining to do so, he suggested that I might use the knife I carried in my belt, the one with which the bullock had been killed the night before. He was quite disappointed when I refused to undertake the operation.

Another man, a pure Arab from the desert, Sidi Hashem by name, who had made himself very much at home in our tent, and had only, with the greatest reluctance, allowed himself to be turned out when we went to bed the night before, asked me if I could do anything for his wife, who, to his great sorrow, had not borne him any children. I suggested that possibly the fault lay with him; but he said no, he had already a child by another wife. The Mohammedan religion allows a man four wives, so I told him I was afraid there was nothing for it but to get another one: it was the infliction of Allah.

'No,' he said, shaking his head, 'I have had this wife ten years, and she is the best woman in all my country. I do not wish to marry any other'—an example of conjugal attachment not too frequently met with among his Moorish neighbours.

He then asked me if I had any poison, but I told him I had brought none from the ship. I wondered to what use he intended to apply it, but rather suspected, from remarks that he let fall, that he was desirous of removing his other more favoured spouse.

The morning wore on, and as the natives saw no sign of a further consignment of rifles, they began to get very angry and make a noisy demonstration round our tent. As the excitement increased, I sent for some of the *Ait Arbain* to explain to them that the guns would come as soon as the sea calmed down, but that if they didn't behave themselves they wouldn't get any at all. They feared, or pretended to fear, that we meant to break faith with them, but we pointed out that the fact of our being there and pitching our camp amongst them was the best guarantee they could have that we meant to carry out our promises. They were very much like children to whom a new toy had been promised, crying because they couldn't have it at once; but we succeeded ultimately in appeasing them.

Shortly afterwards I made the discovery that a shirt of mine had been stolen from the tent during the night, as also a tin of milk and a teapot. It was then our turn to become indignant, and, as the most terrible threat I could think of at the time, I vowed I would give no more medicines until the articles were returned. Some said that they had seen a boy with the shirt, and undertook to get it restored to me. An examination of the tent showed that there was a small gap in the canvas on one side through imperfect pitching, and we therefore set to work to rig it up properly, and make ourselves secure from similar depredations in future.

The chiefs then complained that a great number of people in the camp had come from a great distance, and were starving for want of food. We told them that that was no fault of ours: we had no food for them, and they had better return to their own homes; they hadn't come to do any trade, and we didn't want them to remain at Arksis. The 'Forty' grasped this simple fact after some argument, and told the people to go back home. On this, most of them went away when it got towards sunset, many of them coming again in the morning, but the 'Forty' themselves remained in the camp. They appointed a slave to wait upon us, fetch water from the well, etc.; but as they subsequently entertained doubts as to his honesty, he was replaced by one of their own tribesmen, Ibrahim Jinan, the fisherman.

'Mr. Garden,' as his surname implied, and as we soon learned to call him, was a character. With his little, round, close-fitting woollen fishing-cap, he looked as if he had just stepped out of 'The Arabian Nights,' especially when, his work being finished for the time being, he was taking his ease squatting on the top of a provision-box, and smiling like a Japanese idol. He was the happy possessor of a proper fishing-rod and reel, and still had some fish-hooks which had been given to him by 'Curti'; but he begged of us to bring him some more when next we came to Arksis, which we promised to do. He would catch us fish, and bring us fowls and honey from his own house, and was faithful to the last. His reward was a piece of cloth and my revolver.

In the afternoon of that day, all expectations of a boat coming ashore being given up, Beyerle proposed to me that we should go for a walk, and explore the neighbourhood. We were curious to see what was on the other side of that wall of hills that bounded the plateau. We set out, but were promptly stopped, and it was more or less delicately conveyed to us that we were virtually prisoners. When the tribe had all had their rifles—*their* rifles, mark you—then we could do as we liked, and they would show us where the gold was to be found in the ground. Where the copper was to be found did not need much looking for, as not 100 yards from our tent both Beyerle and I picked up a pocketful of specimens of the metal which would have shown, I am sure, a very satisfactory assay.

I have met several people who are convinced that, in addition to its extreme fertility, Morocco possesses a boundless wealth in gold, copper, zinc, lead, antimony, etc. But the Moors, with that ridiculous fanaticism which characterizes them, are strongly opposed to any mining operations, on the ground that what God has concealed let no man reveal, and so far no one has succeeded, or is likely to succeed, in obtaining from the Sultan a concession to 'work' any portion of his territory for mineral wealth.

The Berbers, however, are not so fanatical in their religious ideas as the Sultan-ridden Moors, although they acknowledge the Sultan as head of their faith, and it will probably one day be proved that there is in Sus a rich, undeveloped field nearer than the Transvaal or Klondike, and set, not amid the Arctic snows, but in a veritable earthly paradise.

This restriction on our movements was decidedly annoying, but there was nothing for it but to acquiesce with what grace we could. But it was extremely irritating, whenever we took a stroll down to the beach or the head of the cliff, to find two or three fellows close upon our heels, with their watchful eyes ever keenly fixed upon us. Beyond this, however, they showed no signs of hostility. On the contrary, with some of them we were on very good terms.

Indeed, that very afternoon, while we were having our green tea, we invited Sidi Hashem, and Sid el Embarak o-Jama—one of the 'Forty'—to have a glass with us. Under the genial influence of the beverage they became very amiable, and told us that they were our friends, and, as they had broken bread with us, they would at all times protect us. Sidi Hashem swore solemn fealty to Beyerle, and Embarak o-Jama took me under his protecting ægis. It was the custom of their country, they said. In token of this understanding, Embarak made me a present of his flint-lock gun, and said he would also give me two daggers.

He had a hankering after a metal travelling-knife, a sort of 'all-in-all' fitted with corkscrew, tin-opener, horseshoe-picker, etc.; but as this was also my dinner knife, cutlery having been overlooked when we came ashore, I promised to give it him when we could go back to the yacht.

When night came on, in consideration of favours received, and in anticipation of benefits to come in their capacity as mediators and pacificators, we allowed them to share the shelter of our tent, with our faithful servant, 'Mr. Garden,' at the door. They asked for a candle, as they would keep awake all night on watch, and in return for this obliging offer the least we could do was to provide them with a light. But we had hardly got comfortably settled in our canvas cots when a sudden gale sprang up, which continued all night, the rain pouring down in torrents, some of it even finding its way inside the tent. The tent swayed ominously at times as though it would collapse altogether, and that very likely would have been the case had not the duteous 'Mr. Garden' gone out and made fast the pegs which the tent-ropes were tearing out of the ground under the strain of the wind.

We rose the next morning about 7.30, to find that the storm had abated somewhat; the rain had ceased, but the sea was still rough. There was the same nonsense about the rifles as the previous morning, and, to appease the natives, we went to the head of the cliff and waved a white flag—a handkerchief tied to the end of a flint-lock gun—and fired three shots, which was the pre-arranged signal in case of danger. We felt sure, however, that it was only waste of energy and powder, as the surf was far too high to allow any boat to land. What was far more to my liking, I went and had a dip in the cove, which Sabbah told the people was a signal to the yacht to come, and the idiots believed it, although the beach was invisible from the sea. About ten o'clock, however, steam was observed coming from the escape-pipe, and our first thought was that the *Tourmaline* was going to move in from the anchorage she had taken up during the night; but we were doomed to disappointment. The waves from our post of observation on the heights seemed bad enough, but to those on the deck of the yacht they would appear much more formidable.

In the course of the morning, with an air of great secrecy and mystery, some of the 'Forty' came to our tent, and told us they had received important news. They were accordingly invited inside. Shuffling off their slippers—for the Moslem never treads on a mat or a carpet except in his bare feet, but leaves his slippers at the entrance—they squatted down, and produced two letters, which they stated had just come in from other tribes. Sabbah put on his spectacles, and slowly translated them. They set forth the desire of the tribe to trade with the Christian, but, in addition to the customary form of greeting and valediction, the two effusions struck me as being remarkably similar in expression. I put the letters in my pocket, thanked the chiefs, and invited them to *shurub atay*.*

The drinking of tea in Morocco is a solemn function, and every pretext is seized upon by the Moors for indulging in their favourite beverage. The charcoal-stove and kettle are the indispensable, and frequently among the poorer classes, with the exception of a

* Drink tea.

grass mat, the only articles of furniture in a Moorish room. A round brass table, with the requisite number of small glass tumblers and a teapot, are brought in, and the host officiates. A handful of green tea, usually of the kind known as 'gunpowder,' is put into the pot, and a small quantity of boiling water is poured in. The teapot is then shaken, and the liquid, of a dirty green colour, is poured out and thrown away. This is called 'washing' the tea, and is supposed to remove the poison which the tea-leaves absorb when rolled on the copper slabs before being put upon the market. After this a great lump of loaf-sugar is put into the pot, which is then filled up with boiling water. No spoon is used to stir the pot, the sugar being dissolved by the tea being poured backwards and forwards into one of the glasses. This operation being repeated several times, the host then takes a sip to see if the tea is sweet enough—the Moors all like it like syrup—and then all the glasses are filled. The guests all sit round, and the host hands a glass to each. With a muttered 'Bismillah,' the tea is consumed with a loud sipping noise and much smacking of lips. To drink it as we should drink, say, a whisky-and-soda is considered the worst of bad form. Meanwhile, the pot being emptied, the host has put in more sugar, and filled it up with more water, and so on, the guests replacing their glasses on the tray as they empty them. At least three glasses are *de rigueur*. To profess satisfaction with one or two would be discourteous to your host. Conversation is general, and among the less religiously observant, a cigarette or a pipe of *kif** is indulged in.

The Susi are no less addicted to the habit, and under

* Native tobacco.

Sabbah's guidance the etiquette of this business was soon learnt, and we were able to dispense hospitality in proper form.

At the conclusion of the ceremony, the chiefs rose and took their departure. When they had gone, Beyerle, who had learned something of the wiles of the Mohammedan during a long residence in Egypt, turned to me, with a meaning look upon his face, and said:

'Did you notice anything about those letters?'

'I thought the wording of them both was very much alike,' I replied. 'Why?'

'Let me have a look at them,' he said by way of answer, and I accordingly spread them out on the table. 'There! do you see that?' he exclaimed. 'Those two letters are written on the same sheet of paper, torn in two. They have got the same sort of lines on them; and look, the two pieces fit where the paper has been torn. The d——d scoundrels!'

'By Jove! you're right,' I assented; 'and the hand-writing is the same, too, when you come to look at it. What a fraud!'

Our first impulse was to go out and tax the 'Forty' with this barefaced attempt to foist a forgery upon us, a shameless forgery concocted and committed in our very camp; but on consideration we decided that our wisest plan was to give no sign that we suspected anything. The incident, however, troubled us a great deal, and gave rise in our minds to the gravest fears that the natives did not mean business, as we understood the word, at all. We began to be anxious, too, about the state of the weather, and to speculate as to what might be our position, unless a change for the better took place soon. We knew that there were a number of hostile natives about the camp, and there was no telling what these devils might get up to.

Reflection on these points was not a pleasant occupation, so I took refuge in writing up my diary. But I was not allowed to forget that I was the *tabib*, or doctor, of the place, and I was constantly interrupted by patients. My shirt and our teapot had been returned by one of the 'Forty,' and I had therefore no valid excuse for refusing to dispense such relief as lay in my power. One man, who had made us a present of a couple of fowls in the morning, brought his little girl in the afternoon to see if I could do anything for her. She was simply covered with the most loathsome sores—the sins of the fathers visited upon the children—and it was pitiful to think that I could do nothing for her. I didn't tell the father so—he wouldn't have believed me if I had—so I just gave her a cooling draught and some ointment, and sent them away in peace.

The presence of Sidi Hashem in our tent was also a disturbing factor, all sorts of people coming continually to see him. He called himself a *shiekh*, and wore a green *sulham*, the colour affected very much by saints, sherífs, etc., and whether it was for ghostly comfort or more material benefit, I don't know, but he seemed to be in great request among the tribesmen. Indeed, it became a positive nuisance, and finally we got angry, and told this dignitary of the desert that if anyone wanted to see him he must go outside to talk, and not fill our tent with all the scum of the camp.

I half expected some violent retort, but he merely looked mild reproof from out his dark-brown eyes, as he sat among the saddles in the corner, and, with an expressive gesture, asked his 'friend' Beyerle for a cigarette. Except where their religion or their parentage is introduced, these people take insults very quietly. Courtesy is wasted upon them—indeed, it is generally misinterpreted for cowardice; but order them about like dogs, and they respect you in proportion as they fear you.

As night approached, the wind increased, until by midnight it was blowing with hurricane force, and we several times feared our tent would come down. All through the night our man 'Brahim Jinan was on the alert, frequently going outside to see that all the pegs were firm. Several of the 'Forty,' too, came sneaking in during the night, on the pretence of keeping watch, but really in search of comfortable quarters. With four fowls also in the tent, two of them lusty roosters that didn't forget to let you know when sunrise was approaching, we were not exactly lonely.

CHAPTER VIII.

DAMP DAYS.

An execution—The etiquette of eating—Sidi Hashem and his 'magnificent barb'—How a Susi sleeps—A bedraggled camp—Our commissariat department—Grinding corn—We go mussel-fishing—The wreck of our launch—A false alarm, and its moral—The Moslems at prayer.

I GOT up the next morning breathing slaughter.

'Wring that noisy rooster's neck, Sabbah—the white fellow—and we'll have him boiled for dinner, being Sunday. What with the jabbering of the natives and the crowing of these infernal fowls, there's no getting any decent sleep.' And the offending fowl was promptly executed.

Out of deference to the susceptibilities of the natives, however, Sabbah did not wring his neck in the approved European fashion, but cut his throat with a knife after the manner of the Moslem. To make an effective job of it he completely decapitated the luckless bird, and his astonishment at seeing the fowl execute a *pas seul* in a wild, gory dance of death before rolling over on his side was comical to witness.

The first news we had was that the gale had blown down one of the tents in the night. The natives had not had the sense to put it up again, but had just lain under the canvas till daylight. When morning came they asked us to fix it up again for them, but we told them that if they couldn't do it themselves, or were too lazy, they didn't deserve to have one to live in, and left them to their own resources. The rain was still pouring down in torrents, the sea was rough, and we observed with some alarm that our supplies were getting low—a combination of circumstances that was calculated to somewhat depress our spirits.

Some of the 'Forty' had managed to get some meat from somewhere, and, having boiled it, asked to be allowed to eat it in our tent, which we granted. Among the Moors, as with the Spaniards, it is the custom for anyone having a meal to invite any bystanders to share it, and, meat being a luxury at Arksis, the object of these people was to prevent there being any bystanders. The pan in which the meat had been cooked was brought in and set upon the ground. The chiefs sat round it in a circle, and with a hasty preliminary 'Bismillah' plunged their right hands into the smoking dish. In Morocco, the left hand is never used whilst eating, and, contrary to the tea-drinking etiquette, conversation is never indulged in. For about five minutes it was serious business, the men tearing at their food like famished dogs, and finishing up by drinking the water in which it had been boiled. The bones were then given to the servants, or thrown to the starving mongrels that prowled about the camp.

In the afternoon Sidi Hashem ordered his negro slave to saddle his horse, as he was going home for a day or so. This, by the way, was, acccording to Sabbah, the same animal that had been brought for the Major to ride, on the occasion of his first visit.

But then, in the Major's poetic language, it was 'a magnificent barb, bedecked with trappings of green velvet and gold.' As we saw it, it was certainly the best horse in the camp, and might have fetched 20 dollars in the market at Mogador, but the harness was of the meanest and shabbiest description. As for velvet, I doubt if Sidi Hashem had ever seen that material, and gold was a commodity with which he was barely on nodding terms. He had already given his dagger to Beyerle, but now that he was going home he wanted it; he might require to *use* it on the way. A gun and a knife to these children of Nature are like a walking-stick to an Englishman. You rarely meet a Susi or a Moor in the country without one or both—or in the towns, either, for the matter of that. Perhaps he noticed the look of disappointment in Beyerle's face, for he promised to bring back a knife from his house, and also some bread and honey for us. Certainly bread and honey would not have come amiss, but as he rode away towards the hills I thought his back-view was the best.

At any rate, our tent was much quieter after he had left, though we had a new arrival to take his place the same afternoon. This man, Khabib by name, was a tall, fine-looking man, who looked as if he did occasionally wash both his body and his clothes. He also possessed that rare gift among the Berbers, a melodious voice. He presented me with a dagger, and did not ask for it back again at any subsequent time, and in return I offered him a collapsible air-pillow. He looked at it for a time, asked if it was made of *halûf*,* and carefully watched me blow it up. Then he smiled, showing a double row of glistening

* Used indiscriminately for pig, wild-boar, bacon, or pork.

teeth, and said he had no use for it, as he didn't lie down to sleep. I thought he was joking, but he proceeded to show me how he wooed the God of Slumbers, and I found out afterwards that most of his kind adopted the same attitude. Squatting down on his haunches, with his back against some support, he embraced his knees with his arms, and leaning his head thereon, he would be as comfortable as a Christian in a feather bed. A Christian would get cramp in his legs in a very few minutes, but a Susi can sit like that for hours together, without having any desire or inclination to alter his position.

The bad weather still continued, and the next morning our camp had a very damp and bedraggled appearance. The pole of one of the remaining tents had snapped in the middle during the night, and the tent which had been blown down the previous night, and which had been rigged up again by the natives after a fashion, was blown to ribbons. But still a arge number of men remained in the camp, rather than go to their homes and wait for fine weather. We had not enough tents to shelter them all, but many of them contented themselves with building a rough stone wall, horseshoe shape, as a protection against the wind, and lighting a fire of brushwood for warmth. The rain, which generally fell at night, they did not seem to mind, though they looked forlorn and dripping objects in the morning.

We had no great anxiety yet concerning our food-supply, as we had brought from the yacht several boxes full of canned meats and vegetables, and though we had exhausted our original stock of groceries, nearly every day some or other of the natives would bring us bread, green tea, honey, sugar, etc. The bread was made of barley and water, without leaven, and baked in an earthenware bowl over a charcoal-stove fire. The 'loaves' were really barley pancakes, varying from an eighth of an inch to an inch in thickness, but very unpalatable. The grinding of the corn is done by the women, probably in exactly the same manner, and with exactly the same kind of implements, as by the Jews 3,000 and 4,000 years ago. The method is primitive in the extreme. A flat stone, more or less circular, with a short wooden peg fixed in the centre, is placed upon a fine grass mat, cloth, or other receptacle for catching the flour (!), and on the top of this is placed another similar stone, but with a hole in the centre, through which the lower peg is placed. A wooden handle is fixed into the upper stone near the edge, and by means of this the woman turns it round and round, the corn to be ground being put down the hole in the middle, the flour finding its way out at the edge. Hair sieves are used for refining, but in the country districts such luxuries are seldom indulged in, the result being that the coarser kind of *khubs* tastes like a mixture of musty barley, chopped straw, and sand.

But in the circumstances in which we found ourselves it did not behove us to be fastidious, otherwise we might have found fault with the water, which, owing to the recent heavy rains, was the colour of milky tea, and left as much sediment at the bottom of the cup as would a dose of Gregory's powder.

Beyerle suggested that for a change of diet we might collect some mussels which covered the rocks at low-tide. I was agreeable, but we had hardly got down to the cove beach when 'Mr. Garden' and Khabib appeared, and volunteered to show us where the best were to be found. It would have been quite impossible for us to follow them, as, to reach the spot, it was necessary to go along the side of the cliff, hanging on to the rock in some places by the hands and bare toes. But they came back with quite a successful haul, in return for which I offered Khabib a white silk handkerchief for his wife, but, not being bright coloured, it found no favour in his sight.

When we got back to the plateau again, we went to the edge of the cliff to see what the *Tourmaline* was doing. The wind was blowing a gale from the north-west, and we noticed that the yacht had gone much farther out to sea, but even there she was pitching about very badly. The launch, too, had not been taken in, but was still afloat, though a long way astern we thought.

'They've got her out on a long cable,' I remarked. 'I wonder they haven't taken her aboard; but I suppose it has been too rough to unship her engines.'

But Beyerle, gazing steadily seawards, exclaimed:

'She's not at anchor, nor in tow; she's broken adrift.'

And sure enough, as we watched, we could see her coming gradually nearer the shore.

'I believe the yacht is not at anchor, either,' I said. 'Look, she has got steam up. Perhaps she's going to try and pick the launch up again before she drifts ashore.'

But no, she turned her nose to the westward and steamed far out to sea. We continued to watch the launch coming slowly in upon the turning tide, and hoped that it would be thrown upon the sandy beach, and not against the rocks. It seemed such a pity it should be destroyed. We had all been so proud of the trim little pinnace, with its smart brass funnel, dainty bow-plates with the Yacht Club pennant, and its tiny Union Jack. And now it was doomed. It was like watching the drowning of a favourite dog, and being powerless to help. Nearer and nearer the breakers she came, now rising on the crest of a wave, now disappearing for a moment in the trough of the sea; and as we were straining our eyes to follow her, she suddenly vanished. In her place we saw a barrel floating rapidly inshore, and knew that our bonny launch had foundered. Never more would she rouse the admiration of the good folks in Arrecife, or dodge in and out among the yachts at Cowes.

The barrel drove ashore among the rocks a little way down the coast, but it was too late to get it, as sunset was rapidly approaching. On our return to the camp we told the chiefs what had happened, and used the incident as the text for a sermon. They ought to be very grateful to us, we told them, for risking the perils of the sea to come and open trade with them on such a dangerous coast, and they should be ashamed of themselves for grumbling, because we did not land rifles in a bad sea. They listened meekly, not to say stolidly, and were like good children for the rest of the day.

About nine o'clock that night, just when we were thinking about turning in, and some of the 'Forty' whom we could not keep out of our tent were already huddled up dozing, there was a sudden alarm. Two men came rushing to the door of our tent in a great state of excitement, and said that they had heard the neighing of horses not far off. Scarcely were the words out of his mouth before the Sbooyas were on their feet. Daggers were hastily slung over their shoulders and their long guns grasped, and of course we joined them in 'belting up,' so as to be ready for any emergencies.

It proved to be a false alarm, but Sidi Mulud, one of the leading spirits among the 'Forty,' took the opportunity of pointing a moral. Our big riding-boots had from the first been a source of wonderment to him, but that anyone should take his clothes off to go to sleep was a quite incomprehensible proceeding to him. If all the Inglíz did that, in case of an enemy attacking them, he said, they would all be shot before they could get their boots on. We could only reply that if we lived in the same dread of our enemies attacking us as these fellows do, perhaps we should sleep in our clothes too. And indeed we did that night, not so much to be in readiness in case of a surprise, but in hourly apprehension that the tent would be blown down by the wind, which had by this time risen to a perfect hurricane.

And a strange sight it was in the faint candlelight to see five or six long-robed Mohammedans suddenly rise up, and turning towards Mecca, and uplifting their hands, commence in a chanting monotone to recite their prayer to Allah. One would generally say the prayer aloud for the benefit of the lot, and they would all bow and prostrate themselves to the ground at the proper moment, which occurs about half a dozen times in the course of one short prayer. The Koran enjoins that before praying the true believer shall wash his hands and feet, his forearms and his mouth and ears; but water was scarce at Arksis, and these hypocrites would go through the solemn farce of putting their open palms on the ground three times as though dipping them in a bowl of water, and perform all the action of ablution!

With the exception of drapers' shopwalkers at home, I have never seen any people more systematically indulge in the habit of washing their hands with 'invisible soap and imperceptible water.'

CHAPTER IX.

TREACHERY AT WORK.

The *Tourmaline* disappears—We discuss our prospects of getting home—British prestige in Morocco—A boar-hunt without the boar—Wreckage—An impudent request—The weekly market—The yacht sighted again—Welcome and unwelcome guests—A native barber at work—Thieves again—Muley Abdallah gives us bad news—Treachery in the camp.

WE didn't feel quite so refreshed on waking the next morning, a circumstance which we attributed to the fact of our having slept in our clothes. The tent had weathered the storm without breaking a rope or up-rooting a peg. But where was the *Tourmaline?* In all the wide expanse of sea that lay beneath us, not a sign of the yacht was to be seen.

'I wonder if she has gone to the Canaries for a surf-boat,' I said, trying to put the best complexion on matters.

But Beyerle gave utterance to the thought that had flashed across my mind. 'Suppose she has been wrecked in the gale?'

'I can hardly think that likely,' I replied. 'After the hammering she got in the Channel and the Bay, I think she could stand anything in the way of mere weather.'

We couldn't shake off a feeling of uneasiness, all the

same, and fell to discussing what we should do if the poor old *Saucy Cat*, as we had been wont to call her on board, had been drowned like her kitten the launch. She might have dragged her anchors in the gale, and drifted on to the rocks, in which case she would have gone to pieces in an hour.

The chiefs said they could not take us overland to Mogador, as we should certainly be stopped by the Sultan's troops as soon as we crossed the border, even if all the tribes in Sus were friendly. We said we didn't care for the Sultan's troops, as they would not dare to lay violent hands on English travellers. (For the sake of uniformity, I suppose, Beyerle preferred to represent himself as English, and the interpreter tried to do likewise; but the characteristics of his race were too strongly marked in him, apart from the fact that some of the tribesmen had seen him before, and knew him for a Jew in Mogador. Him they dubbed El Arabi.) It was all very well for us to profess indifference to the Sultan's troops, but the Susi knew the Sherifian soldiery better than we did, and we were afterwards to learn the bitter lesson that the name of the English no longer carries with it in certain parts of Morocco the respect and awe in which it was once held. *Civis Britannicus sum* is not a declaration to conjure with in the presence of Moorish Kaids and officials nowadays; indeed, it is not nearly so well calculated to insure respectful treatment as the statement, 'I am an American citizen.'

The chiefs said they would take us to Cape Juby, or part of the way to Agadir, whence they would send a letter for us on to Mogador. We felt really alone, strangers in a strange land; hundreds of miles from civilization, and without mules or horses, and with scarcely a change of clothes. The yacht, in which were centred all our hopes, had disappeared.

One compensating feature was that the natives were that morning particularly friendly, and offered to take us for a wild-boar hunt. We gladly accepted the proposal, as it would afford us an opportunity of seeing something of the neighbourhood, and with an escort of three or four active tribesmen we set off in the direction of Wad-Nun, to the south-west. The flat plateau between the mountains and the sea was thickly covered with the cactus scrub, brambles and rough stones. Here and there it was intersected by deep gullies or ravines that sloped up from the sea, along the bottom of which sometimes ran small streams, which the natives dignified with the name of *wad*, or river. With these active hillmen as guides, the pace, combined with the rough ground, soon began to tell on us, as we were out of condition for want of exercise.

On we tramped for miles, but not a sign of an *abu snau** did we see. For the first time for several days the weather was beautifully fine, and the sun, although it was the month of January, beat down upon us with great strength. Several brace of partridges we disturbed, but they were not the quarry we were seeking. Just as we were thinking of turning back, having gone some miles from the camp, one of the men gave a low hiss, and motioned to us with his hand to crouch down. I thought he had come upon the boar at last, as we had seen his traces several times, but he pointed to a moving object in the bush some half-mile away which I could not quite make out. Following up in a wide semicircle, we advanced with as little noise as possible, but the animal's keen scent had detected our approach,

* Father of tusks.

and presently there bounded into the open plain 800 yards away a fine gazelle. Seizing a Mannlicher from one of the natives, I took a rapid aim and fired, and at the same moment a shot from Beyerle's rifle rang out. Both shots missed, and the graceful animal disappeared. The noise must have startled his or her companion from its hiding-place, for we just caught sight of another moving pair of horns, but too far off to waste a shot upon.

We took the beach route on our way back, and had barely got down to the shore, when we came upon a party of women, who had picked up some of the wreckage of the launch. Broken seats, a plank here, a piece of the rudder-post there, testified to the completeness of the wreck, the fragments being strewn along the coast for miles.

What a lunch we had when we got back to camp! El Arabi was busying about rigging up a small tent outside our own to be used as a kitchen for us, and the natives were squatting around in circles and chattering, as was their wont. I was dog-tired, and thought I had earned a pipe of tobacco, which was running unpleasantly low.

I was thus indulging at the door of the tent, when a man came and demanded my pair of scissors wherewith to cut his beard—*bezziz*, he said, *i.e.*, by force. He was promptly kicked out by El Arabi, who told him that if he wanted anything from an Englishman the best plan was to ask politely, but to threaten him was a pretty certain way to get himself into trouble. He went unshorn.

The camp was unusually quiet that afternoon, and there didn't seem to be nearly so many people about as usual. El Arabi made judicious inquiries, and learned the cause to be that a weekly market was being held at Tlata, a place some eight or ten miles distant, to which many of them had gone. The market with the Susi and the country Moors is the great event of the week. If they don't want to buy anything, or haven't the money, they can gossip with the Jews and trading Moors, and learn the news of the last market-place, perhaps ten or twenty miles away. And so the news of the country is spread, and the weekly *Sôk* is also the weekly newspaper, or, rather, its Moorish equivalent. Whether the village is the cause of the market, or the market the origin of the village, it is difficult to say, but certain it is that many hamlets and small towns in Sus have no other name than the day of the week on which the market is held. Tlata is a case in point. The Arabic word for three also stands for Tuesday, the third day in the week; and if it were not for the addition of the name of the tribe being added for distinction, as 'Tlata el Sbooya,' the confusion of Tlatas, Arbas, etc., would be hopeless indeed.

Shortly before sunset, when objects at sea, especially upon the horizon, can be more easily seen than in broad daylight under the full glare of the sun, one of the Arabs descried the yacht far out to sea. With the naked eye she was invisible to me, but getting the binoculars from the tent, I found the look-out man was not mistaken. She did not seem to be moving, and had probably only gone out for more sea-room in which to ride out the gale. '"Cheek" is a poor quality unless thoroughly carried out,' was my mental reflection as, on returning to our quarters, we met a number of men carrying ropes and other wreckage from the launch, which they offered to us *for sale*. Of course we had no use for the *débris*, but it was anything but a gratifying sight to see what once had been a smart and natty pinnace turned to the base use of firewood for a Berber camp.

An amusing incident occurred before we finished supper. One of the dogs which hovered round had become quite friendly with us, as we occasionally fed it with bones and other scraps, and would even venture to come and sit by our table. The idea of a dog in one's house or tent is abhorrent to the mind of a Moslem, and the chiefs who were making a hotel of our tent told us that they would not eat if the dog was allowed to remain. Had they been people of fine discrimination, they might have gathered from our reply that, of the two alternatives presented to us, we preferred the company of the dog, but the attractions of the tent proved superior to their prejudices.

When we rose next morning the yacht was still in sight, but a long way out. The weather was beautifully fine, but a fresh north-west wind was blowing, which made the sea too rough for boats to land. A dip in the cove was a temptation too strong to be resisted, and Beyerle and I enjoyed a cool and refreshing swim.

On our way back we came across a native having an al-fresco shave, and we stayed to watch the operation. The razor (!) was a common wooden-handled knife that a schoolboy in a fit of reckless extravagance might give twopence for, and no soap or brush was used. The top of the head being well moistened with water—I didn't see any but salt-water near—the knife was applied, and the short, stiff, black bristles all removed until the man's head was as bald—and as rough—as a shark's skin. Then the moustache had to be trimmed. This consists of shaving the upper and lower portion, leaving only a thin line of hair running the length of the lip, which is then clipped close to the skin with the scissors. The beard, which generally seems to grow in scrubby patches, is left untouched. Altogether the result of these tonsorial operations is hardly pleasing to the European eye, though, considering the travelling population that accompanies all these people, Moors, Berbers, and Arabs alike, the shaving of the head is a practice that has much to recommend it.

On our return to camp we found that two of our buckets had been stolen. We immediately reported the matter to the 'Forty,' at the same time intimating that two powder-flasks which were in our tent would be retained as security until our property was restored, and all intruders rigidly excluded from the tent. The buckets were returned that afternoon.

In the evening Muley Abdallah and Embarak o-Hamed—one of the men who had negotiated the treaty with the Major at Mogador, and who appeared to us to be only half-witted at times—came to our tent and signified their desire for a private conversation. Green tea was accordingly prepared, and 'Mr. Garden' posted outside the door to keep out intruders, and over their cups, or, rather, their glasses, they told us that the Sbooya tribe was not friendly with Sidi Hussein ben Hashem, and did not like to hear the mention of his name. Whether a letter had been sent to him, as promised, our visitors could not—or, any rate, would not—say, but we drew our own conclusions.

It was plain to us now that these people had lied to us throughout; no letter had been sent, and our staying on there in the hope of meeting either ben Hashem or Dakhman was only a waste of time. The object of these people was evidently to get possession of as many rifles as they could by false pretences, and in the meantime to prevent our having access to any more business-like tribe. I was heart-sick at their lying and treachery, but there was nothing to be done but to keep up the farce, discuss the prospects of trade and the future of Arksis as a thriving port, and take the first opportunity of getting on board the *Tourmaline*. I had had my fears for some time past, but now there was no room for doubt.

Sleep 'that knits up the ravell'd sleave of care' is often tardiest when we want her most, and all through the night my dearly-longed-for rest was broken by the cries of the guard to the sentry outside, and the latter's dismal howl that all was well. That is how it may have struck him, but to me things seemed to be anything but 'all well.'

CHAPTER X.

NAVAL MANŒUVRES.

A reconnoitre from the *Tourmaline*—The arrival of the *Hassani*—A disappointment—The *Hassani* goes in pursuit—Novel method of communicating at sea—An attempt is made to board the *Tourmaline*—The chiefs agitate for rifles—More naval manœuvres—A pitiable spectacle—The Susi open fire on the *Hassani's* boats—A warm quarter of an hour—Sabbah loses his appetite, but finds his tongue.

Thursday, January 13.—We had now been a week ashore—the time we had had to wait on board before we could land.

El Arabi wakened us with the news that the *Tourmaline* was close in, and that a boat was coming ashore. We hurriedly dressed whilst Sabbah excitedly commenced to pack up the camp-beds and other things, as if the boat had already landed. Anxious to avoid arousing the suspicions of the natives as to our intentions, I told him to desist, and going outside the tent, I saw the boat turn round before she reached the mouth of the cave, and make her way back to the yacht. The Captain himself was in the boat, but he evidently considered the breakers still too big to risk a landing. The proximity of the yacht, however, was some sort of comfort, and we observed with satisfaction that the boat was not hoisted on to the davits again, but run out astern, to be ready for another attempt at high-tide, no doubt. But it was anxious waiting, especially as to us on the cliff it seemed as if the sea was going down every minute, and that a boat could land in safety.

Hours passed by, but still there was no sign, so Beyerle and I took a stroll outside the camp to look for snakes. It was a very hot morning, just such a day as would be likely to tempt the reptiles to come out and bask in the sunshine; but before we got far afield a Sbooya came running towards us to say that a steamer was in sight, and pointed away to the northward. We could see nothing, but, returning to the tent for the glasses, could just make out on the far horizon a faint curl of smoke. This was not the track of any trading steamers: their course lay far away to the westward. It could only be the *Hassani*. And as she came nearer we could make out three masts, and then a dark clumsy hull high out of the water, and knew that 'the Sultan's navy' was bearing down upon us.

The *Tourmaline* did not appear to have observed her approach, so, going to the head of the cliff, I fired several shots from my revolver to attract attention. Still she made no sign, so I took a Mannlicher and fired three shots which could be heard a mile or two away. That they evidently heard, for presently steam was seen issuing from the winch, betokening the lifting of the anchor. 'Now surely they will send the boat,' I thought. 'The sea is quite calm, and at her slow rate of steaming the *Hassani* will not be here for an hour yet. It is only twelve o'clock; we shall have our next meal on board the yacht.' And as we watched we saw the boat being hauled alongside.

But what a disappointment! Instead of being manned to go ashore, it was hauled upon the davits, and before we had recovered from our astonishment the yacht had swung round and was steaming out to sea. We could only look at each other in blank dismay, scarcely able to believe the evidence of our senses. It was stern fact none the less. We felt with the London coster whose barrow was overturned by a bus, the contents being rolled all over the muddy street, that 'there weren't no bloomin' word fer it.' Beyerle merely remarked: 'I think we had better go and get our lunch.' And finding wisdom in the proposition, I walked back with him to the tent.

Meanwhile the *Hassani* had altered her course as if in pursuit, and, with the Moorish ensign flying astern, ran up the signal, 'I wish to communicate.' When the yacht had passed the three-mile limit, and was no longer in Moorish waters, but upon the 'high seas,' she turned to meet her pursuer and ran up the answering pennant in reply to the *Hassani's* signals. We noticed, however, that the yacht's stern was kept steadily turned towards the Sultan's boat, and could picture the Major at the Maxim, with his eyeglass in his eye, and his hand on the string ready for emergencies.

Tacking and dodging was the order of things for some time, and then at two o'clock precisely a boat containing the chief officer and about a score of armed men was lowered from the port side of the *Hassani* and pulled towards the yacht. The Captain's orders to his chief officer were to 'board the steamer, and tell the commander he had to follow the *Hassani* to Mogador'—an order that was even more improper than it was ridiculous, seeing that neither the Captain nor

THE HASSANI CHASING THE TOURMALINE.

any of his officers knew the name of the yacht, nor had taken the trouble to inquire what was her business on that coast. But the gallant officer was prepared for anything, even piracy, and at the same time that his boat sheered off from the port side, another from the starboard side of the steamer, manned by about thirty men also armed, shot out beyond the bow and pulled rapidly towards the *Tourmaline*. When within about 200 yards, Captain Graham rang the telegraph 'full speed ahead' as a gentle hint that he had no liking for such methods of communicating at sea, and the boats of course were soon left far behind. Making a wide détour, she came up again close under the *Hassani*'s stern, and Captain Graham from the bridge sang out, 'If you want to communicate, send an officer in a boat without armed men, and I'll talk to you;' but as Captain Siebert afterwards naïvely admitted, 'as he didn't let my boats come near, I didn't take any notice.' He was in the service of the Sultan, and preferred the methods of the Moor to those of the mercantile marine in which he had been trained.

Realizing that the pursuit of the *Tourmaline* was not only a waste of fuel, but an undignified and inglorious display, Captain Siebert brought the *Hassani* to an anchor right off the entrance to the cove, and not half a mile away, while his boats still cruised about to prevent communication from the shore. But the yacht hung upon her flanks like a hound upon a boar, and fired a round from the gun to sea as a warning to the *Hassani* that she was armed. All this manœuvring and dodging about, however, had made a very bad impression upon the Sbooyas, as they had fully expected a fight, and came to the conclusion that the yacht was afraid to tackle this great lumbering old transport. We of course derided the idea, and told them there was a gun on the yacht that could blow the Sultan's steamer out of the water, and added further, for obvious reasons, that if a shot from the gun were to be fired on our camp it would kill about 100 men.

'Why doesn't your steamer fire on the Sultan's, then?' they retorted.

The idea of meeting your enemy—as they regarded the *Hassani*—and not firing at him was incomprehensible to them; and, indeed, it was difficult for us to give an explanation that would be satisfactory to them. They told us, however, not to be afraid: they would not allow any boat from the *Hassani* to land. But it was the meaning of the tactics that had occupied the whole of the afternoon, and not the fear of a landing-party from the *Hassani*, or any other such remote contingency, that agitated our minds. Both steamers were then within the three-mile limit, and if the *Tourmaline* was engaged in a lawful enterprise, as we believed, why did she not signal to the *Hassani* that she had Europeans ashore and meant to take them off, daring the Sultan's steamer or boats to interfere at their peril? Of the effect of such a message there could be little doubt, as one vessel carried a three-pound quick-firing gun, while the other was unarmed, and each knew the offensive equipment of the other. But the curtain of night was rung down upon this serio-comedy in which the members of our company had played anything but distinguished parts, if we critics on the cliff were any judges. A rocket was sent up from the yacht as soon as it was dark, and we couldn't help thinking that no better illustration of recent events could, under the circumstances, have been devised than that of the rocket and the stick.

At sunrise next morning the tribe were all astir, and making a great noise with their prayers. It was evident that something was afoot, and we were not long in learning what it was. The chiefs were very uneasy, being of opinion that the visit of the *Hassani* was only the herald of a raid by Kaid Giluli, and they began to agitate again for rifles. They wanted us to take our canvas boat and row out to the yacht, but we pointed out to them that we should never reach there, as there were three of the *Hassani's* boats patrolling between the *Tourmaline* and the land to cut off all communication. We should simply be captured, we said, and then we should be unable to help them at all. Not that we minded being captured, we argued, as we should only be handed over to the nearest British Consul, but they would be no nearer to their rifles.

This only appeared to partially satisfy them, and they spoke of taking the boat themselves. We told them they were perfectly free to do so if they chose, but we accepted no responsibility in case they lost their lives. In the first place, the boat was a very frail one, utterly unfit for the sea, and would almost certainly be swamped before it had gone 100 yards from the cove; and, in the second place, the men in the *Hassani's* boats would be sure to fire on them as soon as they saw that any attempt was being made to communicate with the yacht. The best they could hope for would be capture—and they knew what that meant for *them*.

This reasoning brought them to their senses somewhat, and a solemn council of war was held in our tent to consider the best plan to be adopted under the circumstances. As usual on these occasions, there was far more talking than listening, but after many absurd suggestions, a proposal was made that had at least the merit of common-sense. This was that they should beg, borrow, or steal a surf-boat from Ifni, take a crew of half a dozen men, and row out to the yacht under cover of the darkness. It sounded all right, but, having learnt something of the Ah-Sin-like characters of these people, I expressed the belief that such a thing as a surf-boat was not to be found anywhere along their coast, or they would have brought it to Arksis long before then. My incredulity was received by the chiefs with lofty, calm disdain, and presently I saw Khabib and his brother arm themselves, mount horse, and ride off north-eastwards.

Before he went off, I scribbled a hasty note to the Major, telling him the position of affairs, and begging him to lose no time in sending relief. I had not much faith in its being delivered, but I sent it on the off chance.

All the morning the yacht had been going through the same evolutions as on the previous day—moving up and down, cruising round the *Hassani*, but doing nothing definite. Anything more exasperating for us to watch could not well be imagined. With the arrival of the Moorish steamer the day before, the sea had fallen to a perfect calm, but the prospect of relief seemed now farther away than ever.

About noon the yacht commenced making signals again. A long message it was, too, to judge from the number of flags that ran up the halliards and were hauled down again. But the *Hassani* made no reply. It was a message ostensibly for us, to tell us that the *Tourmaline* was going up the coast, but really intended as a ruse to draw the *Hassani* a few miles away from Arksis, and then double back at full speed to effect our rescue. As the yacht could steam about two knots to the other vessel's one, this was an excellent plan, provided only the *Hassani* would fall into the trap.

The signal flags were scarcely hauled in before the yacht, going at half-speed, was steaming northwards; and, to our surprise, a few minutes later up came the anchor of the *Hassani*, and she started in pursuit. But only for a little while. The suspicions of the lethargic Teuton had perhaps been aroused, and he returned to his old position, his boats resuming their vigilant patrol, whilst the yacht was nearly lost to sight upon the horizon.

From a council-chamber in the morning, our tent became a medical consulting-room in the afternoon. Numerous patients with all sorts of complaints came trooping along in one melancholy file. Among them 'Mr. Garden' had brought his cousin, and wanted me to see her. She would not come through the camp to the tent, so I went out with him, and found her on the outskirts by a thorn-bush. A young girl of fourteen or fifteen years of age, she had been married *two years*. Her limbs had got no flesh upon them, and though she ate ravenously, she was just a living skeleton—altogether a pitiful spectacle. On returning to the tent, I was warned by Harúsh—Sidi Mulud's brother—not to go so far away again, as there were several Susi in camp belonging to other tribes who were friendly with the Sultan; and as the *Hassani* was off the cove, they might be tempted to make an unpleasant demonstration.

What a pity it was to be a prisoner on a lovely cloudless day like that! I thought; and then I fell into a train of reflections that were none too agreeable. Suppose the tribes had been ill-disposed towards us: it would have gone hard with us indeed. The *Tourmaline* might as well be at the Canaries for all the assistance she was to us. We flew our signals of distress, and, though the sea was calm, she came not. On the contrary, she went farther away, while the *Hassani*, in the meantime, took up a position commanding the entrance to the cove; and it seemed likely that we should be there indefinitely, or until one steamer or the other ran short of coal, and had to go away to replenish.

Shortly after four a man came into the tent to report that the *Tourmaline* was returning. With the aid of the glasses we watched her come along pretty close in, but still to seaward of the *Hassani*. The latter had three boats out manned and armed. One was a large surf-boat capable of holding twenty or thirty people, and the other two were ordinary ship's boats. The yacht passed the *Hassani*, and resumed her old attitude —her stern towards her sentinel.

As we watched to see what the next move would be, a crack from a flint-lock rang out sharply, and a puff of white smoke showed that a shot had been fired by one of the Sbooyas, crouching behind the shelter of the rock on the summit of the cliff, at one of the boats that had come imprudently near. Immediately there burst from all three boats a chorus of reply, and before we had time to realize what had happened, we found ourselves in the midst of a skirmish in earnest. Our tent was a conspicuous mark from the sea, and, judging by the number of bullets that came whistling round us as we watched the fight, the Sultan's soldiers had not overlooked so excellent a target.

Suddenly the boom of a cannon sang over the sea, and like a flash the thought came to us that at last the yacht had opened fire ; but a ball of smoke that rolled away from the forecastle deck of the *Hassani* showed that it was her signal-gun that had been fired. The scene that followed in camp would have been amusing to watch if the situation had not been so serious. Like one man, the natives that were unarmed made a rush for the tent where the Mannlichers were stored— they had not been distributed by the 'Forty,' but deposited in one of the tents—and for a moment or two a rough-and-tumble scramble ensued for the possession of the coveted weapons.

Meanwhile, the fire from the boats was hotly returned by those on the cliff who were already armed, but their aim was erratic. Occasionally the water would spatter round the boats where the bullets struck the sea, but I saw no vacant place at the oars. Our own position was rather warm, too, as we were quite without shelter, and bullets were plentiful as raindrops in a summer shower, now flying over our heads, with that peculiar whistle which has to be heard to be properly comprehended, and which, once heard, is never forgotten, and now burying themselves in the ground or cactus scrub at our feet. We might have retired to the rear out of the range of fire, but both Beyerle and I felt that it was necessary to show all the courage we possessed, even to foolhardiness, in order to counteract the very unfavourable impression made upon the Sbooyas by the *Tourmaline*.

In the early excitement of the fight we had not been noticed, but after a time some of the natives came rushing up wildly and hurried us towards the tent. I thought at first their object was hostile, as their gesticulations and excited jabberings were by no means reassuring. It turned out, however, that their anxiety was merely for our safety, as they had, they said, made themselves responsible for our lives, and would defend us to the last drop of blood in their veins. This sounded very pretty, but we didn't relish being forced against our will to remain in the tent, squatting on the floor Moor-fashion, all the time able to hear everything and see nothing. However, a few minutes later the firing ceased, the boats withdrawing beyond range of all but the magazine rifles.

The sun, which all day long had shone in unobscured magnificence, sank in splendour in the sea. The Union Jack, which drooped limply over the stern of the *Tourmaline*, was taken in; the flag of the Sultan —so appropriately blood-red—was hauled down on board the *Hassani*, and the riding-light on the foremast gleamed like a star aloft. Half an hour later the short tropical twilight had faded into darkness, the stars above crept shyly out from behind their curtain of blue, the sea had crooned herself to sleep, and over the face of Nature stole a gentle and impressive peace.

We had had our share of excitement for the day, but the wants of animal man were not to be neglected, and we had leisure then to think about getting some supper. Sabbah, however, was too utterly overcome to set his thoughts upon so commonplace a matter. I had caught one glance of him during the skirmish, and saw 'Funk' writ large across his pallid face. To say that he was white would scarcely be correct, for his dark olive skin, half covered with a week's growth of beard, could not absolutely blanch, but it was 'sicklied o'er' with a sort of greenish hue, and his trembling lips and twitching fingers only too plainly bespoke the fear that paralyzed him.

'By ——' he exclaimed, with a profanity which generally characterized his most casual utterances, 'the Major —— coward; by —— he is! Why doesn't he fire on the *Hassani* and sink her? Let me get on board the yacht, and I never come ashore again. I wouldn't be here but for you,' he added, turning round on us, as if we were the cause of all his misfortunes; but, considering his then state of mind, both Beyerle and I treated his ravings with no more notice than if they had never been uttered, and he subsided in a corner of the tent, breathing maledictions upon everybody, and cursing the evil fate which had brought him to the country. Not even the sight of a succulent boiled fowl, in the cooking of which Beyerle, myself, and Ibrahim had all lent a hand, could tempt his usually vigorous and healthy appetite. Poor Sabbah! he had no stomach for a fight; but how many of the Children of Israel have? So we had a *souper à deux*, and, as we intended to be up at dawn, we turned in at nine o'clock, only taking our coats off in case of a night attack, and with our revolvers under our pillows as usual.

CHAPTER XI.

EL ARABI TO THE RESCUE.

A signaller's narrow escape—Our situation becomes grave—The chiefs wish us to retreat inland—Discussions thereon—I receive a letter from the Major—We resort to stratagem—More rifles landed—A night vigil, and a quarrel—Muley Abdallah tells his story—Sabbah disguises himself and leaves camp—His return—A rotten boat.

SLEEPING in riding boots is not the most comfortable thing imaginable, but we managed to pass a very fair night, and a few minutes after sunrise next morning found us outside the tent. The Susi were, however, ahead of us, and as soon as we appeared immediately commenced jabbering and clamouring for us to make signals to the yacht to come in and land rifles. This childish foolery made me very angry, and I told them curtly to make their own signals. One simple-minded native thereupon procured a boat-hook, and, tying a piece of white calico to the end of it, took up a prominent position on the cliff-head, and commenced to wave his signal with frantic energy. What is generally recognised as a flag of truce is evidently treated with scant respect in Morocco, for the signaller had scarcely been a minute at his self-imposed task, when a couple of shots whizzed past him, one of the bullets passing through his clothes, but leaving him untouched.

Our situation became rapidly more serious. For some days past supplies from the natives had been falling off, and with our breakfast that morning we had come to the end of our bread. In this emergency we appealed to Muley Abdallah for some. He said he was in the same case, but he would send for fresh stores. Shortly afterwards a deputation of the 'Forty' came and told us it was no longer safe for us to remain encamped there; we must pack up our things, and go with them to one of their houses in the interior.

This was what it had come to! A courier had come in and reported that there had been fighting two or three days' distance.* The Sultan's troops would be down upon us any day—to-morrow, perhaps—and we should be between a good many devils and the deep sea. We held a hurried consultation as to what was best to be done. The idea of 'the interior' took Beyerle's fancy greatly; he wanted to see what the country was like. I, too, had a strong desire to see what was hidden behind the screen of hills, but I felt that, cut off from the sea, we should be, in a sense, cut off from civilization. Inland was an unknown, uncivilized country, and beyond, the desert. The natives said they would leave a watch there, and if any boat should come ashore from the yacht, would send us word immediately. But then there were the tents, instruments, etc., belonging to the syndicate. It was not proposed that we should take them with us, as there

* Distance is always reckoned in these parts by days, and not by miles or any arbitrary lineal measure. A day's journey is reckoned about forty miles.

were no mules available, and who would look after them if we deserted our post? No, we must stay; and we returned that for answer. If the Sultan's troops came, they must come, and we would see the issue of it. The idea of an armed resistance was quite out of the question. Easily defensible as was Arksis from attack by sea, against a land assault no place could be more defenceless. Besides, what hill tribesmen ever fought a battle in an open plain from choice? They could retire to the hills if they liked, we told them; but we would stay at Arksis, and the Sultan's soldiers would think twice before they attacked a peaceable English camp, or laid violent hands upon those they might find there.

The Sbooya chiefs intended otherwise, however. If Giluli came, they said, his troops would kill or capture everyone they came across—Mohammedan or Nazarene, Sbooya or *Ruomi*.* They had made themselves responsible for our lives, and under no circumstances would they allow us to fall into the hands of the Sultan. If all other means of escape were closed, they would pass us overland to Senegal, Timbuctoo, or some other place whence we could travel home in safety. Alluring prospect, certainly, but we were not our own masters by a long way, and eventually we came to the conclusion that it would be better to give in to their plan with a good grace than to refuse and be carried off by force, which they would not have scrupled to use.

With no light heart, therefore, we set about the business of packing what things we most should want and could be crowded into the compass of a few handbags and portmanteaus. By noon everything was

* Generic term applied to all Europeans.

finished and we were ready to start. Then they told us they had changed their minds. Another courier had just come in and contradicted the story of the fighting. Giluli was not yet on the war-path. We had better stay where we were. Then I spoke words to them which, if faithfully translated into Arabic, must have caused them no little astonishment; but they showed no sign in their impassive features. I asked where our bread was, and they replied that they had sent for it. But where they had sent, or when their messenger was expected back, could not be ascertained; so, tired of waiting, we had a vegetarian lunch for a change, composed of tinned asparagus, washed down with the water in which it was preserved, our buckets being as dry as our tongues.

In the afternoon a man arrived from Sidi Warzuk, a village on the way to Ifni, and reported that Khabib had got two surf-boats from the latter place, and succeeded in reaching the yacht, and some rifles and cartridges had been landed. Half an hour later a letter was handed to me, addressed to 'Commander Grey, K.C.B., Camp Erksees,' in handwriting which I recognised as the Major's. Eagerly tearing open the envelope, I read the following:

'S.S. YACHT TOURMALINE,
'15 *Jan.*, 97.

'DEAR GREY,
'The first boat went off with ten rifles and four cases cartridges, and, to our horror, made straight down the coast towards the *Hassanie*. We thought at first we had been had. However, they have just made the shore. Another boat is now alongside, with men I know in her. Let me hear from you this after-

noon or to-morrow, or, better still, one of you come aboard and report what has taken place.

'If the money is right from Sidi Hosein, we could with these boats unload rapidly at night while the weather keeps right, but it is no use unloading unless the cash is arranged for.

'Let us hear from you by this channel to-morrow at latest.

'Yours sincerely,
'A. GYBBON SPILSBURY.'

The irony of it! 'Come aboard and report what has taken place.' That would be 'better still,' no doubt. But the Major didn't know that we were unable to move a dozen yards from the tent without an escort, and were not allowed to go up or down the coast at all. My letter to him had clearly not been delivered, but his note to me afforded a first-rate opportunity for a stratagem. Summoning the chiefs, I gave them a rather free rendering of the Major's letter, which Sabbah translated to them, saying that he was very anxious to land all the rifles while the weather was fine, but that he wanted us all three aboard to help in unloading, and he would be at the same place at sunrise on the morrow, when he would expect to see us.

As if that settled the matter, we rose to set out at once, with or without an escort; but they said we must wait for the men to return with the rifles and cartridges that had been landed, as they were not sure that the way was safe. Any excuse was better than none, but this bugbear of hostile neighbouring tribes was beginning to lose the charm of novelty. The fact was that the idea of acting immediately upon the instructions contained in a letter was utterly foreign to their notions. A letter to them was like a heavy meal to a snake—it was absorbed slowly, and digested at still greater leisure—and it was necessary that an hour or two, at least, should elapse before they could think of bestirring themselves.

We chafed inwardly, but it was not long before the men returned from Sidi Warzuk with the report that they were unable to carry the rifles and cartridges, and had therefore put them in a safe place of concealment near the surf-boat, and they wanted fifteen or twenty men to go back at once and fetch them. A party was soon formed, and we proposed to accompany it. The chiefs, however, said we had better wait till after sunset, as in our European clothes we should be recognised as Christians by the tribesmen on the road, and it would lead to trouble. Beyerle, on hearing this translated, completely lost patience, and broke out into something strongly suggestive of certain clauses of the Athanasian Creed in German. He was for accompanying the party at all hazards, but I urged upon him that it would only lead to a quarrel, which it would be unwise to provoke, if there was any prospect of attaining our object by diplomatic methods. He gave in, but sorely against his will, I could see, as he watched the party hurrying off.

Sunset came, but still there was no sign of movement among the chiefs. Asked when they would be ready to start, they replied that it would be impossible to go now in the dark; we should not be able to see our way. Could anything be more exasperating? First it was too light to go; then it was too dark. What other excuse would they invent next? We had better wait till the moon rose, they said, and then we should go; we should be at Sidi Warzuk long before sunrise. And finally it was so arranged, they swearing by their beards, their necks, and the tombs of their ancestors, that we should start at moonrise; and with that we were fain to be content.

Meanwhile we were still without bread, and we had realized for some hours past that asparagus is a more dainty than sustaining diet; so we made shift with a fried tinned sausage apiece and a cup of cocoa. There was no fear of the chiefs accepting our proferred hospitality, as the sausages were made of the accursed *halûf;* but curious eyes were cast upon the cocoa, which was evidently a beverage they had never seen before. Green tea they knew; *atay negra* they had also heard of; coffee they had a nodding acquaintance with; but what was this? Our stock was small, and our need was great; and I hope we may therefore be forgiven for the deception which led them to believe that the strange liquid was a composition of which the chief constituent was pigs' blood.

Our beds were all packed up, and the chiefs, and others who were to form our proposed escort, had taken advantage of the extra room in the tent to occupy every available space, squatting themselves down in all sorts of attitudes to sleep. What time the moon would rise we were uncertain, having no almanac; but we knew it was about half waned and would therefore not be up before midnight.

At 9.30 the long-expected bread arrived, and we profited by the occasion to cut open a tin of tongue, and fortify ourselves for our night march. When we should get our next meal, and where, we knew not. Shortly afterwards some of the men came back from Sidi Warzuk again, and reported that the rifles and cartridges that they had left there, in a safe hiding-place as they thought, had been stolen, or, at any rate, removed by someone else. On hearing this piece of intelligence, the Susi seemed to think that the best thing under the circumstances was to go to sleep, which they accordingly did. For us sleep was not to be thought of, as we wished to make certain of being ready to march when the time should come. The hours dragged slowly along. Midnight came, but still no moon, and every minute seemed like ten. At last, towards one o'clock, a pale phosphorescent glimmer of light seemed to illumine the outline of the eastern hills, and a few minutes later the silver horn of the moon rose over the top. The Susi all round us in the tent—twenty in number—were fast asleep; but we lost no time in arousing them. They, however, strongly resented their slumbers being thus rudely disturbed, and an angry row ensued. Everyone was now thoroughly awake, and began shouting and screaming at the top of his voice.

A weird scene it must have been, the tent lighted only by a solitary candle in a watchman's lantern, the wild-looking Susi in their long, drab, ghostly robes, Sabbah in a cycling suit, and Beyerle and I in khaki, armed to the teeth with dagger and revolver. Beyerle, having a spare revolver, had traded it for a dagger, and certainly he had succeeded in getting the best one in the camp in exchange for his firearm. I had the one Khabib had given to me, which, though not possessing perhaps so highly chased a sheath, was a no less murderous-looking weapon. One tall Susi from Dlimin, the son-in-law of El F'kir Embarak, cried out that we should not go aboard the yacht till they had had their 2,000 rifles.

'Yes,' screamed his father-in-law in a thin, cracked voice, 'you are my prisoners.'

'Where is the money for your ransom?' frantically demanded another.

I didn't recollect having seen his face in the camp before, so I turned angrily to Sidi Mulud, who seemed to be the calmest of the 'Forty' present, and asked him if *that* was their object in bringing us to Arksis, and preventing us returning to our ship; but he indignantly denied the suggestion, and endeavoured to lend colour to the genuineness of his repudiation by ordering the offending Susi out of the tent.

Still, the upshot was that they said they would not allow us to go to Sidi Warzuk, as the Imsti tribe (to whom Ifni belonged) were not friendly, and if they saw us they might attack us. We replied that if they didn't care to run the risk we would, and we meant to go; and suiting the action to the word, we threw down the baggage we had in our hands, and marched out of the tent into the moonlight. The Susi followed, and their opposition then assumed a more active form. A flint-lock gun that I was carrying was wrenched from my grasp, Beyerle and Sabbah were both seized, and further resistance being useless, we surrendered to *force majeure*, and marched disconsolately back to our tent. The beds were all packed up; the tent was crowded with evil-smelling, verminous natives, with not six feet of room anywhere to stretch one's self; so we spent the rest of the night squatting on the matted ground, with saddles and bags for pillows, the cold night air of the hills chilling our stiff and weary limbs, and denying us the refreshment of sleep. And thus the hours wore on to dawn, and another morning's sun rose in splendour to mock our captivity with its brilliant rays.

Early in the morning Muley Abdallah, who had not been present at the previous night's scene, came to our tent looking very downhearted. Poor old man! I couldn't help feeling sorry for the old fellow, for, from what he had let drop on several occasions, I had gathered that things were not altogether *couleur de rose* with him. He was already growing feeble, and walked with difficulty, leaning on a stick ; but his dress and manner showed him to be of superior kidney to the Sbooya rabble, not excluding any of the appropriately named ' Forty.'

He sat down on one of our camp chairs like a Christian, and, signing that he wished to speak with us alone, opened the ball by saying he had heard of the dispute the night before. He much regretted it, because he feared it might lead to trouble. We begged him to explain, and, deeming the moment opportune, besought him, with promises of ulterior reward, to tell us the real truth as to our position. Did the Sbooyas mean trade, or robbery? and what was the meaning of our being kept close prisoners as we were? Of course, it was not to be expected that he would give us a direct answer offhand to these questions: he was a Moor. But he entered into a long account of how he had been induced by Ratto to leave Mogador, where he had a good business, and come to Arksis, where he was told the Christian was going to open a port, and he would be able to do a good trade with both the English and the tribes. Emptying 5 pesetas on to the table, he told us, with tears in his eyes, that that was all that was left of 500 dollars which he possessed when he left Mogador ; and that he now saw he had been deceived, and that trade with these tribes was impossible. He feared to return to Mogador, as he would be sure to be thrown into prison for aiding the Christians to enter Sus; and he was, on the other hand, unable to remain in Sbooya. The tribe did not mean honestly by us, but wanted to get all the rifles they could without paying for them, and then, when there was nothing more to be got, send us away—or worse. But if we would help him, he would help us. If we would promise to take him to the Canaries, or to Tangier, or some other place in Morocco, and get him a certificate as a British-protected person, he would, on his part, assist us by every means in his power to get aboard the yacht.

It took him a good deal longer to say all this than it has taken me to write it, but I have only given the gist of it. What he said was rambling and diffuse, and interspersed with many references and appeals to Allah, and when he had finished we rose and shook hands upon the compact. Then he told us that the chiefs were minded that we should send a letter to the Major telling him to take the yacht to Assaka, some six miles down the coast to the south-west, where the landing was better and we could get aboard. We should then contrive some excuse to get him on board also, and after that we could deal with the Sbooyas as seemed best to us. Meanwhile he advised us to promise them anything they should ask for, to keep them quiet and well disposed. And, taking up his stick, the old man hobbled out of the tent, and we were left to our own reflections.

Was this another ruse, or was the old Sherif telling us the truth? We couldn't tell, but time would show; and meanwhile there was no harm in writing another letter to the Major setting forth our desperate position, and asking him to go to Assaka as the chiefs suggested.

That letter despatched, we lay ourselves out to propitiate the 'Forty'—they were well named 'Forty,' but there was a word missing—and discoursed, freely and at length, upon the quantity and quality of the revolvers we had on board the yacht, which were intended as presents to friends such as themselves. By this system of indirect bribery we appeared to have at last succeeded in getting together a section of the 'Forty,' including Sidi Mohammed and El F'kir Embarak, to favour the project of our going aboard; and in the afternoon our hopes were further strengthened by our interpreter telling us that the 'Forty' had asked him to don a Moorish *jelaba* and go on a mule with a message in person to the yacht. After their previous conduct, this seemed a strange request for them to make; but Sabbah told us that when the men had gone the day before to bring away the rifles and ammunition that they had hidden, they found that they had all been stolen—by some of the Imsti tribe, they believed. Their desire to change the landing-place was therefore easily to be understood.

I talked the matter over with Beyerle, and we debated for some time as to whether he was the best one to go. I didn't believe in the theory of danger on the road, but I knew how strong would be the temptation to him, once on board, to stay there; and if he should not return, the position of Beyerle and myself would be rendered much more difficult and dangerous. At the same time, if there should be trouble on the road, he would be more likely to escape observation in his Moorish disguise, and speaking the language, than either of us. Moreover, it was out of the question that I should go, and, hearing my determination, Beyerle, with a chivalry and pluck which he showed throughout, determined that he would keep me company. And so it was resolved; and after giving him full instructions, and exacting from him a most solemn promise that, come what might, if humanly possible, he would return on the morrow, we watched him ride away, the hood of his *jelaba* drawn over his eyes to hide his unshaven head.

To our dismay, however, he returned about half an hour later, saying that the Major must have already received my letter, as the yacht was steaming southward, and he was afraid we should get aboard and leave him behind. Besides, the people on the *Hassani*, he said, had evidently seen him, for as soon as he started off, she followed him up the coast. As a matter of fact, however, the yacht had only moved a little nearer to her position of the day before, where she had met the surf-boat from Ifni; so, after a hurried meal, he was despatched once more on his errand. The *Hassani* rolled idly in the gentle swell about a mile from shore, with her boats alongside unmanned, and apparently taking no notice of the yacht that was edging closer inshore, a few miles to the northward, to communicate, as we hoped, with our messengers.

An hour after sunset Sidi Mohammed, who had been one of the party forming Sabbah's escort, returned to camp, and reported that the latter was on board the yacht with two of the Susi. It was then too dark to follow the movements of the *Tourmaline*, but we waited with brighter hopes and greater patience for the next step towards our relief. It was a strange position to find one's self in: an Englishman and a

German in a country scarcely before trodden by the foot of a European, cut off from civilization by natural and political barriers, and inhabited by an ignorant and warlike people, as childish as the savage, yet as wily and deceitful as the Oriental, and whose religion taught them that killing was no murder—at least, so far as a Christian was concerned—but, rather, a sure passport to the paradise that awaits the faithful. Neither of us could speak more than a sentence or two of Arabic, let alone the bastard dialect Shlhah which they speak; but we turned our eyes to the sea, where rode the dainty little vessel in which were centred all our present mortal hopes.

While indulging in some such reflections as these, the strains of a London music-hall song rose on the night air in a voice that could never be mistaken, and presently the door of the tent was pushed aside, and Sabbah stood before us.

'Why, I thought you were on board the yacht!' exclaimed Beyerle and I simultaneously.

'No,' he said; 'the boat they got was rotten, big holes in it, and I had to nail pieces of wood outside and cover it with pitch. And then the sailors wouldn't row in her, although I promised them 10 dollars each if they would take me to the yacht, and 50 dollars to the captain, and give them a revolver each when I got on board. They no good.'

'Well, how is it you've only just got back?' I asked.
'Sidi Mohammed has been here an hour or so.'

'Yahs, the old fraud, he took my mule. I went riding on the mule all right, right up, and when I wanted to come back I found he'd taken my mule, and I had to walk all the way, about six miles, by ——' And he glared at the offending but impassive chief.

This was disappointing news, but disappointments came to us with almost every hour of the day. Still, we would make another attempt in the morning to persuade the 'Forty' to let us all go, on the pretext that we knew all about the mending and rowing of boats, and if they feared enemies *en route*, we could disguise ourselves as El Arabi had done. The latter told us that what the men in camp had said about hostile tribesmen on the way was quite correct, though how he had acquired the knowledge, except by intuition, did not transpire. He was, however, much impressed by the fact, but he had aye a keen scent for danger.

As we had not had our clothes off for two nights, and had had little or no sleep for the last forty hours or so, we once more indulged in the luxury of pyjamas and camp-beds, and enjoyed a good long night's rest.

CHAPTER XII.

THE ATTACK ON THE CAMP.

El Arabi gets his instructions, and leaves camp—An ominous quiet—We dispense hospitality—El Arabi gets on board the yacht—Fatal dallying—A hot skirmish—'Mr. Garden' proves his loyalty—Our flight, pursuit, and escape—A painful ride—Peace and war—A peculiarity of Sus—We are told the result of the fight—Capture of El F'kir Embarak's grandson—The old chief's house.

IT is wonderful what a difference a good night's sleep will make in a man. I had gone to bed the night before dispirited and disheartened at repeated disappointments, but when I awoke, my spirits partook somewhat of the brightness and freshness of the morning air, and I early sought an interview with the more active of the 'Forty,' to endeavour to get their consent to the plan we had formulated the night before. But they would not hear of it. El Arabi should go again, taking with him plenty of men to help row the boat, and one or two of the chiefs would accompany him, but Beyerle and I must remain in camp.

It was something to find them in the same mind for two days running, so I thought it best to agree, with only so much discussion as would make them the more tenacious of their scheme, and by nine o'clock or so

El Arabi, having provided himself with wood and tools for any further patching of the boat that might be required, was ready to start.

He was instructed to take on board with him as many of the Susi chiefs as he could persuade to accompany him, and leave them on the yacht, as a set-off against Beyerle and myself, and to ask the Major to steam away to Assaka at once, without landing any more rifles or cartridges. As the yacht passed the camp, she was to let out an escape of steam from the pipe, and fly a green flag from the mast-head if all was well. We were then to make preparations to proceed to Assaka, where we would camp in the open for the night, lighting beacon-fires at sunset to show that all was well ashore. If they saw the fires, a boat was to be sent ashore at sunrise, and we would be on the beach to meet it; but in any event Sabbah was to rejoin us the next day—if not at Assaka, at Arksis.

Alas for the best-laid schemes! El Arabi left camp with a party of natives, and all through a perfect morning we anxiously watched the yacht, and when, towards eleven o'clock, we saw her draw closer inshore, and a boat creep out to meet her, our hopes began steadily to rise. But I was not quite easy in my mind. There was an ominous quiet pervading the camp, scarcely more than 100 men or so being about the place. I took advantage of this circumstance to take a few snapshots, concealing my purpose from the Susi, as they, like all Mohammedans, have a strong religious objection to being photographed. But I was still puzzling over the depletion of the camp, when I suddenly bethought me of an incident which had occurred two days before, but to which I had not paid much attention at the time. A boat from the *Hassani*, well manned, and fitted with a sail, had been seen scudding northwards. I had asked the meaning of it at the time, but the explanation of the natives, that the boat was carrying the body of a Moorish soldier who had been shot in the skirmish the day before, for burial ashore, seemed to me rather too thin for acceptance. It now flashed across me like a revelation that her destination was Aglu, or Agadir, or some port whence a message could be sent to the Sultan's troops, to arrange a concerted attack on Arksis by sea and land.

By way of a diversion, I made some green tea, and offered hospitality to Muley Abdallah, Hassan the notary—whom I greatly mistrusted, but desired to propitiate—and Muley Hamed, a nephew of Muley Abdallah's, who had accompanied him on his travels, and had rendered us several little services in the camp, particularly in the way of foraging. Both Beyerle and I had by this time acquired considerable fondness for that poisonous and deleterious beverage, and did not require the exigency of Moorish politeness to persuade us to drink our three glasses apiece. It was a Providential inspiration. In the strength of that tea much was to be done that afternoon.

Shortly after mid-day the yacht was on her way southward, 'full speed ahead,' and when abreast of the camp, a green flag fluttering at the peak, and a little white puff from the steam-pipe, told us that all was well, and soon afterwards a number of men returned to camp, and reported that El Arabi was aboard with nine or ten of the natives. Before Sabbah left, he had arranged with one or two Susi to accompany us to Assaka, and carry our baggage—such as we were taking—and one of them came up to me at that time to indicate that he was ready. I went to see how Muley Abdallah and El F'kir Embarak were getting on, as they were both going to accompany us, but found that they had not finished loading their mules. '*Schwei, schwei*,'* said Muley Abdallah, turning both the palms of his hands upwards with a gesture that only a Moor can make, and in my impatience I cursed them for their sloth and their damnable infatuation for the fatal doctrine of *mañana*. Every moment I feared that they would say they had changed their minds, and I was hot-foot to be on the move. But what avail were maledictions in an unknown tongue? Whether they ever really meant to take us to Assaka I now shall never know; but if they did, their foolish dallying on that memorable morning cost those two old men, at least, many miserable days in the bitterness of captivity and the gall of fetters, racked by long rides upon the accursed camel, starved and goaded by brutal Moorish soldiery, only to be set free at last by a merciful, but pitiful and wretched, death by the roadside to mark the track of a 'victorious' Sultan's 'tax-collecting.'

Beyerle was no whit more patient, I think, than I, and in this fever of unrest an hour went by. Then, on a sudden, several shots rang out from the hills across the plain—one, two, three. Beyerle suggested that some of the natives were trying their new possessions, and, indeed, the reports had not the sound of a flint-lock; but I thought otherwise, though I kept my counsel. Shortly afterwards there were sounds of firing to the northward, and in the valleys that cleft the hills to the eastward, and from the *Hassani's* boats, which had now come close inshore, there came a hail

* By-and-by.

of bullets; and then I knew that what I had feared would happen had come at last.

Wild confusion followed. One of the 'Forty,' unarmed, came riding into camp in hot haste, jumped out of the saddle, flinging the reins over the neck of his panting horse, which stood on the instant, and rushed wildly into our tent, shrieking, '*Medva, medva!*'[*] and flinging his arms aloft like a raving maniac. Harush had just before then taken away the flint-lock which Sid' Embarak had given to me, and not another weapon of any sort was to be seen. Suddenly his eye lighted on the two cases containing the Major's and Beyerle's sporting rifles, which lay on the ground in the tent, and, like an enraged tiger, he flung himself upon them, and began tearing at the straps, screaming the while at the top of his voice. By signs I tried to show him that the cases were locked, but he continued to claw frantically at the unyielding leather, the picture of baffled rage.

Just at that time another man rushed in and made a grab at my portmanteau. Recognising him as the man that Sabbah had chosen to carry my bag to Assaka, I let him have his way. Seizing me by the arm with his other hand, he tried to drag me out of the tent after him, shouting, '*Gomo, gomo!*'[†] I glanced round to see where Beyerle was, but he was not in the tent. I had been so taken up with watching the man's frantic efforts to get a rifle that I had not noticed Beyerle go out. Outside, however, I saw how things were. A large squadron of cavalry, the advance guard of an army, was already on the plateau engaged in a hot skirmish with the tribesmen, and more horsemen were pouring through the defiles in the hills. Running

[*] Gun.   [†] Come along.

towards the tent was the faithful 'Mr. Garden,' beckoning vigorously to me to come along. He had noticed that I had stayed behind, and had, at great risk to himself, turned back to fetch me. A little way ahead I espied Muley Abdallah and El F'kir Embarak mounted on mules, and Beyerle on foot just behind them, waiting for me to join him.

We all set off at a good trot; but while those on the mules kept to the level plateau, we headed southwards, scrambling down one side of an intersecting ravine and up the other. We were going in the direction of Assaka, and it would be a race between us and the pursuing Moorish cavalry. In a very short time the hiss of bullets startled our ears, and as they struck the ground with a 'pitt,' or lodged in the cactus scrub at our feet, it sounded like the patter of hail upon a pavement. Every now and then, as we dipped into a gully, the shots would come whistling overhead, or humming up the ravines from the sea.

And we were running for our lives! The sun, which even in January in that country is very powerful, beat down upon us with its burning rays, and the perspiration burst from our pores and trickled down our faces. For half an hour we struggled on, picking our way along the tortuous paths between the cactus growth, our heavy riding-boots weighing on our feet like lead. Glancing back now and again, we could see that the small body of horsemen in pursuit, about twenty in number, gained upon us but slowly. The short prickly undergrowth, that we had so often anathematized, now stood us in good stead; for if it made the going difficult for us, much worse was it for the horses, and every time their riders fired a shot they had to come almost to a halt to avoid a fall while taking aim.

"WE WERE RUNNING FOR OUR LIVES."

[*To face page* 134.

The men with the baggage had disappeared in the first ravine we had come to, striking off to the right as if making for the beach, there perhaps to hide in some of the caves until they could make good their escape under the friendly cover of the darkness, and there were left with us only Ibrahim Jinan and two other tribesmen. In their light clothing and slippered feet they never seemed to tire, and urged us on with words that we could but dimly comprehend. Beyerle, who had a pair of field-glasses slung over his shoulder as well as a large-sized Webley revolver, passed these over to one of the natives to lighten his weight. I handed my revolver also to 'Mr. Garden,' but retained my two daggers. The first skirmish we had rather enjoyed than otherwise, as an exciting break in the monotony of our camp life, but this ignominious helter-skelter was a different affair, and bore too strong a resemblance to a man-hunt for my liking. A bullet is not a pleasant visitant at any time, and if it takes you in the back it is still less to an Englishman's liking. So when, in the next ravine, Beyerle called out to me that he would rather surrender than go on like that, I was almost of his way of thinking. The Moorish soldiers could not fail to recognise us as Europeans, and we could wait their coming and take our chance. That did not suit our Susi companions, however, who, seeing us lagging behind, turned back and urged us on again, one of them accompanying his exhortations by raining blows on Beyerle's back as he would a tired mule.

A few paces farther, and Beyerle, who had shown signs of giving in several times from sheer exhaustion, called out that he could go no farther. Just then I descried some mounted men at the foot of the hill a few hundred yards ahead, but whether friends or enemies I couldn't tell; but they served as a spur to our flagging energies, although I was wellnigh spent myself. Taking my comrade by the hand, I dragged him along for a few more paces, our limbs becoming wearier with every step. The perspiration was running down our faces, and we were panting with the unwonted exertion like a couple of tired dogs.

Again Beyerle cried out that he could go no farther, and, seating himself on the ground, urged me to go on by myself.

'You can still run, old fellow,' he said; 'you go on and save yourself. Leave me here—I'm done.'

'No,' I replied; 'if you stay, I stay too, and we'll see it out together;' and I waited whilst he recovered his breath a little.

Looking towards our pursuers, I saw that they were scarcely 200 yards behind, and they seemed to have ceased firing, pausing as if irresolute whether to go on or give up the chase and turn back. The *Hassani*, I could see, was steaming southwards after the *Tourmaline*, but we were quite out of range of her guns. The men at the foot of the hill were stationary too, and appeared to be friendlies, as they were signalling to us. Seeing this, I called Beyerle to pull himself together for one more effort, and, seizing him by the hand, raised him on to his feet and dragged him along. As we approached the little party, we saw, to our great joy, that there were two led mules for us. Poor Beyerle was so done up it took four men to lift him astride his beast, and it was with the greatest difficulty that I scrambled into my saddle by standing on a cactus bush. A sorry beast she was, in truth, with her bones nearly bursting through her skin, a very scarecrow of an animal, but to me at that moment she was a priceless boon, even though delicacy might forbid the subject of teeth in her presence.

I had then leisure to observe the party we had so opportunely fallen in with, and saw it was composed of Muley Abdallah, his nephew Hamed, El F'kir Embarak, and about half a dozen tribesmen. Turning round in my saddle, I could see that our pursuers were being attacked from the hills on their flank, and were too busily occupied in looking to their own lives to have any time for us. They were in full retreat towards Arksis.

For the best part of an hour we had been running. It was a near thing, but we were saved! And then began the long wearisome climb over the mountains towards the villages inland. Both our animals lacked stirrups, and after the long run we had had, the weight of my legs dangling over the mule's sides soon began to give me considerable pain in the groin. The bridle consisted of a single twisted leather rope with a loop at the end, and I found some little relief by resting first one foot and then the other in the loop, twisting the line round the pommel of the Moorish saddle on which I sat.

As we reached the summit of the first hill, about 1,500 feet above the level of the sea, a panorama of the most beautiful character was unfolded before our gaze. One range of hills succeeded another as far as the eye could reach. On the slopes of the hillsides, and down in the valleys below, patches of green and brown showed that cultivation was by no means neglected, and the little homesteads and tiny *duars*, or villages, dotted here and there, gave this romantic scenery enough animation to deprive it of absolute wildness. Timber was by no means abundant, a few argan trees—a tree that suggests a cross between a stunted oak and an olive-tree—being the only specimens. Water was also lacking, not a stream or rivulet being visible in spite of the heavy rains of a week ago. Droves of cattle and sheep could be seen here and there, and the green barley was just showing above-ground. What a different spectacle from that which we had just witnessed on the other side of the crest of the hill! Peace and war divided only by a line of hills.

For hours we rode on, the tribesmen having left us, as soon as we were in safety, to hurry back to the fighting. I noticed that all the villages were built on the summit of a slope or high up the hillside, the walls surrounding them giving them the appearance of forts, and I learned that such a situation was chosen to afford a better retreat in case of attack by some neighbouring tribe, or their old hereditary enemy, the Sultan of Morocco. In that one fact can be read the history of Sus.

On the way we met Sidi Hashem, the man of many wounds, hurrying on his way to the scene of action; and a little later our party was reinforced by several stray tribesmen, who reported that the Sultan's troops had been beaten off with considerable loss by the Sbooyas, and were in full retreat northwards, but that they had captured the grandson of El F'kir Embarak, and taken him with them.

The sun was setting as we descended into the last valley, and shed a crimson radiance over the lovely scene; but darkness had set in, and the evening star was twinkling in the heavens before we had climbed the final slope and reached our destination. Half dead with fatigue, we slid from our saddles scarce able to stand, and, passing through a low doorway, found ourselves in a sort of compound where mules, donkeys and horses were hobbled and tethered. It was too dark to see much, and I was wondering why our guides had brought us into this stable, when a door in another wall was opened, and, crowding through the hole—for it was barely 4 feet high—we found ourselves in a long, narrow room, dimly lighted by a solitary candle. Then I realized that these were their 'houses.' The courtyard was for the animals, the mud hovels for the human beings; but the only entrance to the one was through the other.

Of furniture there was no sign, except a couple of grass mats whereon these 'luxurious' people squat when they take their simple meals, or huddle themselves up for sleep. The room in which we found ourselves was 7 or 8 feet wide by about 25 feet in length, the mud floor of which was slightly raised at one end. It was innocent of any window or other ventilation that I could see than the doorway through which we had entered, while the roof was formed of thick branches of trees laid crosswise, with the interstices filled in with mud, And this was the residence of El F'kir Embarak, one of the Sbooya 'Forty,' and a signatory to the 'treaty.'

Into this den, where Muley Abdallah and his host were already making themselves comfortable, a broken earthenware bowl was presently brought, in which dry twigs were laid, and a fire lighted to boil water for tea. The smoke from the wood fire, however, soon became so dense that our eyes began to smart, and we were compelled to seek the fresh air again to avoid being choked.

While standing outside, one of the men came, and, divining that we were not entirely charmed with our apartment, conducted us to another house close by, which he eulogized as *bserf miziàn*—very fine; and the next time we saw the fugitive chief, the links that bound us to him were not those of host and guest, but the more material chain that fettered us as fellow-prisoners of the Sultan.

CHAPTER XIII.

IN THE HOUSE OF THE WOLF.

We are lodged in Mulud's house—We make the acquaintance of his son, and of ' Morocco kangaroos '—Close prisoners—'Twixt hopes and fears—News of El Arabi—Flight of Muley Hamed—We suspect treachery—An unpleasant pantomimic performance—We are searched and robbed—A trying ordeal—We are handed over to the Moors—A midnight march—Sidi Hassan.

FOLLOWING our guide, we passed out the way we had come in, and presently found ourselves before another mud erection very similar in appearance to the one we had just left. There was the same corral for the animals, into whose accumulated dung our feet sank at every step, but this palatial residence boasted two stories instead of only a ground-floor. Passing up a flight of stairs made of mud faced with wood, we climbed through a trap-door, and emerged into a room somewhat wider, but not so long as the one we had just left, the walls of which had once been white-washed. It boasted two cupboards let into the wall, and a window with folding shutters, and instead of the primitive roof before described, this one was formed of planed pine boards. From one end of this room a hole in the wall, arch-shaped but without a door, communicated with a smaller room, or cubicle, where two mats and a carpet were spread for us, and a small oil-lamp, of the kind that was probably in use at the time of the virgins of the parable, shed scarcely more than sufficient light to make darkness visible. A close scrutiny of the walls showed that the room was already inhabited, and we looked forward with apprehension to a night of anything but undisturbed repose.

After an interval which seemed to us an age, some bread was brought up to us, and a kettle of water on a charcoal brazier. This *khubs* is much less palatable than the Scotch barley bannocks which R. L. Stevenson stigmatized as an 'inglorious form of bread,' and requires some strongly flavoured sweet like wild-honey to overpower the nauseous taste, mere butter or meat simply serving to accentuate its unpleasant flavour. However, we had had no food since eight o'clock that morning, and when they brought us up a tin of tongue that had come from our stores at Arksis, we fell to with an appetite little short of ravenous.

The house we were in was Sidi Mulud's, who came to do the honours and prepare the tea, in drinking which he and his son joined us. After this meal, we smoked a pipe of native tobacco which he gave us, our own stock having been exhausted some days before, and then, worn out with fatigue, we stretched ourselves out to rest, the younger Mulud, an evil-looking youth, sharing the same apartment. To rest, but not to sleep. I think the 'Morocco kangaroo' is the largest and the hungriest of all the family *Pulex irritans*.

We were glad when morning came, and looked forward with pleasure to going out and basking in the sunshine which was bathing the fields outside; but we found we were closer prisoners than at Arksis, and were not allowed to leave our two rooms. We were even forbidden to show ourselves at the window, and, not understanding much of their language, were unable to ascertain the meaning of these restrictions. Our thoughts turned to Sabbah, and we wondered how he had fared. Doubtless, we thought, they on the yacht had seen something of the fight, but Assaka was six or seven miles from Arksis, and we had no doubt that a boat from the *Tourmaline* would come ashore for us. Then it flashed across my mind that there would be no beacon-fires, and they would know we were not there. Perhaps, however, some of the natives would go down to the coast and signal for a boat, and some means would be found of getting us unobserved to Assaka. Speculating thus 'twixt fears and hopes, I noted with uneasiness that no food was brought us, so we made a wretched breakfast of the remains of our supper of the night before.

At the sound of horses outside the temptation to go to the window and look out was too strong to be resisted. Two or three horses were there all ready saddled and tethered, and we cheered ourselves with the hope that they were to take us to the coast, but hour after hour passed by, and no move was made. They told us we must wait until a messenger should come and report that the road was clear. Muley Hamed came up about mid-day, and took away the blanket which had covered us the night before, and which belonged to Muley Abdallah. This did not look as if we were going to spend another night in that house, and we regarded the incident as a hopeful augury, especially as we gathered from his words and signs that El Arabi had come ashore with a little man with a big moustache and another *N'zarani* (Christian). The big moustache might apply to either Watling or

Last, the second officer, but we could glean no further information.

Four o'clock came, but still there was no sign, and we began to feel sure that treachery was at work. We knew that Sabbah had got aboard the yacht, and would tell the Major that our position ashore was fraught with considerable danger, and, if he did not come himself, he could at least send some of the Susi from the yacht with a message. But he had promised faithfully that he would return, and, from what Muley Hamed had said, we had no doubt he had come ashore. If so, where was he? Perhaps he was waiting for us at Assaka, and we should go to join him after sunset. Speculate as we might, however, we could not shake off our feeling of uneasiness. Shortly before sunset, as I was peeping through the window, I noticed an old man in green robes that I had not seen before, and drew Beyerle's attention to him. He was squatting on the ground, and a small circle of men sat round him. By the looks on their faces, and the going to and fro, we concluded that something was in the wind, but what we could not make out. Several horsemen galloped up to the village, and away again, and looking across the fields, we observed one or two mounted men posted in different directions on the crests of the surrounding hills like vedettes. There they remained until, the sun going down, it was impossible to see them any longer; and shortly afterwards young Mulud came up with a lamp, and we retired into the inner room.

With the exception of Muley Hamed's one visit, we had been alone all day, and now we asked for food.

'*Artini khubs o asel. Walu makla*' (Bring some

bread and honey; we have got no food), I said to him. A vacuous expression came over his ugly face as he repeated in a tone of astonishment: '*Asel?*'

I thought he hadn't understood what I meant, so I repeated the word, varying the accent; but he smiled meaningly, and, instead of going to bring us anything to eat, sat down and commenced to talk. It was a one-sided sort of conversation, and most of it was lost upon us, but his frequent allusions to the *Moros* were not reassuring, especially when accompanied with the significant gesture of drawing his hand across his throat. He also went through a pantomimic performance of taking his clothes off, which I interpreted to mean that we were to take off our own clothes and don those of a Moslem in order to reach the coast by the aid of disguise, while Beyerle was inclined to read it as a hint that we should have to discard the garb of a Christian, and adopt the robe and religion of the Moor, unless we preferred to have our weazands slit. The latter was the less cheerful interpretation, but I was ever inclined to take the hopeful view of things, even though what I have taken to be the sunshine has too often proved to be but indifferent gaslight. He was a repulsive-looking scoundrel, and, becoming more and more familiar, at last roused me to a fury of anger, and springing to my feet, with fists clenched, I left him in no doubt as to what would happen if he persisted in his infamous behaviour. He got up to leave us, and I asked him where his father was, or Muley Abdallah; but motioning us to lie down and go to sleep, he went out with a villainous grin upon his ugly face.

'I don't like the look of this,' said Beyerle. 'I wonder why Muley Abdallah hasn't been all day.'

'I don't understand it, either,' I replied. 'I wish

one of us knew their infernal language, and then we could find out what they're up to. Anyhow, you try and go to sleep now, and I'll keep watch for a while. I don't think it's safe for both of us to sleep at the same time; you don't know what these devils may do.'

'All right, old chap; you wake me when you're sleepy,' he answered; and, blowing up a little pocket air-pillow of mine, he stretched himself out on the mat, and turned his face to the wall, while I sat and waited to see what would happen.

In about half an hour young Mulud came back, and, saying that we were going to the steamer, asked me for my dagger. Under the circumstances I thought the weapon was better in my possession than his, and gave him his answer by slinging the rope which held it over my shoulder. Then he attempted force, but, finding that useless, he soon desisted, and left us alone again. Scarce five minutes elapsed before he was back once more, and, saying something about *al vapor*, signed to us to get up and follow him. We hardly dared to hope that we were really going, but anything was better than this state of suspense, and we jumped up with alacrity. Descending through the trap-door, at the foot of the stairs we found Sidi Mulud himself, who led us across the courtyard, signing to us not to make a noise. It was pitch dark outside, there being no moon, but no word was spoken. Opening a door, he motioned us to enter, and we found ourselves in a room similar to the one in El F'kir Embarak's house, and lighted by a candle stuck on the raised mud platform at one end. Sidi Mulud stayed outside, but his son followed after us, and closed the door. Two other men were in the room, and without ceremony we were told to hand over everything we had in our possession.

So this was to be our fate, I thought—to be stripped and murdered in cold blood by these treacherous scoundrels. Wild thoughts rushed through my brain in that terrible moment. Life is dear to most men, and the idea of being slaughtered like sheep in a shambles filled me with a fierce revulsion. I took the measure of our strippers. They were three in number; we were two. That was nothing. If I passed the word to Beyerle, and we agreed to make a fight of it, by a sudden onslaught we could dispose of two of our adversaries before they had recovered from the surprise of the attack. But even if we were to despatch the three of them before they could raise an alarm, what were we to do? where were we to go? It was probable that we should not get beyond the outer courtyard wall; but if we did succeed in getting clear away, what then? Ultimate capture was certain, and then perhaps a worse fate still would be in store for us. Moreover, perhaps they did not intend to kill, but only to plunder us; but young Mulud's gestures with his hand and throat recurred to my mind, and filled it with ominous foreboding.

All this flashed through me in an instant, though it takes some time to tell, and I settled it in my mind that we should gain nothing by resistance. We were utterly and absolutely in their power. There was nothing to be done, therefore, but to wait the issue with courage—in such a manner as we should not afterwards be ashamed to remember if we should survive. The Susi themselves meet death with a calm and dignified fortitude, consoling themselves with the reflection that 'it is written,' and I scorned to think that an Englishman—or a German—should show a front less firm, or an upper lip less stiff.

'*Gibu el cumia*' (Give me your dagger), said my searcher, and I handed it over to him without a word. Then every pocket was turned out, and watch, money, priceless photo-films that could never be replaced—everything—were taken from me. A gold signet ring on my little finger was difficult to draw off on account of my fingers being swollen, and the stripper, not to be baulked by such a trifle, drew his dagger and was going to cut off the offending digit, but I placed it in my mouth, and got the ring off without further trouble. Beyerle was more fortunate in that respect. Seeing what was happening to me, he drew his own ring off without attracting attention, and concealed it in the palm of his hand, while his stripper was busily engaged in trying to hack off the brass buttons of his khaki coat, which presumably he took to be gold. Turning towards me he remarked, 'Cocky, they are going to butcher us.'

'Yes,' I replied, 'I think they are. Buck up, old man, buck up!'

Poor fellow! He suffered from a weak heart, and I saw that the strain of the terrible ordeal was beginning to tell on him.

The man that was stripping me was still busy hacking at my buttons, when to our intense relief—for anything was better than this awful suspense—there was a knock at the door, and Mulud himself appeared in the doorway. Making a sign to us, we followed him into the darkness outside. Across the filthy courtyard he led us, and out into the open. There awaiting us stood a man on horseback and two on foot. None of the men did we recognise as any of those we had seen in our camp, and the horseman struck me as being better mounted and better dressed than any

Sbooya we had seen. Without delay we set out on the march, the mounted soldier leading the way, Beyerle and I and Mulud following immediately behind, and the two other men bringing up the rear.

'Where do you think they are taking us to, Cocky?' said Beyerle—'Cocky' was his favourite appellation when addressing me. 'Do you think they are going to shoot us?'

'I haven't the faintest idea,' I replied, 'but I don't think they're going to shoot us, because, in the first place, it's too dark for them to see properly; and in the second place, if there was any picnic of that sort in hand, they would have it in the market-place in broad daylight, I fancy, so that all the people could turn out and see the fun. I can't make it out at all.'

I tried to glean from Mulud what all this portended, and whither we were going, but I could make nothing of his replies, except that I caught the words *mat mud*, and knew then that our lives were to be spared, at any rate for the time being. He also kept repeating the word *labas*, signifying 'all right,' to which we could honestly and fervently reply, *Hamdulillah* (Thank God).

Presently another horseman joined us, and we marched on in silence. We found out from the new arrival that he came from Fez, and then it dawned upon us that we were on our way to be delivered over to Giluli. That's what young Mulud meant when he kept on saying '*Moros*' with that fiendish grin of his, but what did that accursed gesture of his imply? Was this only a postponement of our execution? The next few hours would solve the riddle.

After about an hour's tramping, we came to a halt on the hillside, along which ran the semblance of a path or track. The night wind blew cold and made us shiver, starved as we were for want of food, having tasted nothing that day except the remnant of the previous night's barley bannock for breakfast. For nearly twenty minutes we waited there, until another horseman made his appearance. We were evidently picking up the scouts we had seen posted on the hills in the afternoon. Here Mulud left us, returning the way we had come, but spoke no word to us.

On we staggered again over the rough and unknown road, now following the dried-up course of a hillside stream, at other times climbing over great boulders. I noted our direction by the stars, and observed with a little satisfaction that, though we didn't keep on one straight course, still we were trending always towards the coast. After some hours' marching we halted before a house such as we had last left, and one of the men knocked at the door. It was not opened, but a voice replied from within, and it was soon evident we had come to the wrong place.

Another quarter of an hour and we had reached our destination, a tumble-down mud building of the usual kind, and the door was quickly opened in response to our knocking. Inside the room, which was reached through the customary stable-yard, were grouped some six or seven Moors, squatting in a circle, conspicuous among whom was the same venerable *shiekh* in the green *sulham* that we had seen from the window in Mulud's house. The others addressed him as Sidi Hassan, and I afterwards learnt that he was the notary of the Kaid el Bashir, Governor of the Sbooya. A grass mat was spread on the floor, and a camel-hair rug was given us to cover ourselves, and the remainder of that hideous night was spent in snatches of fitful sleep.

CHAPTER XIV.

EL ARABI COMES ASHORE AGAIN.

How El Arabi got on board the yacht—How his news was received—Mr. Henfrey's plan of campaign—The relief-party selected—Betrayal and capture—El Arabi appeals for mercy—The march inland—A halt on the way—A heated discussion—De Reya's cheerfulness under adverse circumstances—An act of kindness—A bad prospect—An unpalatable meal—The march resumed.

MEANWHILE, what had become of Sabbah, and how had he fared on leaving the camp on the morning of the attack by Giluli's troops?

On arrival at Sidi Warzuk, his first care was to patch up the worst leaks in the boat with the materials he had taken with him, and then get a sufficiently numerous crew together to row the boat out to the *Tourmaline*. There was some difficulty in this on account of the crazy condition of the craft; but by promising fifty dollars to each man, he got together a crew of eight to pull the oars. An offer of 200 dollars and twenty pieces of cloth failed to induce the owner of the boat to steer; and, in truth, the largeness of the bribe, especially coming from a Jew, might well have awakened suspicions in his mind, as well as in the minds of the other natives, to whom a sum of fifty dollars represented untold wealth.

When all was ready, Sabbah himself took the tiller; but they had not got far from the beach when the heavy surf almost capsized the boat, and they put back for assistance. Sidi Khabib, who was one of the volunteers, called out to a relative of his who was on the beach, and who knew something of the management of a surf-boat, and, with his help as steersman, the boat was successfully navigated alongside the yacht. Up they scrambled like cats, as soon as the boat was made fast, and their childish glee at being for the first time on board a *vapor Inglíz*, and the curious things they saw there, drove out of their minds for the time being their promised reward; and in a very short time the pangs of sea-sickness made them forget everything except their present miseries.

The position of affairs ashore was quickly related to the Major by Sabbah, and orders were given immediately for the surf-boat to be hauled up on to the davits, and for the yacht to be got under way for Assaka. The Susi were then taken into the chart-room, and those of them that had weapons were required to leave them there. No sooner had the steamer commenced to move, however, than they were all seized with qualms of *mal-de-mer*, and they were quickly removed forward, where, under the shelter of a sail rigged up as an awning, they squatted on the deck, looking the picture of abject misery. As the yacht passed Arksis, the agreed-upon signals were made, but none on board saw or heard anything of the firing which took place ashore so soon after.

The real state of affairs was concealed from the crew, who, however, gathered that all was not as it should be; but in the saloon nothing was talked of but this unexpected and unpleasant development, and the best means of getting Beyerle and myself back to the yacht in safety. Of the small quantity of spirits that had been taken aboard only a few bottles of rum were left; but as this was the first mate's favourite beverage, he, at any rate, was under no necessity to practise the virtues of total abstinence. All his martial ardour seemed to have been aroused by Sabbah's news, and he had settled in his own mind all the details of the plan of operations that was to be adopted. On leaving the saloon, where the Major, the Captain, Watling, and himself had been sitting chatting after dinner, he encountered de Reya, with whom he had made one or two voyages before.

'Now, my boy,' he said, 'are you ready for a fight? I've just been talking it over with the Major, and we've settled it all how we are going to get the two gentlemen from shore. I shall go in the boat with the Moors—of course I shall be armed—and Mr. Last and you, and some of the others, will bring up the rear in the gig, in case you're wanted. Of course, I shall be armed,' he repeated, producing a formidable-looking revolver from his capacious pocket; 'and I'm a dead shot, you know. You're not afraid, are you, de Reya?'

'Not me,' said de Reya. 'I'll go with you, sir.'

'That's all right. I thought I could rely on you,' he remarked; and, regarding the matter as virtually settled already, he went down below, just to have another little conversation with the steward before turning in.

But things wore rather a different aspect in the cold light of early dawn, and the idea of going ashore did not seem to have the same exciting fascination as it did the previous evening. Before the first faint streaks of dawn were showing over the eastern hills, the Major was on deck giving his final instructions. It was decided that Sabbah should go in the surf-boat with five of the Susi, leaving four of them on board the yacht as hostages; but on hearing this, Sabbah requested that he might be allowed to have two of the crew to help row back, in case they were successful in bringing us off from shore, and, this being agreed to, the Captain selected Last, the second mate, and de Reya for that purpose. The Major had already had a talk with Khabib, who, from what we had seen of him ashore, had struck us as one of the most loyally inclined towards us, and asked him, unwisely as subsequent events proved, to render every assistance in his power to get Beyerle and myself and Muley Abdallah on board the yacht, as he was not going to let the natives have any more rifles except in exchange for cash or goods, but was going back to Mogador. The Major no doubt did it for the best; but to take thus into his confidence an ignorant and fanatical tribesman, who had only his own ends to serve, was surely the most certain method of inviting treachery. And so it befell.

Day was now breaking, and as the *Hassani* was observed bearing down upon the yacht, there was no time to be lost. Handing a Union Jack to Last, with instructions to hoist it on the boat, the Major ordered him to return to the yacht immediately if we two were not at the rendezvous on the beach, and, armed with a Marlin rifle each, the two sailors and El Arabi stepped into the boat with the five Susis, and put off. As the boat was rowing towards the shore, the *Hassani* came up, and lowered one of her boats, full of armed men, in pursuit. The Major therefore cleared for action, and signalled, 'I shall fire on your boats if you persist in coming alongside.' This had the desired effect, for, truth to tell, the Moorish officers and soldiers on board the Sultan's steamer were in a very wholesome funk of what might happen if the 'powder began to speak' from the little quick-firing gun on board the yacht, the voice of which they had already heard.

Meanwhile, a party of natives ashore could be seen on the cliff carrying a green flag, which had been used from the first as a signal that all was well, but as the boat grounded on the beach, it was surrounded by the natives ashore, who waded up to their knees in the surf, while the Susis in the boat sprang out, crying, 'The Christians have cheated us! the Christians have cheated us!'

Our men were immediately pounced upon, and their Marlins snatched from their hands before they had had time to realize what was happening. With the muzzle of a gun under their ears, the two sailors then had their pockets rifled of everything they contained, and were then ordered to march inland, an order that was explained and emphasized with blows from behind.

Finding themselves outnumbered and overpowered, the two sailors went along without resistance, but Sabbah for a few minutes fought like a wild-cat whilst he was being despoiled of his weapon and property, even his boots being taken from him. Then his courage failed him, and falling on his knees in the sand, he burst into tears, and, wringing his hands, cried out :

'My God, we are prisoners! Where are our brothers? Take us to our brothers!'

'You shall see your brothers,' said one of the men, with a grin, giving him at the same time a prod in the back to make him get up on to his feet.

The Hebrew has never in any age been remarkable for personal courage, and in this particular representative of the race the utter lack of that quality was such as not to excite pity, but provoke contempt; and, as he realized his perilous situation in all its horrors, he made one more piteous appeal to his captors for mercy. They might do what they liked with the other two, but let *him* at any rate go back to the yacht, and he would give them heaven only knows what reward. But the Susi, like all Mohammedans, are largely endowed with physical courage themselves, and admire nothing so much as that attribute in others, and the spectacle of this grovelling Jew, who recked little of what became of his companions so long as he could save his own skin, aroused in them only feelings of the utmost contempt. Pointing his gun at him, one of the natives threatened to shoot him on the spot if he didn't get up, and, fearful lest the man should carry out his threat, El Arabi rose to his feet with trembling limbs, and quaking fear at his heart, and followed after the others up the hillside.

His companions, who were now some distance ahead, shouted out to him to follow, and endeavoured to bring him to his senses and screw his courage up; and with their exhortations, aided by the spurring on of the natives from behind, he soon came up to them. The leader of the gang, one Barkat, seeing him lagging behind in his stockinged feet, lent him his own slippers, and the party moved on at a rapid pace, and the sea was soon hidden from view behind the crest of the hills.

All through the long morning they trudged without food or rest. They had left the yacht before breakfast time, and had not taken the precaution to eat anything before leaving, an omission they now sorely regretted. About mid-day a halt was called, and the three captives were taken into a native tent, made of some coarse fibre roughly woven, and pitched by being thrown over some short sticks fixed upright in the ground. Here two women ground up some barley with their primitive mill-stones, and some bannocks were baked over a charcoal fire, but the bread was so nauseous as to be scarcely eatable — especially to the two sailors, who had never tasted the like before.

After a rest they were marched on again, and their captors told them that they were going to meet their Christian friends, who were in a house farther inland. Towards three o'clock a large house, somewhat resembling a fort, was reached, and they were taken into a large room on the ground-floor, on which a couple of grass mats were spread. There was no window in the room, and Sabbah begged that the door might be left open to let in the light. This was granted, and there being no guard set immediately over them, they spread one of the mats on the ground in the courtyard, and lay down in the sun. From this spot the sound of clamouring voices outside could be easily heard, and Sabbah soon made out that a heated discussion was going on as to what fate should be reserved for the captives. Some were in favour of selling them as slaves to tribes in the interior. Fortunately for them, the two sailors were unconscious of what was being said, but to Sabbah, who overheard and could understand most of the conversation, the mere suggestion was appalling. Possibly he had not heard of James Butler, who was captured thirty years before, and the horrors he went through during seventeen years of slavery in Sus, but he was acquainted with the character of the people, and had doubtless had related to him, at some time or other, the story of the Spanish captive who had been crippled in a peculiarly horrible manner to prevent his escaping. A bullock is said to have been kept for several days without water, at the end of which time the unfortunate prisoner was placed on its back as if he were going to ride it, his feet being firmly tied under its stomach, and the animal was then led out to drink. The effect on the wretched victim's limbs may be more easily imagined than described. A cold perspiration broke out all over Sabbah at the bare thought of what his fate might be among this savage people, but he did not communicate his fears to his companions, one of whom, at any rate, was endeavouring to keep his spirits up by humming snatches of comic songs that were then the popular ditties of the London music-halls.

Others of the tribesmen were in favour of handing them over to the Sultan's troops if a good bargain could be made with Kaid Giluli, and a heated wrangle ensued.

Presently a woman passed through the stable-yard —for such it was—and Sabbah begged of her to get them a rug, wherewith to make themselves a little more comfortable, and she very kindly brought them a good thick native-woven blanket with which they covered themselves. Tired out with their long tramp, and utterly unconscious of the doom that threatened them, Last and de Reya fell fast asleep and remained in that state of happy oblivion until long after the sun had set and the stars were shining overhead. Sabbah, however, was too full of apprehension to sleep, but strained his ears to learn what was to become of him and his companions. He was not much cheered when a woman came to him and said in accents of pity rarely heard among those people, 'I am very sorry for you, poor boys! Why have you come to this savage country? Don't you know that the people here would kill you for a *billion*?* You will never see your own country and your friends again, for they are going to kill you.'

Scarcely had she gone before a man came and led the three captives to a room at the top of the house, where the sounds of the dispute, which was still going on below, but faintly reached their ears. At times it seemed probable that the argument would be settled by a resort to arms by the contending factions, but nothing of the sort occurred. And meanwhile, under cover of the warm rug which the kind-hearted woman had lent them, the two sailors slept on and took their rest, whilst Sabbah endured the tortures of a waking nightmare. At midnight a man entered the room with a dish of some dirty-looking mess called *tshisha*, which is a sort of coarse porridge made of broken barley and water, and only imperfectly cooked. Hungry as they were, and accustomed to the none too delicate fare provided in the forecastle of merchant ships, this horrible pig-food was, however, too disgusting to eat, especially as it had to be scooped out of the bowl with the fingers and squeezed into semi-adhesive balls before being passed into the mouth.

After this interruption they were left alone again

* A *real billion* is a Spanish coin nominally worth 2½d.

until the early morning, when they were roused up and taken outside once more. What had been decided overnight Sabbah was unable to ascertain, but under a strong guard they were marched on, whither they knew not.

CHAPTER XV.

BEFORE THE KAID.

We learn our destination—The march resumed—Mohammedanism and Truth—We meet El Arabi again—Our fate in the balance—Kaid el Bashir settles it—Concerning Kaids generally—A Sultan's tax-gathering—Raiding in Sus—Kaid Dakhman uld Bairuk—Arksis again—An ambitious suitor—Kaid Said el Giluli—An unsatisfactory interview—News of the *Tourmaline*—Captain Siebert prophesies—A novel substitute for tobacco—We are searched and thrown into chains—An unpleasant companion—Cheerfulness in adversity.

WHEN Beyerle and I woke to the consciousness of our new surroundings, the sun had not yet risen, though the first streaks of dawn could be seen through the cracks in the rickety door, but the Moorish soldiers in the house were already astir. It was some comfort to hear the sound of each other's voices, and to make sure that we were still alive, and had not played a prominent part in a butchering performance the night before. The old *adul*, with his white beard and green *sulham*, looked quite a model of venerable benignity as he sat at the other end of the room with his legs crossed and tucked under him. From him we learnt that the least of many anticipated evils was about to happen—we were *en route* for Giluli's camp, to be handed over to the Sultan. In the hands of even this semi-civilized potentate, or any of his officials, we felt that our lives, at any rate, would be safe, and the restoration of our liberty only a matter of formality, and such time as would be occupied in delivering us over to the nearest British Consul. While waiting for breakfast, Sidi Hassan was inclined to be conversational, and, producing various articles, principally weapons, desired to be informed as to their country of origin. Daggers and guns are made in Morocco by the Moors, but the people themselves show a higher appreciation of *Ruomi* manufacture, especially British, and to tell them that the blade of their dagger is Inglíz is to add considerably to their pride in possession, and pleasure in life generally.

In the midst of this inspection of armoury a dish of *tshisha* was brought in, which the soldiers vigorously attacked, passing the bowl on to us after they had eaten their fill. It was nearly twenty-four hours since we had divided the remaining half of a barley bannock in the house of Mulud, and we were right hungry, but my gorge rose at this unpalatable food, and neither Beyerle nor I could eat more than a mouthful or two. Moreover, it was the first time that it had been forcibly brought home to us that fingers were made before forks, and it was not much encouragement to us to reflect that the Sultan of Morocco himself eats his food in the same primitive manner.

Shortly after we had finished 'breakfast,' a messenger arrived on horseback, evidently the bearer of news for which we were waiting, and we were ordered to get ready to move. The impression we had formed the night before, that the men into whose hands we had fallen were of a better class than the Sbooyas, was strengthened by daylight. They were better dressed, blue Melton cloth of English manufacture taking the place of native-woven material, generally used by the Sbooyas for their *sulhams;* and their general appearance was less suggestive of the wild and turbulent hill-man. As soon as the horses were saddled, the door of the stable-yard was opened, and we were ordered to march. We set off again across the hills towards the sea-coast, about a dozen men accompanying us, some on foot and some on horseback.

A brisk walk in the fresh morning air was quite exhilarating, and struck the happy medium between the comparative confinement of our camp at Arksis and the race for life from the field of battle; but we should have been more satisfied in our minds if we had known for certain whither we were trudging. We had been told that we were going to be sent to the Sultan, but we had been long enough in that country to have learnt to accept no statement as true unless confirmed by several persons at different times, and then only to receive it with reserve. Truth is not a quality that can be ranked among the virtues of Mohammedans, who seem to act upon the principle of never telling the truth if a lie will serve their purpose as well. Indeed, it is recorded of a former Sultan that, being one day upbraided by a European for not having kept a promise that he had made, he angrily retorted, 'Am I a dog of a Christian that I should be the slave of my word?'—an elegant Oriental way of expressing it.

According to our reckoning, we seemed to be marching in the direction of Assaka, and we endeavoured to extract some information from one of the men who seemed inclined to be not unfriendly, but he only pointed ahead and said something about *sahabi* (friends). Then I remembered what Muley Hamed had told us about El Arabi coming ashore with a man with a big moustache and another, and I guessed that we were on our way to meet some of the *Tourmaline* men.

After about an hour's tramp, we came to the top of a high hill, from which we could descry the sea some miles off, and shortly afterwards we saw advancing towards us a large party of armed men, mounted and afoot, among whom Beyerle immediately recognised Sabbah in his cycling suit. On approaching nearer, we saw that he was accompanied by Last and de Reya. On coming up to us, Sabbah gave vent to a yell of joy. He had fully made up his mind that we had either been killed or sold into slavery, and that he had looked his last upon us. Of course they were all curious to know what had happened to us since Sabbah had left us at Arksis, as we were to learn how they had fared since they had come ashore; and when the tale was told, we all agreed that our experiences were pleasanter to relate than to undergo.

When the two escorts had joined, there was quite a numerous company, most of them armed with the *m'kahla*, or long-barrelled flint-lock gun, though some of the men, the cavalry especially, carried Martini-Henrys. This meeting had evidently been pre-arranged, and after a very brief halt the march was resumed in a direction at right angles to the one Beyerle and I had been following up till then. We had not gone far, however, when another handful of cavalry came up at a gallop, and, wheeling across our path, called a halt. An excited squabble immediately began, but in the babel of voices that arose it was difficult at first to make out what all the noise was about. It appeared, however, that some were for taking us one way, and some another. One man grabbed de Reya by the collar, and attempted to drag him along by the side of his horse, and I feared that our little party was about to be separated. This was not at all to our liking, and we meant to stick together if possible; so we all followed in the same direction. Meanwhile, the two contending parties seemed to be preparing for a fight for the possession of us, and every moment I expected to hear the powder 'speak,' so quietly drew on one side to be out of the line of fire, and called to the others to do the same. Just at this juncture a youngish-looking, clean-shaven man, whose complexion was quite fair in comparison with that of the dark-skinned Susi and Moors, by whom he was surrounded, rode out of the press, and galloped up to the man who was still grasping the collar of de Reya's coat. Some of the flint-locks were already levelled, and every moment I expected to hear the crack of a shot, and see an empty saddle, but with a fine air of authority he demanded that we should be surrendered to him. The cool audacity of the deed had completely disarmed them, and before they had recovered from their surprise we were marching along again in the wake of our new custodian. He proved to be Sid' el Bashir, whom the Sultan had recently appointed Kaid of the Sbooyas.

There is something very laughable about these appointments of the Sultan in Sus. There are not many of them, it is true, and such kaidships as there are nominally can scarcely be considered as 'offices of profit under the Crown.' No salary is attached to the title, and as the Susi have always refused to pay taxes to the Sultan or his nominees, and have resisted any attempt to collect them by force of arms, there is no chance of the Kaid enriching himself by plundering the *Kabilas** after the manner of such dignitaries on the other side of the Atlas, since he has no force at his back.

Resistance to the Sultan and his Kaids is by no means uncommon in Morocco, but dire and speedy vengeance is wreaked upon the refractory tribe, when the 'Commander of the Faithful' descends with an army like a murrain upon the land, and, in their expressive phrase, 'eats it up.' The pretext for such an incursion may be well founded—such as the dismissal by the Beni M'Gild tribes of the Bashas that were appointed to their districts by the Sultan, after handling those functionaries in no gentle manner—or it may be the more trivial one of suspected disaffection, but the punishment inflicted is the same.

In the early part of this year (1898) the Sultan, with his army of 20,000 or 30,000 men, visited the province of Shawia, and the memory of the imperial visitation will long remain imprinted on the minds of the unfortunate dwellers in the land on account of the horrors and outrages committed by the Sherifian hordes. Unfortunately, in this country the innocent always suffer with, and too often *instead* of, the guilty. The ablebodied frequently manage to make good their escape when a raid takes place, but the old men and the boys, the women and girls, are left to the tender mercies of this Nero of the nineteenth century. And so it was in this case, but Muley Abd-el-Aziz was in no mood to be baulked of his vengeance, and there

* Tribes.

followed scenes of rapine, pillage, and bloodshed which aroused feelings of the greatest horror and indignation among the European residents throughout the land, long accustomed as they are to stories of such fiendish cruelties.

The grain season had given every promise of being an unusually good one, but the growing crops were ruthlessly demolished by the Sherifian troops, who set their horses, mules and camels to feed upon them. Their cattle, and everything portable belonging to the unfortunate tribespeople, even to their ragged clothes, were carried away; large numbers of innocent men were murdered, their heads being salted and sent to various towns in the sultanate, there to adorn the gates surmounted on poles; many more were taken prisoners, while their houses were destroyed; and the families of these victims that were left behind found themselves in an almost complete state of nudity, without shelter or food, and with death from starvation staring them in the face, as they had nothing but roots to feed upon. Thus was the ruin of one of the most fertile of Moorish provinces accomplished, as if the only object of the Sultan and his advisers was to destroy all the sources of wealth and prosperity throughout the country.

The fate of the wretched captives was, if possible, more terrible still. With their feet riveted together, they were sent on the backs of mules or camels to fill the foul dens of death which the Moorish officials call 'prisons,' in various towns throughout the empire, and it is estimated that, of the 6,000 or so prisoners taken during the campaign (!), less than 4,000 reached the place of incarceration allotted to them, and many of those arrived looking little better than skeletons, and frequently were flung half naked, dead and dying, into the panniers on the backs of the mules.

That these things should be done by an uncivilized barbarian would not be so astonishing; but when we remember that the Sultan of Morocco maintains diplomatic relations with all the Powers of Europe, and that his army is drilled and led by a Scotsman who once held Her Majesty's commission in the British army, and who has on various recent occasions been the recipient of marks of favour from his country and his Sovereign, we may well stand aghast, and pause to ask ourselves if we have not some indirect participation and responsibility as a nation for these revolting atrocities, to which we have to turn to Armenia or the Sudan for a parallel.

In Sus, and in a lesser degree in the mountainous districts of the Riff, these things are not so easy of accomplishment. On account of the nature of the country, the advance of a large body of troops is a slow affair, and long before the punitive expedition—or rather I would call it the raiding-party—has arrived in the district of the objective tribe, the tribesmen have had an opportunity of hiding their property and betaking themselves to the hills, whence they can carry on a very effective kind of guerilla warfare in comparative safety. On these expeditions the Sultan himself never accompanies the troops, generally leaving the work to some loyal Kaid in the neighbourhood, who takes with him the men of his own tribe, accompanied by a few of the Sultan's military officers. But every attempt to subjugate these tribes to the Sultan's domination, and to impose Moorish Governors upon them, has left matters precisely where they were before, with the exception that both sides are a little poorer in numbers, and the Moorish prisons a little richer. Dakhman uld Bairuk, the powerful chief of Wad-Nun, may perhaps be considered as a solitary exception, but he, instead of paying tribute to the Sultan, is understood to receive regular subsidies from him, given, probably, with the double object of securing his assistance in the event of any encroachment upon Sus territory by foreigners, and of discouraging any possible ideas he may have of joining in a concerted rising of the Sus tribes to proclaim the independence of the country, and dispose once for all, by force of arms, of the absurd pretensions of the Sultan of Morocco.

And so this Kaid el Bashir was a Governor nominated by the Sultan, but utterly without the power of enforcing his decrees. At the same time, I couldn't help but admire his pluck and spirit in this affair, as, rifle in hand, he threatened to shoot the first man that dared to interfere with him or disobey his orders.

We trudged on for some hours, halting only once at a well to drink. About mid-day we came to an opening in the hills, and below us lay Arksis once more. But what a different aspect it wore from what it had done forty-eight hours before! Our old camping-ground on the head of the cliff was covered with the tents of an army numbering, at a rough computation, some 5,000 men. Horses, camels and mules innumerable were cropping the short, sparse vegetation of the plateau, and the blue and white of the soldiers' *sulhams*, with here and there a red *tarbush*, or fez, lent colour to the scene, while the long, bright barrels of thousands of guns flashed in the sunlight.

Close inshore, right under the lee of the cliffs, lay the *Hassani* at anchor, and we knew then that the fight of Monday, which the Sbooyas had told us had ended in the flight of the defeated Gilulis to Ifni, had resulted very much in favour of the raiding invaders.

At the head of this gully a halt was ordered, whilst a bullock was slaughtered and sent as a present and conciliatory offering to Kaid Giluli; and in the meantime we rested and chatted with our escort. Sidi Hassan, the venerable *adul*, was one of the party, and was anxious to improve his knowledge concerning things English. From things he drifted on to persons, and expressed a desire to marry one of the daughters of the Queen of England. I told him that that could easily be arranged, as so important a personage as himself was the suitor, and that on my arrival in England I would inform one of the Princesses, and she would doubtless take the first steamer for Morocco. I had not the least doubt that the ignorant and self-sufficient old fool was serious, and considered himself quite an eligible *parti* for a Princess of the Royal House of England; but before the next week was over we heard that, being suspected of treachery, he had taken flight, but had been pursued and sent to find a bride among the houris of Paradise.

After waiting about an hour, a messenger came back from the camp, which seemed so close but was really about a mile and a half away, and reported that all was ready for us to be taken before the Kaid. Considerable interest was manifested by the soldiers on our arrival, and as we neared the Kaid's tent two long lines of soldiers were drawn up to keep a clear passage. Through this lane we marched, Beyerle and I leading the way, and the other three bringing up the rear. At the entrance to the tent, which was somewhat larger than the one we had occupied, we saw, to our great joy, a couple of men in European dress, whom we rightly guessed to be officers of the *Hassani*, as we knew that the Captain, at any rate, was a German. Inside the tent we found about twenty Moors ranged in a circle, evidently awaiting our arrival, and on the floor in the middle a large grass mat was spread, on which we were invited to sit.

Squatting down in the Moorish fashion, I faced the Kaid, whom I had no difficulty in recognising, both from his dress and the position he had taken up. A fat old man of between sixty and seventy years of age, with a short, white, pointed beard and fair complexion, he gave no suggestion of being the fierce and intrepid warrior that the stories of the Sbooyas had depicted him; yet it was said that in battle he displayed the activity of a young man and the courage of a lion. His face wore an almost benevolent expression, and I thought I detected the embryo of a smile upon his thin lips as we ranged ourselves before him. But what struck me most was that his eyelids were darkened with *kohl* just under the lashes, his cheeks were painted like those of some old Jezebel of the streets at home, and the tips of his nails were stained brown with henna. His dress was superior to anything I had yet seen in the country; his *jelaba* was of cashmere of the finest possible texture, having almost the appearance of white silk, ornamented with a broad olive-green scarf, over which he wore a *sulham* of dark blue Melton. On his bald or shaven head, of course, he wore a large white turban. Such was Kaid Said el Giluli.

The Kaid asked which of us was the chief, and I told him the chief was on board the steamer.

A man in a red fez was indicated to me as an interpreter, but I soon discovered that his familiarity with English was much less than Sabbah's; and the latter was therefore employed as the intermediary between the Kaid and myself in the interview which took place.

'On what grounds,' I demanded, 'have our lives been endangered by the firing of your soldiers, has our property been taken away from us, and our liberty been interfered with in that we are brought here as prisoners?'

'You have come to Arksis without the Sultan's permission,' was the bland reply, as if that explained everything.

'Is Arksis in Sus?' I asked, and the indulgent smile that overspread his fat features was meant to be sufficient answer. I pressed for something more specific, and he said:

'Of course it is; you know that.'

I pursued my geographical inquiries:

'Is Sus part of the Sultan's dominions?'

'Yes, of course it is,' was the ready reply.

'Very well, then,' I said, 'we do not need any special permission of the Sultan to come here, as the treaties between your Sultan and ours provide that every British subject has "the free and undoubted right to travel and to reside in the territories and dominions of his said Majesty, subject to the same precautions of police which are practised towards the subjects or citizens of the most favoured nations,"' and produced from my pocket a printed pamphlet to impress him with the fact that I was speaking 'by the card.'

'I know nothing about treaties,' he retorted; 'you have come to Arksis without the Sultan's permission.'

And this was the head and front of our offence. Not a word was said about the landing of arms, or anything else, the mere fact of 'coming to Arksis without the Sultan's permission' being in his mind, apparently, a crime of so heinous a character as to dwarf all other considerations, and to justify the punishment even of death. The self-confessed ignorance of the man annoyed me, and, moreover, boded no good fate in store for us, so I decided to try the effect of bluster.

'You may not know anything about treaties,' I said, 'but your master the Sultan does; and he has agreed with our Sultana that any English who may be found in his dominions, either in time of peace or war, shall have perfect liberty to depart to their own country without interference; and if you have got any complaint to make against us, you had better put us on board the *Hassani*, and take us to the British Consul at the nearest port, which is Mogador. Meanwhile, for what has already taken place, and for any other harm or injury which you may do to us, I shall hold you and your master the Sultan responsible.'

I shot the bolt, but it fell harmless on that self-sufficient mass of pachydermatous obesity.

'No,' he said, with his blandest and most child-like smile; 'you wanted to see the country: I will show you the country. You shall go to Morocco City, and then you can see the lions.'*

---

* It is a prevalent belief among the Moors that lions are to be met with at the foot of the Atlas Mountains, but I don't think there is any authentic report of their existence so far north.

Finding argument with the old fellow but a waste of time, I rose to my feet, and, addressing Captain Siebert of the *Hassani*, asked him if he would take us to Mogador.

'I can do nothing,' he replied. 'I had already done my best with the Kaid, before you came, to persuade him to allow me to take you to Mogador; but he would not listen to me. He is going to send you to the Sultan; but you will be all right. You are very lucky that you have come into his hands, for those people you were with are savages, and would probably have killed you. My engineer was caught by them some years ago, and was nine months before he was rescued. He had a very hard time.'

Turning to the Kaid once more, I asked him if we would be supplied with what food we required, and he answered, 'Oh yes;' and added in a tone of inquiry: 'You will pay for it, of course?'

'How can we pay for it when all our money has been stolen from us?' I asked. 'Let us go on board our own steamer, and we shall not need to ask you for anything, but meanwhile it is a long time since we had anything to eat or drink, and we are very hungry.'

'All right,' he replied; 'there is plenty of food in the camp, and you will be very well treated until I hand you over to the Sultan. Would you rather be sent with a special escort now, or wait a few days here to see if your steamer comes back?'

'We would rather wait a day or two for the yacht if you will let us send a message; otherwise we would prefer to go by special escort as quickly as possible.'

And the interview being concluded, we were shown

into another tent that was already occupied, where we were regaled with tea and bread and honey and a bowl of rice, all of which we much relished, as none of us had had a square meal since Monday night, forty hours before.

During the time that I had been talking with the Kaid, Beyerle had been carrying on a conversation with Captain Siebert and his chief engineer, Mr. Sievers, in their mother-tongue. They had told him that the *Tourmaline* had left the coast about two o'clock the previous day, evidently bound for the Canaries, and we were glad to think that by this time the news of our capture had already been flashed along the wire, and the first steps taken towards securing our release. The *Hassani* was going now to Cape Juby down the coast, and then to Mogador. Beyerle asked the Captain to notify the British Vice-Consul there of our capture, and wrote our names down in the Captain's pocket-book, and he promised to perform that small service for us. Furthermore, on Beyerle asking him if he could send us anything to drink, as we had not had for some days past even water that was not either thick with clay or swarming with visible red worms, he readily promised to do so. Any idea of our reaching Morocco City or Mogador in fourteen days, he said, must be put aside. It would take us two or three months, as these people never hurried, and Giluli wouldn't send any special escort. He was going to exterminate the Sbooyas first. There were seven camps all round the place, and the circle would be gradually drawn in so that not a man could escape, and every man, woman and child in the tribe would be slaughtered and their houses burnt: not one stone would be left upon another.

'You will see,' he said, 'the Kaid will take you with him; he will not let you out of his sight.'

All this Beyerle related to us while we were regaling ourselves in the tent which we thought was going to be our new quarters. But we were soon to be unpleasantly undeceived. We had scarcely finished our meal before we were taken out and shown into one of our own tents that they had pitched for us. It was the one that we had used as our kitchen, during the time we had been ashore. It was barely large enough for two to sleep in with comfort, yet five of us were crowded in there. Moreover, it was rotten and ragged, gaping rents appeared in many places, and its inner sides were blackened and begrimed with the smoke of many wood fires. On the ground was spread a grass mat which only covered half the space, and on this we sat and endeavoured to be as cheerful as the circumstances of our case would allow.

Barkat, who had lent Sabbah his slippers, came to claim his property, and on Sabbah handing them to him, to our astonishment the man calmly took out his knife, cut off some small strips of leather from the sole, which he put into a pipe made out of a mutton bone, and commenced to *smoke* it. But half an hour had not elapsed when a fresh prisoner was brought in, the grandson of El F'kir Embarak, whom we had heard had been captured in the battle on Monday. He was only about fifteen or sixteen years of age, although he had an 'old' face, such as is often seen on young gaol-birds at home, and the only clothing he had on was a filthy shirt, so ragged that it was a perfect marvel how the thing held together. I was sorry for the lad as he sat there huddled up with his knees to his mouth and shivered with the cold. At the same time he was not a welcome companion, and I protested against any Susi being put into our tent, as it was already much overcrowded, but no notice was taken. I began to think that our treatment was not going to be as good as we had been led to expect, but we were all cheered by the arrival of a hamper from the *Hassani*, brought in by the steward of the steamer, in whom we recognised Giluli's would-be interpreter. Lager beer, wine, spirits, and, above all, a box of fifty cigars, met our delighted vision, and we were loud in our praises of Captain Siebert's generosity and hospitality to an unfortunate countryman in distress.* The cigars were particularly welcome, as we couldn't raise a pipeful of tobacco between us, and we were just settling ourselves down to enjoy the luxury of a smoke and a drink of lager beer, when we were interrupted by the entry of two or three soldiers, who immediately set to work to search us, and relieve us of anything that might be found upon us. It was not a very profitable haul they had, as Beyerle and I had already gone through one plundering process, and the other three had not overburdened themselves with portable property on coming ashore. Beyerle again succeeded in concealing his signet-ring, but was despoiled of his diary, which he begged hard, but in vain, to be allowed to retain. That note-book ultimately found its way into the hands of the Sultan, who caused it to be translated from French, in which it was written, into Arabic, and who was, I hope, edified by what he found there set down. I was more fortunate in that respect, as mine was concealed, with a pencil,

* The incident was subsequently robbed of some of its charm by Captain Siebert presenting a pretty stiff bill to Beyerle on his arrival in Tangier.

in an inside pocket of my khaki jacket, which was buttoned up, and it never occurred to my stripper that I had anything there. My pipe also escaped capture once more, and my tobacco-pouch, which had been returned to me by young Mulud as *haluf* (pigskin).

The tattoo of drums and a flourish of trumpets in front of the Kaid's tent announced sunset, and, to our dismay, brought our gaolers once more to our tent, carrying chains and irons, which they flung down with an ominous clank. We were not long left in doubt as to the object of these accursed fetters, for without any ceremony or ado they proceeded to put round the neck of each of us a heavy iron collar which opened on a hinge, and was fitted at each end with two large projecting flanges pierced with eyelet-holes. When the collar was adjusted round the neck, an oblong iron loop was slipped over the two projections, thus closing the collar, and a long chain passed through the eyelet-holes, the ends of the chain being brought together and fastened with a padlock, which was placed outside the tent under the eye of a guard. Instead of a collar, an anklet was fastened round the leg of the Susi boy, and in that manner the six of us were chained together. We protested vehemently against this indignity, but they jokingly told us that as we were so near the sea the Kaid was afraid we might escape and swim away to our ship. They assured us that this was the lightest chain they had, and threatened that if we grumbled any more about it they would put the heavier one on us. Finding further protest useless, we asked for a rug to cover ourselves with, as the nights were decidedly cold, but a vicious tug at the chain, which hurt our necks, was the only response.

IN CHAINS.

Perhaps it may be thought difficult to extract humour from such a situation as we found ourselves in, but we looked at one another, Beyerle in his six feet two, and Last in his five feet ditto next to him, with the collar nearly up to his ears, and when de Reya said, 'Look at Tajer* Last: his clothes don't fit him,' the ludicrousness of the whole thing rushed upon us, and we burst into an uncontrollable fit of laughing. 'Well,' I remarked, 'I never thought we should be decorated with the Grand Iron Collar of the Sultan of Morocco; it's a distinction that very few Christians have received in recent years, I think;' and de Reya began softly to croon to himself:

> 'Why did I leave my little back-room in Blooms-bur-ee,
> Where I could live on a pound a week in lux-ur-ee?
> I've got out of the frying-pan into the blooming fire.'

Darkness coming on, we had no option but to make the best of it by huddling close together like so many animals, for the sake of warmth, care being taken by de Reya, who was next to him, to give as wide a berth as possible to Khabib, the Susi boy, who had been beguiling the tedium of the daylight hours by slaughtering his livestock. The boy also had complained of the cold, as he was almost naked, and one of the Moors returned to him for the night the *sulham* of which he had been stripped when brought into the tent.

Lying awake vainly endeavouring to keep warm, the meaning of young Mulud's gestures now came to me. He was trying to tell us that we were going to be handed over to the Moors, and he foreshadowed

---

* Merchant, a term generally applied to Christians indiscriminately.

the chains by drawing his hand round his neck; whilst his pantomimic unrobing was intended to convey to us the information that we should be stripped of our clothes. We had, however, been spared this last indignity. We were in sufficiently bad case without that, and we passed a most wretched night, which did not augur well for our future treatment.

CHAPTER XVI.

THE BEGINNING OF THE RAID.

Breaking camp—A Moorish war-song—The raid commences—
The search for grain—Camel-riding—Arrival at Tlata—We
try to see the Kaid—And are punished accordingly—We are
put on show—A pleasant visitor—A captive's welcome—
Muley Abdallah is brought in—Moorish philosophy—How
Muley Abdallah and El F'kir Embarak were captured.

By sunrise the camp was all astir, and, peeping through one of the numerous holes in our tent, we were surprised to see that many of the tents were being taken down. While we were speculating as to the meaning of this, we heard one of the guards unlocking our chain, and immediately afterwards he came and took the iron collars off our necks, and ordered us to go outside. All was activity and bustle in the camp. Most of the tents had been already struck, and our poor rag shelter was rolled up in a trice by busy soldiers under the orders of a short fat man, who stumped about with a thick stick in his hand, belabouring the lazy, and directing all, and who, in spite of the lame leg that he owed to a Susi bullet, seemed to be all over the place at once. Uld Suka was decidedly an acquisition to such an army as Giluli's. The camels —those most dissatisfied of all beasts, that complain when their load is laid upon them, and eke when it is taken off—were on their knees or on their feet, but all growling and groaning; the men were shouting, screaming and cursing in a perfect Babel of voices, and the whole thing forcibly suggested the decamping of a magnified Sanger's circus.

A slave came running up to us, as we stood shivering in the early morning air watching this strange scene, and brought us each a pancake of bread freshly baked, and made of wheat instead of the black barley which we so disliked. As soon as we had devoured our simple breakfast we were ordered to mount the camels that were brought round for us, the beasts grumbling as they knelt to the burden, and their owners swearing that they were already fully loaded.

By this time only the Kaid's tent remained standing, and a few minutes later that too was struck. This did not look like waiting for the *Tourmaline*, or being sent by special escort, but we had no chance of speaking to the Kaid. The foot-soldiers and the mules and baggage-camels were already moving, and could be seen defiling through the passes in the hills, and the weird strains of the Moorish war-song rose on the air from a thousand throats, '*Allahum salli alaik a Rasul Allah; essla Ala nebi.*'* The horsemen were drawn up in one great hollow square in front of where the Kaid's tent had but lately stood, the red and yellow standards in the centre fluttering in the breeze, and a wilder or more magnificent living picture of barbaric splendour I had never before beheld. All the colours of the rainbow were there: the red and yellow of the standards, saddles and *tarbushes*, the blue *sulhams* of the officers, and the saddle-cloths of every hue and

* O Prophet of God, may God bless you! (lit., pray for you). Blessings on the Prophet!

shade. And the sun shone down upon their flashing weapons, and bleached to a perfect whiteness their turbans and *jelabas*. In the centre was the Kaid himself, apparently haranguing the troops. He finished, and shouts long and loud rent the air. Then they broke square, and set out upon the march. The path through the defile was so narrow in places that not more than two or three could march abreast, and travelling was both difficult and slow. At last our turn came, the Kaid and his bodyguard being just behind us, with a small detachment of horsemen bringing up the rear.

Some of the men riding alongside of us told us that we were only going to travel a few miles that day, to Tlata, where a market was held every Tuesday. On the way we passed two of the large boxes that we had had in our camp, containing canned provisions. The tins lay strewn about the path, or in the dried-up bed of the Wad Gueder, which in the rainy season runs into the sea about half a mile to the north of the cove of Arksis. The tins were unopened, as the Moors would touch the meat of no animal that had been killed by infidel hands, and there they lay thrown to waste, whilst we were starving for want of decent and sufficient food.

To every house sighted on the way a small party of soldiers would gallop up, and rifle the place of everything they could find. In general, the women and young children seemed to have been left behind, while the men had betaken themselves to the hills for safety. Whether any of these were molested in any way I couldn't say, but certainly none was taken prisoner. Barley was what was chiefly wanted, as, with the exception of a few of the officers, these Moorish raiders brought no supplies for the army or animals with them, depending upon what they might find in the enemy's country. The houses were soon ransacked, but the grain had to be searched for in the most systematic manner. The Susi, like the Moors, store their grain in *matamoros*—large holes dug in the ground, the sides of which are lined with a kind of cement to keep the damp out. These underground granaries, which are generally in the courtyards of their houses, are so constructed that the aperture can be closed by placing a flat stone over the mouth, about 2 feet below the surface of the ground, and the hole above is then filled up with earth. When skilfully closed the mouth of the cave cannot be detected, and the soldiers had to probe all over the ground with their ramrods before they could discover the location of these storehouses. In many cases the search resulted in the discovery of nothing more than a few pots of honey, but nothing came amiss to these hungry freebooters.

It was very nearly two o'clock before Tlata was reached, and we were all extremely tired with our camel ride. The baggage-camel is the most uncomfortable beast to ride that can possibly be imagined. The sensation has been likened by someone to that which would be felt by mounting a stool placed on a springless cart driven over a ploughed field. I found it all that, and more. Next to walking barefoot in chains, riding on camel-back is, in the eyes of the Moors, the worst degradation they can put upon their prisoners, the reason being, I suppose, that this lofty perch renders the rider a more conspicuous target for the jeers and missiles of the crowd.

The country through which we had passed was of an exceedingly fine description, but destitute of anything resembling a road, the track in many cases being nothing more than the dried-up rocky bed of a stream, the verdure-clad but treeless hills rising high above us on either side. Argan-trees were the best specimens of timber we encountered, palms not being visible, and though the prickly pear grew in abundance, it is only a bush at best, and is often used as a hedgerow for gardens. Frequently we passed by fields of growing barley, or, rather, passed through, as these uncivilized marauders rode roughshod over everything, their horses trampling the green shoots remorselessly under their hoofs.

Tlata is a small level plain entirely surrounded by hills, with a stream running through it, and would form an ideal camping-ground for manœuvres in time of peace, but to my lay mind it seemed too much exposed to the fire of an enemy from the surrounding hill-tops to be a suitable site in time of war. The market stalls—small rubble erections scarcely large enough for a man to stretch himself out full-length in—stood near the centre, with a large mosque in close proximity, and houses dotted all round the hillsides.

In this hollow our wretched tent was again pitched close to that of the Kaid, and we consoled ourselves with a bottle of lager-beer, knocking the neck off with the edge of a stone for want of a corkscrew. After this luxury we felt somewhat refreshed, and disposed to have a look round the camp, but on venturing to emerge from the tent, we were promptly and not too politely ordered to get inside again and sit down, being forbidden even to stand up and stretch ourselves. This was a little more than a joke, especially during the heat of the day, and by no means harmonized with the Kaid's statement that we should be well treated.

'I wish we could see the Kaid,' I said. 'I don't believe these fellows have got any orders to keep us shut in here in this heat.'

'Go out to his tent,' suggested Sabbah. 'Don't take any notice of these beasts; walk straight past them. The Kaid's tent is just there,' he said, pointing through a rent in the canvas, and indicating a large tent not twenty yards away.

'Well, but it's no use,' I replied. 'I couldn't make him understand what I wanted. You come with me and translate, and I'll talk to him fast enough.'

'All right,' he said; 'go straight out, and I'll follow you.'

Drawing back the flap, I sprang out and made a bee-line for Giluli's tent, disregarding the cries of the astonished guards. But I was stopped before I had gone a dozen paces, and bundled unceremoniously back into the tent, and the next minute one of the guards came in with our necklaces and effectually put a stop to any further vagaries of that sort. The excuse for putting the chains on us the previous day was that we might escape to the sea, which was only a feeble and foolish lie; but this time my rashness and disobedience was considered sufficient warrant. It wanted yet two or three hours to sunset, so, as we had nothing to do, a siesta seemed to be the best thing under the circumstances. There were, however, other people in the camp who had nothing to do, and it occurred to them that a visit to the prisoners would be an agreeable diversion. Most of our visitors came out of mere idle and vicious curiosity, and would just look in with a grin, and, having taken their fill, pass on with a malediction or a jeer to seek other amusement elsewhere. A number of Sbooyas were in camp, too—though how they came to be there without being molested we were unable to guess—and whenever they came near the flap of our tent was thrown back by the guard to enable them to have a better view of the Christians in chains. Of these we took no notice, and their curses died on the air unheeded; but it was hard to look unconcerned when the scoundrels spat towards us. In all this the guards encouraged them, and took evident delight in adding to the weight of our misfortunes and humiliation.

One of our visitors, however, came with other and better motives. He was so fat that he could scarcely get through the narrow opening of the tent, but his kindly, jovial face was like a ray of sunshine in the darkness after the scowling visages that had met us everywhere. And after he had had his chat and gone, he sent his servant with some food, of which we were very much in need. After the stuff we had recently been having, a dish of boiled rice and a pot of green tea was almost an epicurean meal. Perhaps the fact that he had once been the Governor of a province himself, and was now only an officer in the Sultan's army, made him sympathize with those who found themselves in fallen estate, but, anyhow, the name of Kaid Mohammed Bel F'kuk will always be held in grateful and kindly remembrance by five of the Sultan's captives. When I knew him and his country better, I ceased to wonder that he had lost his governorship. A country Kaid in Morocco must needs have a good deal of the brutal tyrant in him to keep his post, and there was nothing of that about Bel F'kuk. Moor and Moslem though he was, Nature had meant him for a kindly and courteous gentleman, and even in that land of cruelty and barbarism she had her way. Allah reward him!

Sunrise saw the camp once more a-bustle, small parties of horsemen forming up in front of the Kaid's tent, apparently for orders, and then riding off in various directions. The guards came in and relieved us of our chains, and I thought we were about to set off on the march again. The Susi boy, however, was not released, a pair of anklets being fastened on his legs which would have effectually prevented him from escaping far, even if he had been so rash as to try the experiment. By dint of a few cautious inquiries we learnt that we were not going to move from Tlata for two or three days, as the Kaid was going to make that place the basis of his 'operations' against the rebellious and stiff-necked tribe. This was great disappointment to us, as every day spent in camp meant a day later in reaching Mogador, or any other semi-civilized place. But there was no help for it; we were simply powerless in the hands of this untutored barbarian, who couldn't even sign his name, but had to employ an *adul*, or scribe, to write his letters for him.

I would have liked to have whiled away the time by writing up my journal, which I had not touched since leaving Mulud's house, but I was afraid lest my book and pencil should be seen and taken away from me. The monotony of our imprisonment was soon varied, however, by the arrival of fresh captives.

The first was an old man with a short white beard, a hooked nose like a hawk's beak, which a prominent chin seemed to be striving to meet, and keen, deep-set eyes. He was hustled roughly into the tent, having run the gauntlet of the soldiers' blows from the Kaid's tent to ours, and Uld Suka, the chief of the commissariat department, whose 'perquisite' he seemed to be, cracked him several times over the bare and shaven head with a thick stick, saying, '*Mirhba, mirhba*,'* and proceeded to chain him up and strip him of all superfluous articles in the way of clothes and portable property.

'I went to cheat the Christians—I went to cheat the Christians,' he reiterated in the tone of one who thought his conduct merited praise rather than blows, but the plea did not seem to commend itself to his captors. He was a man of the Imsti tribe from Ifni, who had seen where the Sbooyas had hidden the fifteen rifles and ammunition which they had landed from the *Tourmaline* in the surf-boats, and when the men had gone away, after depositing them in a safe place of concealment, as they thought, he had obtained assistance from some of his own tribe and removed the lot. Whether to boast of his exploit, or for what other object, I don't know, but he had been foolish enough to come into Giluli's camp, and had been promptly seized.

Scarcely had he been settled on the chain, when we heard that El F'kir Embarak and Muley Abdallah had also been captured, and we began to wonder how many prisoners the Moors intended to pack into our tent, or if, with their increasing numbers, they would find a separate place for the Moslems, and leave us our tent to ourselves. Our speculations were interrupted by the arrival of Muley Abdallah. He hobbled in with the aid of his stick, and seemed too much ashamed of himself to recognise us, or it might be too much taken up with trying to save his things from the despoiling

* Welcome, welcome.

hands of the soldiers. His clean *jelaba*, his *daleel*,* and his turban were soon taken away from him, and his fez was going to follow suit, but he pleaded with them to leave it, as he was an old man, and they returned it to him. His string of amber beads, which he counted as assiduously as a Roman Catholic devotee, he was also allowed to retain. His leather satchel he was, of course, deprived of, and I was not a little astonished to see that it contained no less than ten dollars. This hardly squared with the story he had told us at Arksis, when he emptied five pesetas on the table, as representing all his worldly possessions; but there, what did it matter now? With the world, as he had known it, he had finished. His children would see him no more. The sun would shine with all her golden radiance; the moon would shed her silvery beams, and the stars would twinkle on the white terrace-roofs of his loved home—but not for him. He was a prisoner of the Sultan, on his way to Marrakesh, there to drag out the rest of his wretched days in some foul and dismal den of death, with fetters on his feet, chains round his neck, and hopeless misery at his heart, starved and tortured in body and mind, until a mightier than the Sultan should send the messenger for whose coming in those dark places there is always a glad smile of welcome—the Angel of Death—to break his bonds for him.

Of all this the poor old man was doubtless thinking, as he sat there in a kind of dumb stupor, chained to Khabib on the one side, and Misti, as we had christened him, on the other. Presently he lifted his eyes from the ground, and, for the first time since he had come

* A small book containing extracts from the Koran, which many devout Moors carry about with them as a talisman.

in, looked at us, and raising his hand, palms outwards, with that peculiar gesture which was a favourite of his, and is common among the Moors, murmured, '*Labas! mektub.*' It was a philosophic attempt to console himself and us with the reflection that 'it was written,' and that all would yet be well—if not in this world, in another and a better.

It is a wonderful fatalism that these Moors have. All their troubles are of external origin, they think, and in the shaping of their destiny they have no voice. It is ordained of Allah beforehand, and if trouble befall them, they bear it with dignity and fortitude, reflecting that all earthly effort to prevent it was vain, as 'it was written,' and had to be. And so it happens that when a slave, by one of those strange freaks of fortune only possible in a country like Morocco—a curious mixture of democracy and absolute despotism —becomes Grand Vizier, the people hear the news without surprise, and wait for the next turn of the wheel which shall land him in a Moorish gaol, there to rot like any other unfortunate or unpopular Kaid or Basha, obscure murderer, or prisoner of war. *Mektub!* If it wasn't so serious, it might be comic opera, as witness the reply of a country Kaid who was called upon to explain his conduct in imprisoning several Moors that were under the protection of the British Government. He first of all denied having taken or seen the men, but finding simple lying of no avail, excused himself by saying that it merely occurred to him to order the arrest: *kadera* (fate) decreed it!

We didn't see anything of El F'kir Embarak that day, as he was put into another tent, having begged hard not to be put with the Christians. I wonder if either he or Muley Abdallah ever knew that Uld

Bairuk Dakhman had sold them to Kaid Giluli for 1,000 dollars, after they had taken refuge in Wad Nun, where they had fled from Mulud's house on the afternoon of the day that Beyerle and I had been sold by our worthy host at the more modest price of 400 dollars. And this same traitor Dakhman was once a regular recipient of the bribes of the English Company at Cape Juby before the British Government, in a moment of fatuous and purblind folly, allowed the settlement to pass into the hands of the Sultan of Morocco, and a few hundred miles of sea-coast with it. The day may not be far distant when England will realize that the fringes of the Sahra are not to be counted among the waste places of the earth.

CHAPTER XVII.

THE CAMP AT TLATA.

Close confinement—Kaid Bel F'kuk's generosity—*Kuss-kuss*—Fresh captives are brought in—How a Susi changes his clothes—Our camp at night-time—El F'kir Embarak confesses—Forty hours without water—We are transferred from our tent to a mud hovel—We make a new friend—The fast of Ramadan—Reflections on Mohammedanism—The Moor as a marksman—A soldier's regrets—The force of example.

THE same routine was followed next morning as on the previous days, the chains with which we were all fastened together at sunset being taken off us at sunrise, though the Moslem prisoners were fettered day and night. We were not allowed to go outside the tent except for the most necessary purposes, and then only under an escort of guards. We therefore kept to our tent as much as possible, as we only exposed ourselves to all sorts of insults from the soldiers and tribesmen as soon as we were seen about the camp. Our food-supply was anything but satisfactory, a bowl of coarse *tshisha*, which we had to eat with our fingers, forming our breakfast, unless the soldiers were hungry and ate it in transit from the Kaid's kitchen. This happened on more than one occasion, but Kaid Bel F'kuk, with a generosity that had nothing in common with the 'charity' which, among Christians, is but too often merely a mortgage to be paid off with heavy interest at some future time, generally sent us either a dish of rice or a bowl of *kuss-kuss* from his own private store. His kindness was the more remarkable as we were 'accursed infidels,' and as for hope of reward, the chances were extremely remote that he would ever see us in this life again when once we should have parted.

Kuss-kuss is one of the staple dishes among the better class of Moors, and is made of flour granulated by hand in some peculiar manner, and then put into a bowl with chicken or meat, and cooked by steaming over a charcoal stove. It is not perhaps the sort of dish that would find much favour on the menu-card of a West-End restaurant, but it is at least clean, wholesome, and palatable, though one requires some little practice before one acquires that finished dexterity in rolling up the glutinous granules into a ball with the fingers of the right hand and gracefully jerking it over the thumb into one's mouth. The garniture of meat is generally on the top of the floury pyramid, and it was very mortifying to see these tempting morsels calmly appropriated by the guard at our tent door, with merely a muttered 'Bismillah' by way of excuse or explanation, leaving us only the semolina. If he robbed hungry captives of their food before their very eyes, 'bismillah'—in the name of God—I used to wonder what depths of iniquity he would be capable of in the name of the devil, or whoever corresponds in Islam to this enemy of the Christian faith. However, a complaint to Bel F'kuk quickly put a stop to this mean and petty pilfering, and ever afterwards he used to send his own servant Embarak—Embaraks in Morocco seem to be as plentiful as Joneses in Wales—to 'see that we got it,' as the advertisements say.

Our third day in Tlata saw several new arrivals, and the 'housing of the poor' became a burning question. El F'kir Embarak was brought in, and took his place alongside Muley Abdallah; and El Hadj el Arabi, a thick-lipped Sbooya, with the brain equipment of a rabbit, and Faraji, a negro slave, were also among the unfortunate. The two last-named lived to attain to the dignity of 'witnesses for the Crown' in a travesty of justice which was performed at the British Consular Court five months later for the satisfaction and appeasement of the ignorant and disreputable barbarian whom Her Majesty's Attorney-General for Gibraltar there described as 'our friend and ally, the Sultan.'

There were then in our old rag kitchen ten men and a boy all huddled up together, and when the sun set we were all linked together on one common chain. When we sent a complaint to Giluli about being thus herded together, he facetiously retorted that, as we were such friends with the Sbooyas, he had specially put them in our company, and could not think of parting us. The Kaid was not without a certain grim humour. The supply of Sherifian necklaces—made in Birmingham, like the chain—had apparently been exhausted, as all the recent arrivals were shackled by the feet instead of the neck, and one of our number had also to have the iron round the leg. When it came to the turn of Beyerle or myself, the soldiers made us take off our riding-boots, and pass the night in our stockinged feet, as they had a notion that we might in some mysterious way draw off boot and fetter if fastened over the leather. All our fellow-prisoners, with the exception of Muley Abdallah, who had merely a disagreeable human odour, stank like polecats, the negro slave in particular exuding a perfume that was almost powerful enough to knock a man down. Probably none of them had ever had a decent wash in his life, and as for changing his clothes, that was a habit that Sbooya economy had taught him was a reckless indulgence. A *jelaba* or *keshaba* is worn constantly until it shows evident indications of rotting off, and even then it is not discarded, but another is put on over the top of it. Muley Abdallah is not included in these strictures, as he had learnt something of the decencies of life, probably from contact with European civilization in the coast towns of Morocco.

Small wonder, then, that under these circumstances spots began to break out over our bodies, I, in particular, being in a very bad state. Beyerle also began to suffer from rheumatism, the nights being very cold, and the heat of the day causing a heavy dew to fall after sunset. Even much farther south, in the very desert of Sahra, the nights are often strikingly chilly, although the heat of the day may have been almost unbearable. Against these chills a khaki suit and a cotton shirt are not the most effective protection; and when, added to this, we had to lie on the rough ground with stones for our pillows and no blankets to cover us, it will readily be granted that these were conditions at which the most hardened campaigner might well have grumbled. But Bel F'kuk again came to the rescue, and every evening sent his servant with a large camel-hair rug, large enough to cover our lower extremities, at any rate, else I don't know what might have happened.

What made sleep still more difficult was the noise that went on through the greater part of the night. The singing of the soldiers over their camp-fires, the growling of the camels, the neighing of the horses and the braying of donkeys, made night hideous. As if these were not enough, there was one malevolent fiend that I would unremorsefully have consigned to one of the lower circles of the Inferno, who every night used to give vent to the most soul-scraping imitations of a donkey's bray for the delectation of a select circle of his admiring and noisy friends. Furthermore, a desultory fire was kept up after dark from the hill-tops surrounding the camp by the Sbooyas who lurked among the mountains, like jackals on the prowl for prey. Several small detachments of horsemen were sent out from the camp at nightfall in the hopes of pouncing upon the guerillas, but generally returned without success.

Two days went by without any sign of breaking camp, and we heard rumours that the Kaid intended to stay there until he had got from the Sbooyas all the rifles that had been landed from the *Tourmaline* at Arksis, together with a heavy fine by way of damages for the mischief they had caused. Each prisoner as he had been captured had been taken before the Kaid and closely questioned as to recent doings on the coast, and El F'kir Embarak, at any rate, had made a clean breast of all he knew. And so Giluli knew that fifty repeating rifles were distributed somewhere among the Sbooya tribe, and that fifteen had fallen into the hands of their neighbours in Imsti, and he meant to possess himself of them all, or know the reason why. The fact that the old man had 'split' did not trouble us in any way, except that we reflected that our stay would be more likely to be of two weeks' than two days' duration. I was surprised to hear, however, that he had taken all the blame upon himself. He it was, he told the Kaid, that had brought the Christian to Arksis, and Muley Abdallah had had nothing to do with it. Muley Abdallah had only come to Sus to collect a debt that was owing to him, and was perfectly innocent. For himself, he was going to end his days in the Sultan's prison, he knew, but he didn't care : he was an old man, and would not live long, anyhow. They could kill him now, if they liked, but they should let Muley Abdallah go. I thought it was rather chivalrous of the old chap to try and shield his friend like that, but it was all of no avail. It didn't matter to Giluli whether Muley Abdallah was guilty of any offence or not. He was a prisoner, bought and paid for ; that was quite sufficient, and a prisoner he would remain.

All this time the weather had continued gloriously fine, for which we were devoutly thankful ; for, with our tent all in holes, if it had come on to rain, our condition would have been deplorable indeed. As it was, we had quite enough to complain of without having to endure the miseries of bad weather. For some reason or other the morning meal from Kaid Giluli ceased to make its appearance, and we had to wait till about eight o'clock in the evening before we got our 'official' food—consisting usually of coarse *tshisha*, but occasionally *kuss-kuss* with carrots, though destitute of meat. Our good friend Kaid Bel F'kuk, however, was unremitting in his attentions, and his *kuss-kuss* in the morning and rice in the evening, or *vice versâ*, kept us from actual starvation. Water was as difficult to obtain as if it had been some costly liquor, our keepers being too lazy or too indifferent to fetch it for us. There was no system or regularity about either food or drink, and during these early days at Tlata we learned what thirst meant. For forty hours we were left without water, and our piteous appeals were met always with the same response, '*Dabeji*,'* till we all got to hate the very sound of the word.

What had struck me from the first impressed itself upon the Kaid when we had been at Tlata three days, and the order was given to move the camp from the plain up on to one of the hills forming the side of the basin. The reason given out was that rain was expected; but this was an obvious lie, as there was not a cloud in the sky, nor any other indication of approaching change in the weather. We were among the earliest to move, and were installed in one of the mud hovels that pass for houses in that part of the country. It was very similar in every respect to the one of which El F'kir Embarak was the proud possessor; and, now I came to look more closely, this surely could not be far from the village to which we had escaped from Arksis just a week ago. Yes, sure enough, there was the *duar* on the crown of the ridge to the north-east, perhaps two miles away; and there below was the stream across the stony bed of which Beyerle and I had staggered in the darkness when the soldiers of Giluli had come and led us away, with our hearts full of a foreboding that we might never see another morning dawn.

Any hopes we might have had that we would now be separated from the native prisoners were quickly dispelled; but the room in which we were placed was long enough to allow of the Moslems keeping to one end of the room, while we occupied the other nearest to the door, which served the triple purpose of entrance, window, and ventilation. It was perhaps

* Soon.

25 feet long by 6 feet broad; but Moors pack closely, and we certainly had the lion's share of the space, besides being able to enjoy a good view of the surrounding country and our recent camping-ground. The Kaid took up his quarters in a house immediately backing upon ours, while Hadj Ali, his notary, occupied one in the same courtyard as ours, and immediately adjoining our luxurious abode. One advantage our new lodging possessed over a tent in the open was that we were not nearly so much exposed to the staring of the mob, as the door leading to our courtyard was nearly always closed to all who had no business there. It also gave us the opportunity of making another friend, as will presently appear; but I wondered at the Kaid preferring a dark, unventilated, evil-smelling mud hovel to a clean, well-fitted, and roomy tent in the open air. Our own tent now came in useful as a bolster, being somewhat softer than even the smoothest stones that had hitherto had to serve us for pillows. It was wonderful how soon we had learned to acquire a fine discrimination in the selection of stones for this purpose, a flat one with a smooth surface being eagerly sought for, while one with a slight depression in the centre was a real treasure. After all, comfort is only a question of comparison, and one can indulge in the most philosophical reflections on the luxuries of life—when they are beyond one's reach.

On the day we moved up on to the hill commenced the great Mohammedan fast of Ramadan, when for thirty days the faithful followers of the Prophet must neither eat nor drink anything between the hours of sunrise and sunset, nor gratify in any other way their carnal appetites. Not many of the country Moors are worshippers of 'my Lady Nicotine'; but during the daylight hours of the great annual fast not even the smell of tobacco must be allowed to pass their nostrils. Whenever we happened to be consoling ourselves with the fragrant weed, the more scrupulous of the loiterers round about would hold their *jelabas* to their noses that they might 'avoid even the appearance of evil.' It will not be wondered at, then, that we used tobacco as a means of ridding ourselves of objectionable visitors, when other intimations that their presence was unwelcome proved of no avail. Our Moorish guards were 'old soldiers,' and, like their class in other countries, not given overmuch to prayers or fasting, and contrived to do only so much of either as would save them from getting into trouble in case their shortcomings should be reported to the Kaid.

Their religion, however, does not apparently restrain them from befouling their tongues with the filthiest conversation imaginable; for often enough I have seen men stand upon a house-top, and go through their prayers with all the pantomimic accompaniments of bowing and prostrating which are necessary for the due performance of their orisons, and come down straightway to us and make the most disgusting and revolting allusions and suggestions without a tinge of shame. The conversation in a British camp may not be always of the most refined description; but, then, Tommy Atkins does not come straightway from his prayers performed on the house-tops, figurative or literal, and proceed to besmear his language with the grossest and filthiest obscenities. The Moslem, then, is either endowed with a hypocrisy compared with which that of the British Pharisee pales into insignificance, or else his perceptions of decency are utterly sunk in a slough of swinish sensuality.

Not a sign of a woman was to be found in the camp, the very army-trailers being boys and emasculated men in the early twenties; and vices are indulged in, even by the chiefs and better class, that in most civilized communities are generally regarded as unspeakable. None think it shame; and yet this creed which numbers its followers by hundreds of millions, while allowing practices of the most vile and vicious description, enjoins that during the fast of Ramadan the devout Mohammedan must not allow a drop of water to pass his parched throat, though the sun may be scorching up the very vegetation with the fierceness of its rays, and he must not gratify his nostrils with even the scent of a cigarette smoked by the damned *N'srani*. These words may not wholly apply to Mohammedan countries in other parts of the world, but Morocco is admittedly and undoubtedly the most rigid and fanatical in all the outward observances of Islam. In Turkey and Egypt, for example, a Christian may enter a mosque with impunity, provided that he complies with the formality of removing his shoes; but a British subject, not being a Moslem, who enters a mosque in Morocco is, under the 'Morocco Order in Council,' guilty of a 'grave offence' punishable by imprisonment.

The only other topic of conversation that seemed to have any abiding interest for these vile scoundrels was weapons. They were curious concerning the pattern and qualities of the rifles we had brought with us in the *Tourmaline*, but were quite satisfied that the Martinis which most of them possessed were the best that could be got. For men that were brought up with a gun in their hands, so to speak, their marksmanship was anything but brilliant. It was fortunate for Beyerle and me that it was so, for had we been in front of European soldiers instead of Moors, when we were fleeing from the field at Arksis, the distance between us and our pursuers was at one time so short as to make it practically certain that we should not have escaped to criticise their shooting. The first day we spent in the house at Tlata one of our pursuers introduced himself to us, and told us that had they caught us that day our fate would have been sealed, as the advance-guard had no instructions about Christians, and would have killed us on the spot, and thus insured their admission into Paradise. I chaffed him about the poor shooting exhibition he and his friends had given us, but of course he would not admit that any Christian could have done better. We owed our escape, he said, to the cactus scrub that covered the place. The horses picked their way with such difficulty over the ground that they gained upon us much less rapidly than would otherwise have been the case. He was inclined to cherish a grudge against the physical topography of Arksis, but, after all, he supposed 'it was written' that we were to escape, so it was useless to repine.

We feared that in consequence of our removal we should lose sight of our friend Kaid Bel F'kuk, but his man Embarak turned up as usual in the evening, with a bowl of rice and a pot of tea. He had been too busy packing up, etc., to come in the morning, he said, and wanted to go to sleep early, but the Kaid made him take us our supper first. To eat boiled rice or *kuss-kuss* with one's fingers is an accomplishment to which an Englishmen does not take naturally, so, our cigars being finished, we hit upon the expedient of breaking up the box, and using the unshaped slips of wood as spoons. The plan worked admirably, but it had the slight drawback of imparting to the food a mixed flavour of tobacco and cedar wood.

Embarak had scarcely taken his departure, when Hadj Ali's servant entered the room with a samovar and some tea and sugar. 'So shines a good deed in a naughty world!' Kaid Bel F'kuk's example in practical charity was beginning to bear unlooked-for fruit. The two men were close friends, but hitherto Hadj Ali had been afraid lest Kaid Giluli should see him show any kindness to us, whereas Bel F'kuk, being in a more independent position, was indifferent to Giluli's feelings in the matter. Now that we were no longer under the immediate observation of the old tyrant, Hadj Ali began to do a little towards lessening the severity of our treatment. The very chains seemed lighter and less galling when our hearts were warmed with fresh green tea.

CHAPTER XVIII.

GILULI'S VOW, AND HOW HE KEPT IT.

We make an unpleasant discovery—Chains 'made in England'—We resort to judicious bribery—An English-speaking Moor—Courier or spy?—I write to Consul Johnston—Al-al appointed interpreter—An epicurean meal—'The Spaniard'—The filling of the chain—Death of Kaid Giluli's cook—The Kaid makes a vow—The Moor and his horse—Fire and slaughter—A sickening sight—Mulud's house burned.

THE confinement and scarcity of good and proper food now began to tell upon us. Several of us suffered from skin eruptions, and a close examination of our clothes revealed the unpleasant fact that they were infested with vermin. This discovery made us all feel wretched and depressed, as there was no possibility of getting rid of these loathsome pests; for, even if we were relieved of the unwelcome company of the native prisoners, we had no clothes to put on other than those we stood up in. The Moors seemed surprised that we should make a fuss about so trifling a matter, as not only do they not object to the harbouring of lice about their own bodies, but they go so far as to declare that a man is not a proper well-regulated Moor unless he has them about his person. While on the pilgrimage to Mecca, a Moor neither changes his clothes nor lays violent hands upon his 'bosom friends,' from the day he sets out until he returns. The condition of the new-made Hadj on his return to Morocco is best left to the imagination.

Sabbah had managed to save from the despoiling hands of the soldiers a silver watch and a couple of pesetas, but he had been foolish enough to let the former be seen on one or two occasions since his search. The result was that one of the petty officers, called Kaid Jaah, demanded it. Sabbah refused to give it up, and even resisted when force was applied. In consequence, we were all put in chains in the middle of the afternoon as a punishment. Being asked whether he would prefer the watch or two pesetas, the man said he would rather have two pesetas; so Sabbah agreed to give him the money if he would take the chains off. The bargain was struck, and we were free once more for a little while from those accursed irons. When we grumbled at being chained, the guard retorted that we ought not to complain: the thing was made in England, he said, so it was only right that we should wear it. The marvel to me was that the man didn't keep both the money and the watch.

As it seemed certain that the rest of our portable personal property would be taken from us by one or another of the soldiers, we came to the conclusion that it was best to make a virtue of necessity, and distribute the remaining articles judiciously in return for favours received, or with an eye to possible prospective benefits. Sabbah's silver watch—with which he was most loath to part, as it was the gift of a dead friend—was given to Hadj Ali, and the goodwill and interest of this important personage was thereby secured, to say nothing of the more material advantage of a regular nightly supply of tea and sugar. In those days of starvation in that dry land I came to think that no liquor that I had ever tasted in my life seemed so near the nectar of the gods as that refreshing hot green tea we drank in our captivity. De Reya's meerschaum cigarette-holder went to Embarak, who brought our food from Kaid Bel F'kuk with such welcome regularity. He was a 'sad dog' in his way, this Embarak, and to the vices of the Moor he had added the Christian accomplishment of smoking—on the quiet—and an eighteen-penny cigarette-holder was to him a treasure of priceless worth. Beyerle's gold signet-ring was kept in reserve for more desperate emergencies, should such unhappily arise, but he was lucky enough to retain it to the end. Under these slightly improved circumstances, we were able occasionally to give a glass of tea to Muley Abdallah and the old F'kir, and to forego our share of the solitary daily meal we got from Kaid Giluli for the benefit of all the native prisoners, who, poor fellows! always seemed as hungry as a pack of wolves.

The days dragged slowly on, and brought but little variety, the arrival of fresh prisoners being the principal incident to break the monotony of our captivity. One was a soldier who had been insubordinate to our friend Bel F'kuk, and was put in irons for a few hours to cool his rebellious spirit. When sunset came he was released, but after he had had his evening meal he came back again. This time his visit was a voluntary one, and he brought us some cigarettes, which, while not, perhaps, of the choicest brand of tobacco, we relished with an appreciation born of abstinence.

That same afternoon we had all been rather startled by hearing a voice suddenly exclaim in English,

'Well, how are you?' At the door of the hut sat a rather handsome Moor, with a full black beard. Sabbah recognised him at once as a man that he had known in Mogador. His name was Al-al, and he said he had just come from Mogador with a letter to the Kaid from the Basha of that town.

'Poor people, I am very sorry for you,' he said, when he saw the condition we were in; 'but you will be all right soon. You will be sent to your Consul when the fighting is over. No one ever heard of the Sultan keeping Europeans in prison.'

'Will you take a message for us to the British Vice-Consul at Mogador, if you are going back?' I asked him. 'You know him—Tajer Johnston?'

'What will you pay me?' he asked.

'We can't pay you anything,' I replied, 'as all our money has been stolen from us; but I will ask the Consul in the letter to pay you, and you will be all right. Besides, we will make it worth your while when we get to Mogador.'

He looked rather thoughtful at this, and said, after a pause, that he wasn't sure he was going straight back there. He could, however, get a friend of his to go, he said. He was very tired himself, having walked from Mogador in *four days!* Moorish couriers, I knew, are marvels of speed and staying power, and can accomplish distances with little food and sleep by the way that would astonish a European; but from Mogador to Tlata—over a wild and mountainous country, and a distance which took us afterwards a little over eleven days to accomplish—no, that was drawing the long-bow a little too much, I thought.

When first he mentioned that he had come from the Governor of Mogador, a wild idea flashed across me that perhaps he had come with a message about us; but on second thoughts I knew that that was impossible. Even if the *Hassani* had gone straight there from Arksis there would not have been time for a message to come back; but, as a matter of fact, the steamer had gone to Cape Juby from Arksis, and the news of our capture could not yet have reached Mogador. Then I began to fear that he was a spy sent by the Kaid to hear what we spoke about. When I came to look at him more closely, he had a shifty look about the eyes, and his professions of sympathy had an unreal ring about them. However, I wrote a note on a scrap of paper setting forth our unhappy plight, telling the Consul that we had been put in chains, and were sick of fever and disease, and begging him to use the utmost despatch in securing our release. If it reached its destination, well and good; if not—well, no harm would be done, even if it fell into the hands of the Kaid; short of beating us, our treatment by him could not easily have been made harsher.

Later in the evening we heard that we were to have an interpreter to look after us, who was to ask the Kaid himself for anything we might want. This sounded very pretty, no doubt, but, inasmuch as Arabic was Sabbah's native tongue, we had not so far experienced any difficulty in making known our needs. The difficulty we had experienced was in getting our needs relieved. Still, we hoped that better times were in store for us. Alas for the reality!

The next morning Al-al was at our hovel door soon after sunrise, and told us himself that he had received orders from the Kaid to wait on us, and ' look after us very well.' Anything we wanted, he said, he would ask for, and, though there was not a great variety of food in the camp, he would get us a few things, and cook them himself. We were going, he told us, to Tisnit, which was a large town, and there he would get us eggs, chickens, milk, rice, and Heaven only knows what luxuries we were not going to revel in when we got to this centre of Susi civilization. We began modestly. Beyerle said he was hungry—not an uncommon complaint in those days with any of us —and would like some breakfast to remind him of days gone by. Certainly our new attendant was not more than half an hour in procuring us some loaves of black bread and—wonder of wonders!—honey. The memory of those days in Sus is not an altogether unclouded dream of bliss, but among the recollections that I cherish to this day is the flavour of that ambrosial honey. It clung about our palates with intoxicating sweetness, as the sugary lumps slowly and reluctantly dissolved in our mouths. And, as the sweet stream lingeringly trickled down our throats, we shut our eyes in the pure ecstasy of the pleasure of the palate. It drowned the musty flavour of the *khubs*, which might in the delirium of our sensual enjoyment have been the food of angels; and for some brief moments we tasted the joys of Epicurus. Some clear, fresh water from the stream below completed our repast, and once more we felt that we were men—and were alive.

Seriously, though, all that day our man looked after us fairly well—for a Moor—and we didn't suffer once from thirst. Our guards, far from resenting the new régime, rather welcomed it, as affording them more frequent opportunities of sleeping away the long, empty days.

Another friend we made was the cook of Kaid Hassan, also an officer in the Sultan's army, and a friend of Bel F'kuk's. This cook had been at one time for several years in Spain, and spoke Spanish fluently. We were thus able to carry on a conversation in two languages not understood by our guards, and gain scraps of information as to our probable movements. I would not deny that we also had in view the possibility of obtaining scraps of a more material kind, but the arrangements of Kaid Hassan's kitchen were not such as to allow 'the Spaniard,' as we dubbed him, to exercise that discriminate charity which he would have liked to have shown us. From him we learnt that we were going to break camp on the following Saturday at sunrise—it was then Thursday—and renew the march to Tisnit.

I couldn't help being struck with the fact that, with the exception of Muley Abdallah and El F'kir Embarak, none of the native prisoners taken were men of any account. El F'kir Embarak, who was really only half-witted, was the only member of the 'Forty' that had been captured so far, the majority of the captives being old men that we had never seen in our camp at Arksis. The fact that they were innocent of any crime did not affect Giluli or his marauders. There were the chains, and they had to be filled somehow. The old trick of sending the heads of his own men that had been killed in battle as trophies of victory to the Sultan would not do this time. That had been done by Giluli on the raiding expedition which he had led into Sus some eighteen months before, when he was intercepted, and his forces cut to pieces before he had gone three days' journey from Agadir. The heads had been duly spiked upon the walls of

Marrakesh, but the fraud had been discovered, and Kaid Giluli was for some time under the shadow of his Sultan's displeasure, from which he was only just then emerging.

The prospect of moving camp naturally revived our spirits somewhat, as Tisnit lay to the north, and that way lay also Mogador. Anything was better than lying rotting in that foul den, where we were fed and herded in a manner worse than many a farmer's swine at home—as far as our captor's orders went, at any rate. Our condition must indeed have been deplorable to have excited the pity of some of the Moors themselves, accustomed as they are to witness only too often sights that would sicken a hound, and who, in all their language, have not got the words wherewith to say, 'I am sorry for you.' '*Paciencia! un poco de paciencia*,' our 'Spaniard' would say every time he saw us, and, indeed, it needed all our stock of that virtue to meet the demands that were made upon it.

In the afternoon of the day the 'Spaniard' told us we were going to move, we heard that his confrère who presided over Kaid Giluli's kitchen had been shot by the Sbooyas while riding in the van of a pillaging-party among the hills. The fellow, besides being in the eyes of his master an expert in the culinary art, was always to the fore when there was any fighting to be had. Being Ramadan, there was not much for him to do except at night-time, when he had to cook the supper, and another meal which most of the Moors indulge in during the fast, and which is generally eaten about two hours before the dawn. He had therefore mounted his horse and joined one of the numerous pillaging-parties that were scouring the country round. He had gone to his last fight. A

Sbooya bullet, fired from behind a mountain boulder, had struck him in the chest. His head dropped forward, and he rolled out of the saddle limp and lifeless. The Kaid, on hearing the news, was furious with rage, and as he thought of the succulent stews and the *kuss-kuss*, that none knew so well how to make, he swore a solemn oath that he would burn every house and homestead in the tribe before his vengeance would be satisfied. And he kept his word. Al-al had seen him in his tent, but had not dared to speak to him, and the first result to us was that we went supperless.

The next day being Friday—the Mohammedans' Sunday—we hardly expected much movement in the camp; but the light had hardly crept into the eastern sky beyond the fretted outline of the hills, before parties of cavalry and foot-soldiers were radiating in all directions, bent on fire and slaughter, ravage and rapine, in accordance with the Kaid's commands—a mission entirely to their liking, and which made the life of a soldier of the Sultan, in their eyes, worth living. One of our guards, whom for some inscrutable reason we had nicknamed 'Cocoa,' was anxious to join the foray, but his old white horse, that stood hobbled in the courtyard, was sick, and he was in despair. The Arab is famed in song and romance for the love he bears his horse, and the modern Moor—who, after all, is but a hybrid combination of Arab and Spaniard, Berber and Black, with a marvellous faculty for absorbing most of the vices of all, and forgetting many of their virtues—has inherited something of this sentiment. The care that a European bestows upon his steed he scorns to take. The faithful animal's stable roof is the open sky, and his bed is the dung-heap of the courtyard, or near his master in the tented field, with a hobble on his feet. And if it should rain, what then? If he is not used to the rain at night, says his owner, how will he accustom himself to it by day? and as for brushing him down to give him a shiny coat—pooh! If he is muddy, lead him up to his middle in the first ford you come to. Still, he is a treasure to his master—a little dearer than his master's wife, who can be easier replaced—and so, when 'Cocoa' saw his animal was really ill, he turned in his despair to the hated Christian for help, sharing, perhaps, the superstition which nearly all country Moors possess, that Christian and medicine-man are synonymous terms. To profess ignorance would have been no use: I should not have been believed, but merely thought ungracious. So, assuming as wise an air as I knew how, I examined the poor beast attentively for some time, felt a large swelling in his leg, and gravely shook my head. Then I looked at the man—the hardened, vicious, ugly-looking ruffian—and, lifting my hand to remind him that all things come from Allah, said to him, '*Murid bserf; juge lium mud,*' to convey to him that the horse was very ill, and in two days would be dead. Was it a guess or an inspiration? I know not; but the animal died the following day.

By ten o'clock there was not a house in sight, except the mosque in the market-place and those we were occupying, that was not in flames; and as the day advanced, the smoke from the burning ruins of a score of villages curled up skywards in a mute appeal to Heaven for vengeance on the ruthless invaders. Mud hovels they may have been, destitute almost of everything that makes for comfort among a civilized people; humble and poverty-stricken, mean, contemptible and dirty, if you will—but they were none the less the treasured homesteads of a people 'rightly struggling to be free.' There could be no excuse here that this was a necessary work, inseparable from the march of civilization—for that has yet to be re-imposed upon the Moors themselves—but it was simply a wanton and cruel raid, begotten of a thirst for plunder, and born of a fevered lust for slaughter, upon a people that have ever kept within their own borders, and desire only to be allowed to live in their own way in their own land. Who could look without pity upon a spectacle of such ruthless destruction?

The treachery of the tribe to us was not the Moors' affair, and whether the Sultan has a right to this land of the Berber at all is a very open question; but in that day's savage work could be read the reasons of a once magnificent nation's decay, and the miseries and poverty of its people to-day.

In the afternoon a poor wretch was brought in, hardly able to stagger, and roughly held up by a captor on each side. He was an old man, poorly clad, and with a great gaping wound in his back, caused by a stab with a *cumia*. The point of the dagger had penetrated to the depth of an inch or two just by the shoulder, and his *sulham* was drenched in the blood that flowed from his wound. In spite of this, the poor wretch was roughly flung upon the floor, two iron collars fastened round his neck, and, heavily chained, he was left to die or recover as the seriousness of his injuries might decide. He ate nothing when the supper came—his only craving was for water—and his groans were pitiful to listen to. Presently his blood began to form in pools upon the floor, and trickle in a dark red stream past our outstretched legs. It was doubtful whether he would live through the night. And in this hovel of horrors, chained with the still more unfortunate victims of the ferocity of a barbarous and cursed despotism, who in the extremity of their misery called aloud upon Allah for help, since the help of man was denied them, we had to seek our sleep.

Meanwhile the work of devastation in the surrounding country had continued all day long. Before sunset one of the soldiers pointed out to us a dark cloud of smoke wreathing up from a block of houses on a hill-top that could be seen from our open door. It was the village of Mulud and El F'kir Embarak, and as the sun went down and the silent stars shone out, the lurid flames shot up and outlined every hill and peak for many a mile away, and the house of a traitor was a heap of blackened ruins.

CHAPTER XIX.

ON THE ROAD NORTHWARD.

The order to march is given—Death of a prisoner—Sbooya stratagem—Magnificent country—We leave Sbooya land—Giluli's terms to the Imsti—The Sultan's 'paper-chase'—Al-al leaves us to our own resources—A Job's comforter—The Kaid's generosity—A touching incident—De Reya has a fall—Arrival at El Arba—We have a washing-day and a treat generally—We learn our destination—A venerable patriarch—The three-card trick—Camp beggars.

FOR some days past, instead of asking when we should be on the move again, we had confined ourselves to inquiring how many rifles they had succeeded in collecting. As the last report gave the number as somewhere between twenty and thirty, we had hardly ventured to hope that we should resume the march on the Saturday, as 'the Spaniard' had told us, but, to our agreeable surprise and relief, the order to start was given by the Kaid at sunrise on that day, or, rather, the order was given the night before, and preparations were commenced at daybreak. Al-al brought us some barley *khubs*, and Bel F'kuk, with kindly forethought, sent Embarak with a bag full of small hard biscuits, which we crammed into our pockets to eat on the way.

The same order of march was observed as before.

First the tribesmen on foot; then the mules with the baggage, tents, etc., followed by the horsemen, prisoners, Kaid and his staff, and rear guard. When the native prisoners were ordered to come out into the courtyard, it was evident that the poor wretch that had been brought in the day before would be unable to either walk or hold himself on a mule, let alone a camel. He was faint and weak from loss of blood, and dropped on his knees as soon as he tried to stagger across the courtyard. The exertion caused the blood to flow from his wound afresh, and it would have been an act of mercy to have put a bullet through him and ended his misery at once. Instead of that, one of the soldiers roughly shook him, and, drawing his knife, threatened to cut his head off and send it to the Sultan if he didn't get up and walk. The poor fellow was too far gone for threats to move him, and in a tone of utter indifference merely murmured, '*Wakha.*'* The march, however, could not be delayed by the mere trifling obstacle of a dying man, so while the other unfortunate prisoners were all chained together in one long line by the neck-collars, a fresh supply of which seemed to have been recently unearthed, he, whose only fault had been that he had stayed in his house when others had fled, and endeavoured to save his goods from the hands of marauders, was taken outside and flung upon a dung-heap, while the Kaid, sitting on a house-top, calmly surveyed the scene.

As before, we were mounted on camels, and rode a little way ahead of the Kaid and his body-guard, while the Moslem prisoners walked barefooted or in slippers, urged on by blows and execrations from the soldiers.

* All right.

El F'kir Embarak and Muley Abdallah, either on account of their former rank or present feebleness, were allowed to ride on camels instead of being made to walk. Already a great change was observable in poor old Muley Abdallah. When he was first brought in a prisoner, his clothes were fairly clean. Now they were filthy; his face was begrimed with dust and dirt, and he looked haggard and ill.

As soon as I got an opportunity, I asked what had become of the wounded man. One told me they had left him there, but another afterwards said they had cut his head off to send it to the Sultan. After all, the latter was the more merciful. Left on his dung-heap in the broiling sun, he would die miserably of exhaustion and loss of blood, and tortured with a raging thirst. For hours after the camp had broken up none would venture to approach the spot, and almost before the breath was out of the poor wounded captive's body the crows and vultures which hovered over the army of the Sultan's ravagers would swoop upon him and tear the flesh from his bones.

We had scarcely been an hour on the road, when a block occurred in a narrow gorge in the mountains. We were following the course of a small stream that trickled through a deep valley, the rocky slopes of which rose up on either side to the height of about 1,200 feet. The Sbooyas, knowing the route Giluli would take, had piled up great stones across the narrow pathway in the ravine, and for nearly an hour the march was delayed. Had they gone a step further, and lined the upper slopes of the valley with armed men, while another party barred the retreat behind, Giluli's forces would have been like rats in a trap, and there would have been nothing to prevent a few hundred men from slaughtering the invaders to a man. Of courage they have plenty, but of the art of war these tribesmen do not seem to know the veriest rudiments.

The scenery certainly was of the most wild and romantic description, and Al-al, seeing us admire it, took occasion to remark that we could not have seen it in freedom 'if we had paid £2,000.' With the exception of one or two who had disguised themselves as Moors, we were the first Europeans, he said, to travel across the country; several had tried, but none had succeeded. I much regretted that I had no longer my camera with me, nor any instruments whereby I could ascertain our daily position and make a map of the route; but I had not even a compass, and it was often difficult to tell even the general direction of a day's march, so devious were our courses at times.

When the road was at length cleared, the march was resumed, and burning and pillaging was again the order of the day. Not a house escaped or was spared; and if any of the natives were venturesome enough to show themselves on the hillsides, a small detachment would start off in hot pursuit.

About two hours after mid-day we passed the border of the Sbooya tribe and entered the Imsti territory, and shortly afterwards, from the summit of an elevation, we could catch a glimpse of the sea once more. Half an hour later we reached our camping-ground, and were glad enough to get down from our beasts and stretch ourselves. The Kaid's tent was already pitched and furnished by the time he arrived on the ground, and it was not long before the heads of the tribe came with presents of jars of honey and loaves of sugar, and, by way of surer propitiation, a bullock was slaughtered with due form and ceremony. This was the tribe to which our fellow-captive Misti belonged, and Giluli required them to account for the fifteen rifles stolen from the Sbooyas before he resumed his march. Further, he demanded that a considerable sum of money should be paid to him by the following day, or he would deal with them as he had dealt with the Sbooyas. The envoys of the tribe pleaded hard with the Kaid not to destroy their houses, but those were his terms, he answered: the rifles and the money on the morrow; and, seeing how their neighbours had fared, they used all diligence to save themselves from a similar fate.

We had been told that we were to have the chains put on us so long as we were in the Sbooyas' country, and now that we had crossed the border, we once more protested. Our gaolers replied, however, that the Kaid said we must be chained as long as we were in Imsti, as the tribe was friendly with the Sbooyas— 'our brothers,' as Giluli facetiously described them. We had, however, one boon. Our tent being no longer able to hold all the prisoners, by any process of packing known even to the Moors, we had it once more to ourselves, whilst the natives slept in the open air close by, all chained together. The nights being very chilly, they were allowed to have a fire, and the poor wretches crouched round it in a circle, their toes nearly in the embers, while one or other of their number kept the flames alive until the first gray streaks of dawn put out the light of the stars.

Somewhat to my surprise, the Imsti tribe were equal to the demands made upon them by Giluli, and the rifles were delivered up the next day, together with the required fine and a goodly supply of barley and other useful provender for man and beast. A lot of property that was not voluntarily surrendered was simply appropriated, in some cases a man's all being seized by the despoilers. A woman whose husband had been robbed of all his cattle begged for some of them to be returned to her, but she was driven from the camp. One man peaceably tilling his field was roughly torn from his plough for no better reason than the desirability of securing as many prisoners as possible, or to afford some of the soldiers an opportunity of plunder, and harnessed to the chain. I felt very sorry for this poor fellow. He was absolutely guiltless of any offence whatever, and was as quiet and peaceable-looking a man as his brother Imsti was the reverse; but all is grist that comes to the mill of the Sultan's prisons.

A favourite pastime of schoolboys is what they call a 'paper-chase,' in which the 'hares' indicate the course they have taken by bits of paper thrown out as they run, as 'scent' to the 'hounds.' The track of the Sultan's prisoners on their way from his camp to his prisons is marked by the rough graves of the men that die on the road. This poor fellow never reached Marrakesh. He was one of the 'bits of paper.'

Al-al, by the way, had soon tired of his attendance on us. Some of the soldiers had chaffed him about being a servant of the Christians, and he now avoided our tent as much as possible. We were therefore worse off than if we had never seen him, as our former guards, having been told that Al-al would in future attend to our wants, now refused to do anything for us, even so small a thing as get us a drink of water. They were glad enough to be relieved of the trouble, and now were in no hurry to take it upon themselves again. If food came, well and good; but they weren't going to bother themselves to go and look for it. Al-al himself showed a complete change of front, both in his manner towards us and in his conversation. Kaid Giluli, instead of being the compassionless ruffian that Al-al had painted him a few days ago, was now in that individual's expressed opinion 'a very good man.' The snivelling hypocrisy of the man angered me, and I felt very much tempted to take him by the neck and kick him whenever I saw his long, dark, solemn face. Never by any chance did he bring us any tit-bit of news that he thought would cheer us, but any soldiers' gossip calculated to damp our spirits he would retail to us with ill-concealed enjoyment. 'I have news of you,' he would say in his broken English: 'the Kaid is going to send you to Morocco City. You must go to the Sultan.' This because he knew that all our hopes were centred upon Mogador and the British Consul, knowing that we had a right to demand to be taken to our own countrymen, and that Giluli had no right to take us to the Sultan or any Sherifian authority. 'Put Mogador out of your mind,' he would say—'you will never see Mogador. You are the Sultan's prisoners. He is going to keep you. You will go to Morocco City.'

When Al-al began to ask questions as to the number of rifles we had landed, what kind they were, and so on, I was convinced that he only came to our tent to find out what he could to report to the Kaid; so the next time he came I conversed with Beyerle in French, but he couldn't resist the temptation of displaying his knowledge, and letting us know that he understood something of that language also. After that, there was nothing for it but to maintain a guarded silence when he came. Not that we were conscious of having committed any offence, seeing that we had landed on territory that we believed to be the property of the Globe Venture Syndicate by purchase in due and proper form, but there was no reason why we should afford Kaid Giluli any information on the subject at all. On one of these occasions I asked him what he had done with the letter I had given him to take or send to Mogador, and to my surprise he produced it from his bag. He said he could get no friend of his 'that he could trust' to go, and handed it back to me.

The Kaid must have been in a very good humour at the ready compliance of the Imsti tribe with his demands, for the same afternoon he sent for Sabbah and myself, and, producing a couple of mackintoshes and a pair of leggings, asked if they were our property. The mackintoshes belonged to Beyerle and myself, whilst Sabbah claimed the leggings. They were some of the articles that we had packed in our bags when we were preparing to leave our camp at Arksis for Assaka; and, to my surprise, the Kaid handed them over to us. Mackintosh and indiarubber the Moors generally regard as being made of *haluf*—the hated pig—and as such taboo to them, which I suppose explained Giluli's unexpected generosity (?). Whatever the reason, we were very glad to have the articles back, as they would serve either as pillows or coverings at night, and would be a protection while on the march, if, unfortunately, it should come on to rain at any time. And, indeed, the mackintoshes were put to all these uses before we fell into civilized hands once more.

We made an early start on the Monday morning, the camels, which had been allowed to roam about at will to graze, being soon collected from the hillsides where they were browsing off the sharp thorny leaves of the argan-trees, and other delicacies that they could find.

While we fretted at every stoppage that delayed our arrival at our destination, the day's rest we had at Imsti did us all good, as, after the ten days' close confinement at Tlata, we were not in the best travelling fettle, and the fatigue produced by seven or eight hours' riding on a baggage camel, over rough and roadless country, has to be experienced to be thoroughly realized.

A touching incident occurred very soon after we had got well under way. The road from the camp was at first a broad, well-defined track, and the native prisoners were trudging along, when a young woman suddenly darted into the roadway and kissed poor old Misti on the top of his head. The old fellow did not look as if he and human affection had a very close acquaintance, but even the wild beasts cherish their offspring; and this was his daughter, who probably felt that she was taking her last farewell of him on earth. The salute took but a second; the girl disappeared as quickly as she had come, and the chain-gang passed on in silence to their doom.

If the little incident was pathetic, the next on the road narrowly escaped being tragic. It was about mid-day, and the route all morning had been over hills and down dales of varying declivity. Sabbah and de Reya were mounted on one camel, the former in front and the latter behind; and while climbing the steep slope of a rugged and rocky path, the breast-band of the animal broke with the strain. The packsaddle slid off, and both men were thrown violently to the ground. Sabbah, who was uppermost, was only a little shaken; but de Reya fell heavily, with Sabbah and the saddle on the top of him. He lay there for some time with scarcely a move, and I feared at first that he was seriously injured. Beyerle and I, who were on the same beast, dismounted to attend to him, and in a little while he was able to get upon his feet and walk, leaning upon Beyerle's arm. In falling he had struck the bottom of his spine against a stone, and the accident caused him considerable pain for several days. An examination of several of the camel breast-bands showed that they were in similar danger of breaking under the least unusual strain, and I complained to the Kaid, and requested him to give us mules to ride, as we were not accustomed to riding camels. Had the accident to de Reya been fatal, as it might easily have been, Giluli would have been in some trepidation, having advised the capture of five Christians, and being only able to produce four, even allowing, for the moment, Sabbah's pretensions to such a title. But, like Pharaoh of old, as soon as the danger was over he hardened his heart, and insisted on our riding camels until we should reach Tisnit.

Bel F'kuk, who was near, took an opportunity of trying to console us. 'Keep up your heart,' he said to Sabbah, out of hearing of Giluli: 'it is a punishment from Allah; but it will pass. You will see your own country soon, *Insha Allah.** To-morrow I will ask the Kaid to let you have mules to ride, but I fear he will make you ride the camels. He is a hard man.'

* Please God.

PRISONERS ON THE MARCH.

[To face page 706.

We did not make a long day's journey that day, for by about two o'clock we came in sight of the tents that had gone on in advance, and were already pitched. The halting-place, called El Arba after the Wednesday market that is held there, was a plain surrounded by hills, somewhat similar to Tlata, but of much greater size. The surrounding mountains, too, attained a somewhat higher elevation, the summits being apparently destitute of vegetation, while the lower slopes were by no means bare of verdure.

When our tent was pitched we had a visit from several of our friends, Hadj Ali and Kaid Bel F'kuk among the number. From the latter we learnt that we were going to stay at El Arba for one day, and he promised us that on the morrow he would get us some soap and water, so that we might wash ourselves and our clothes. There was a treat to look forward to! For the last fortnight Beyerle and I had not had our clothes off once, scarcely even our boots, and the others had been almost as long. Water to drink had been difficult enough to get; but water to wash with was an undreamt-of luxury. For my part I was wondering whether an old blunt knife and some sandpaper would not be useful, preparatory to the application of so mild a remedy as soap and water, but, not wishing to hurt anyone's susceptibilities, I kept my idea to myself.

The next day was a red-letter day in the history of our captivity. About mid-day a couple of soldiers appeared at the door of our tent, and told us they had come to take us to Kaid Bel F'kuk. The invitation was obeyed with alacrity, and under their friendly escort we were conducted to a little grove on the edge of the camp, where we found a good-sized tent pitched, and a large mat spread upon the ground. In the tent, which had been pitched for our special benefit, we quickly stripped ourselves of our underclothing, socks, etc., and handed the things to the black slaves that were waiting for them. Our washing-day had arrived at last. I think the operation consisted in putting the clothes into a running stream and treading on them with bare feet, afterwards spreading them on the bushes in the sun to dry. But there was no doubt about the thoroughness of our own ablutions. Bucket after bucket of water was brought by the willing slaves, and not much was left of the cake of soap when we all had had our bath.

By the time we had finished, Kaid Bel F'kuk appeared upon the scene with his friend Kaid Hassan, and milk and boiled rice were brought out. Our host did not partake, but contented himself with watching us, his fat, good-tempered face being wreathed in honest smiles the while. After this green tea was served, and—wonder of wonders!—a box of cigars. Like a good Moslem, he didn't smoke, and I wondered how or why the cigars had found their way into his possession. On examining them I recognised them as the same brand as those we had had from the *Hassani*, and I guessed that the Captain had made a present of them, perhaps when he came ashore. They were not much use to the Kaid, but they were mighty acceptable to us, and the jovial old soul insisted on our taking the box away with us, and promised us another when we should have finished that.

All the afternoon we basked in the sunshine, chatting with the two Kaids on trivial subjects, and endeavouring circumspectly to find out our real destination. We felt sure that Bel F'kuk would not tell us the usual camp fairy-tales, and such a first-rate opportunity of getting at the truth was not to be neglected. From him we learned that Kaid Giluli had sent a courier with a letter to the Sultan, who was with his army fighting near Dar-al-baida (Casablanca), reporting our capture. He also told us that we were going first to Tisnit, where he and the rest of the army would stop; but we and the other prisoners would be sent on to the Sultan's camp with a small escort. That was not quite what we wanted or expected, but there was always a chance of an alteration in the Kaid's plan on receipt of a reply from the Sultan. For my own part, I couldn't get it into my mind that we were going anywhere else but to Mogador, and the rest of the party caught in some degree the infection of my confidence.

> 'Hope for the best; be prepared for the worst,
> And bear what comes like a man,'

always seemed to me a gem of philosophic wisdom, and our circumstances provided a first-rate opportunity of putting those precepts into practice.

The afternoon passed away all too quickly, and we were very loath to return to our tent when the declining sun told us that it was time to go. Still, we took away with us a new lease of spirits, to say nothing of a box of cigars. Moreover, we had washed, we had feasted, and for a few brief hours we had breathed the air of freedom. The same two soldiers escorted us back through the camp, and then proceeded to Giluli's tent to report that we were once more safe under the watch and ward of our appointed guards.

The remaining hour of daylight we spent in observing the life in the camp, and it was not without interest. If anyone wished to have an audience with the Kaid, he intimated his desire to an old patriarch, who was alleged to have reached the truly venerable age of 120 years, and who acted as intermediary. Inasmuch as a Moor can never tell you with certainty how old he is, or the year in which he was born,* I accepted the statement with all reserve, especially as the old fellow did not look a year over eighty, and rode his twenty or thirty miles a day on his mule with the best of them. Among the applicants that afternoon was a young soldier, who complained of having lost not only his money, but also his *jelaba* in his unsuccessful efforts to 'spot the lady' in the seductive *three-card trick!* He wanted the Kaid to order restitution of his property, alleging that he had been cheated, but Giluli, with the rough-and-ready justice of a Kadi, gave him a severe lecture for his folly, and ordered him to receive ten lashes for indulging in the sin of gambling. The punishment was promptly carried out in front of the Kaid's tent, the delinquent being seized and held face downwards by four men, while a fifth vigorously applied a quadrupled leather thong to that portion of his anatomy which we were taught in our younger days was specially designed by Providence for such purpose. That was a verdict for defendant, with costs, with a vengeance. At the same

* While in Sus and Morocco I inquired of several men their age, and they invariably made the wildest of guesses, or fixed the date of their birth by stating that it was shortly before or shortly after a former Sultan did something or other. A man of forty or so would give his age as eighteen or nineteen, perhaps, and in the same breath ask if de Reya (who had no hair on his face, and looked about twenty) was still suckled by his mother. It is quite a common practice among them to suckle their children until they are almost verging on puberty.

time, I couldn't help marvelling that so essentially an art of civilization as the three-card trick should be practised in a Moorish camp, and find its victims as easily among the denizens of Morocco as with the unfledged Cockneys in Epping Forest on a Bank Holiday.

Another amusing thing was to watch the beggars that exploited the camp. Their *modus operandi* was systematic in the extreme. About half a dozen of them would stand in a row in front of the Kaid's tent, and chorus their appeal in a monotonous chant, at the conclusion of which they would all salaam obeisance, and in most cases a messenger would emerge from the tent with a loaf of sugar, which he would hand to the leader of the gang. Then would follow another chant of thanks, which sounded for all the world like the lessons repeated parrot-wise by boys in a Sunday-school, then more obeisance, and the idle loafers would pass on to another tent, and go through the same performance. The abodes of the principal men in the camp were easily found, as throughout Morocco the tents of the well-to-do are almost invariably ornamented with symbols in blue, in rows all round, representing bottles to indicate plenty. The plain white-canvas tent does not impress the native mind like the 'blue-bottle' variety, and was generally passed over by the begging fraternity. Our own tents at Arksis were all of this description—except one soldiers' white bell-tent and our kitchen—and had been appropriated by Kaid Giluli for the benefit of his faithful followers.

When night fell and our usual candle was brought, we fell to discussing the prospects of getting news from the north. Captain Siebert had told us that the *Tourmaline* had steamed away in the direction of the

Canaries, and we knew that the telegraph-wire would be worked from there. The Legation at Tangier would doubtless communicate at once with the Sultan, and we did not doubt that his Sherifian Majesty would order the Kaid to send us at once to Mogador. Calculating the distance and the difficulties of communication, we reckoned that, everything being favourable, we might have news by February 3 at the earliest. Only two days more! And in a lighter frame of mind than we had known for some days we sought forgetfulness in sleep—stones our pillow, earth our bed.

CHAPTER XX.

STILL NORTHWARD.

The laziness of the Moors—The camel in Morocco—Romantic scenery—The women come out to curse us—Khamis Ait Bubka—The vagaries of a saint—A wrestle and its good results—Beyerle falls ill—Giluli's kind message—An imaginative correspondent—I meditate on Kaids in general—Arrival of a courier—The Kaid's plans upset—Al-al has a fit—Concerning *kif*—The lullaby of the ocean.

THE Moors may be a lazy people, and doubtless in the main they are. They have a precept which, as far as my observation in the country went, finds a very wide circle of admirers, who practise it most religiously :

Never run if you can walk ;
Never walk if you can stand ;
Never stand if you can sit down ;
And never sit if you can lie down and go to sleep.

Late rising, however, is not their particular form of sloth. Sunrise generally saw the camp astir, and the morning after our long-remembered 'washing-day' the place was early alive with the bustle of preparation for departure. The gathering-in of the untethered camels began with the first gray streaks of dawn, but nothing seemed to be accomplished without a lot of shouting, screaming, and general vituperation. As a rule, at least an hour elapsed between the time we were roused up and the time we started on the march; and altogether there was a lack of that order and discipline which characterizes the armies of civilization. The selection of the riders for the various camels always gave rise to much heated discussion, the owners of the beasts invariably protesting that their loads were heavy enough without the addition of a 'cursed infidel'; but the wrangle generally ended up with two of us being perched up on the back of the already-loaded animal instead of one. The carrying capacity of the camel, however, is considerable, for a well-fed animal can easily carry a load of 600 or 700 pounds for days together on marches from sunrise to sunset. He maintains a steady pace of about three miles an hour, and threats and abuse, coaxing and persuasion, alike fail to induce the brute to quicken his ungainly 'galumphing' gait. As a courier, he is far outstripped by his biped owner, and as a 'mount' he is a painful ordeal. The rough, mountainous districts of Morocco scarcely suit his tender feet, but he is indispensable. He is the transport service from Tangier to Timbuctoo, from Saffi to Sudan, and without him Morocco would be ruined, bankrupt, starving, in a week.

For the first few hours our route lay through the passes in the mountains, and the scenery was of the most beautiful and romantic character. Lofty crag and verdant valley, gurgling streams and wooded slopes, and over all 'that tent of blue which prisoners call the sky,' unflecked by clouds, and in the midst of which there blazed, in all his undimmed glory, the burnished African sun. Once or twice the path was so precipitous that we had to dismount from our camels and walk—an interlude we all appreciated. Passing a mountain stream in one of the glens, we halted to cool our hands and faces, and drink while we had the chance. The order of procession was at this point Indian file, and Kaid Giluli was out of sight in the rear. The Moors looked on as if they would like to do the same; but it was Ramadan, and they forbore, or contented themselves with drawing in a mouthful of water and spitting it out again.

As we got farther north the country began to show more signs of regular cultivation, the ground being tilled wherever the opportunity offered. During the afternoon we passed near a village, the houses of which seemed to be better built than those in Sbooya and Imsti, and made a little more pretence to architectural design. As we neared the houses our escort called a halt. The prisoners that were on the chains afoot had, with the greater portion of the army, taken a slightly divergent route from that which we were following; but Muley Abdallah and El F'kir Embarak were with our party. Presently some women were heard *lu-lu-ing* at the top of their voices—the peculiar sound the Arab women all over Northern Africa make when urging on their menkind to battle, or welcoming them home from the fight, or other circumstances of an exciting nature. As they approached the soldiers urged them on to curse El F'kir Embarak, as an enemy to his country, and they responded with vigour and apparent earnestness. They would probably have *lu-lu-ed* with more sincerity had they witnessed the Susi driving the defeated invaders back across the Atlas, but the Arab woman has always a strong leaning towards the winning side. Their anathemas, however, were not confined to the Sbooya chief, who looked as if he didn't hear, but were also directed towards us Christians. Not understanding what they said, we could easily appear indifferent, but Sabbah was unable to control himself. He happened to be on foot, and, stooping down, picked up a stone to fling at the women; but one of the horsemen, realizing his intention, quickly rode up, and persuaded him to desist by presenting a loaded rifle at his head, and, urging our animals forward, the women were soon left behind.

It was nearly four o'clock when we arrived at our next camping-ground, a place called Khamis Ait Bubka, where barracks had been built by the late Sultan Muley Hassan for his soldiers on their raiding excursions southward. We were not put in there, however, but occupied our tent as usual; while the Moslem prisoners had a native tent, which was practically a large camel-hair rug, propped up here and there with short supports just high enough to enable the occupants to crawl under. I was so dog-tired when we arrived, being with difficulty prevented from falling asleep on the camel's back, that before our tent was pitched I had thrown myself down on the ground and gone fast asleep. While thus unconscious, I had rather a narrow escape from an unpleasant accident. A *buhali*,* seeing us, began to amuse himself by throwing large stones at us, one of which dropped just past my head. The crowd were hugely entertained, and of course didn't dream of interfering with a 'saint,' who was gesticulating wildly and screaming curses; but Kaid Jaah, with more sense, informed Giluli of what was going on, and the lunatic was persuaded to desist. A number of people came to curse and stare

* Fool, and therefore saint.

at us when we were installed in our tent, but we were becoming more assertive as we drew nearer to civilization, and ordered or drove these unwelcome visitors away as occasion demanded.

Looking through the holes in our tent to watch the sun set, I observed a man with a stick walk up to the Kaid's tent. He had every appearance of a *rakàs* (courier), as besides his long staff he carried a wallet on his back, the usual outward and visible signs of a courier in Morocco, and had a travel-stained look about him. Not much importance was attached to the incident, though, as we calculated that there had not yet been time for a message to have come from the Sultan about us, and letters were constantly coming and going, in and out of the camp.

That evening was the first time we had a meal of meat, Kaid Jaah, who had lately altered his whole demeanour towards us, sending us in a bowl of stewed mutton, which he said was from his own supper. If that were so, then his leavings were almost enough to give four hungry Christians and a Jew a sufficing meal; but in any case we were extremely grateful to him. Before we were chained up at sunset he had invited me to wrestle with him, and I had succeeded in throwing him; and I believe this was his way of showing his appreciation.

When night fell, poor Beyerle, who had for some days suffered considerably from rheumatism, began to show symptoms of fever. His lungs were in a bad state, the night dews and exposure having brought on a severe cold, which I feared was going to turn to congestion. In this extremity Al-al was despatched to the Kaid to ask for a rug to cover, if not all, at least one of us who was sick. This interesting savage, after asking what was the matter, replied that if his lungs troubled him they could easily be cut out. Not long after this happened some of the London daily papers printed a communication, supplied by 'the trusted and zealous correspondent of the Moorish Government,' in which the following sentence appeared: 'I am glad to hear that the prisoners are being well treated, and I fancy Giluli is too prudent a man to lay himself open to complaints of undue hardship.' Some of this dormant prudence perhaps awoke after he had sent this message to us, and fearing possibly that unpleasant consequences might happen to him if one of us should unfortunately succumb to his 'good treatment,' he sent an old canvas sack which bore the legend: 'Brunner Mond and Co., Silvertown, E.,' stamped upon it. As a covering for five men it was obviously inadequate, but it was just large enough to wrap round Beyerle's chest, and, after all, was perhaps the means of saving his life. But where did 'the trusted and zealous correspondent' get his information from?

The night air was cold there in the heart of the hills, and we shivered in our misery.

'The savage!' I exclaimed, when Al-al brought back the message from the Kaid, and an unholy hope of vengeance, vague and intangible, rose up within me. I sought comfort in reflecting how few of his order die in their beds, or even live to enjoy the riches they amass by their robbery and extortion. There is a Nemesis that seems to tread upon the heels of Moorish Kaids. There is the sword of Damocles for ever over their heads, suspended only by the slender thread of a capricious Sultan's pleasure, and perhaps the dark doors of the prison of Marrakesh would yet open to receive Sid Said el Giluli in the chains to which he so lightly consigned others.

'This is very punishment,' said Sabbah, ' by —— it is. I was a —— fool, I was, to come ashore again after I got on board the *Tourmaline*. If I'd known Giluli was there, I'd never have come ashore—not me!'

No one made any further remark, but I fancied I caught the air of ' Why did I leave my little back-room in Bloomsbury?' as de Reya whistled softly to himself.

All the next day we rested at Khamis. In the morning Al-al came to the tent and told us that a courier had arrived the previous evening from the Sultan, with a letter about us, but he didn't know what the purport of it was. I asked him how the man could have travelled from Shawia, away in the North of Morocco, in so short a time, and he said that the courier had orders to go day and night. He had taken the French steamer from Casablanca to Mogador, and thence overland to Khamis in three and a half or four days, sleeping only just an hour or two in the night-time, with perhaps a rest at mid-day. Still, it wasn't possible that this could be an answer to the letter Giluli had sent from Arksis. Perhaps the Legation at Tangier was at work.

'Which of you is the German?' asked Al-al, after a pause.

' German?' I said; ' what are you talking about? We are English.'

Beyerle had passed as English all along, and he wished the fiction to be maintained; but I thought it strange that Al-al should ask.

Shortly afterwards Kaid Jaah came in and told us

that a letter had come from the Sultan to Giluli, telling him to send us to Marrakesh without delay. As the information was vouchsafed to us without our asking, and, moreover, agreed with what Al-al had said, we were inclined to believe it, except that for Morocco City we read Mogador. Al-al looked as if he had lost a dollar and found a peseta. On inquiring the cause of his trouble, I learnt that the Kaid wanted him to take a letter to the Sultan at Shawia, but he was tired, he said, and did not want to go. This man began to be a very fair barometer for us. When he looked gloomy we might be sure there was good news for us, but when other tidings came he seemed to be more cheerful. Truly the subtle workings of the Moorish mind are well-nigh unfathomable.

It had been the intention of Kaid Giluli to take us by devious routes to a number of places in Sus, to show us off as trophies of his victories, before he went to Tisnit; but the receipt of this letter from the Sultan altered his plans, and the order was given to resume the march on the morrow.

When the first silver of the dawn was in the eastern sky, the camp awoke. The mountains began to be less imposing in height, and cultivation to be more general. For the first time in the country we saw the graceful, slender date-palm, underneath whose waving shadows nestled a milk-white *kubba*, or saint-house, that gleamed snow-like against the bright green of the valley's livery of early spring.

During the afternoon Al-al, who was riding a mule, suddenly swayed, and would have fallen from the saddle had not Uld Suka seized him by the *sulham*, and held him up as he was fainting. I heard a cry, and, jumping down from my camel, turned back to see what was the matter. I found the man foaming at the mouth in an epileptic fit. He had had nothing to eat since the early morning meal, about 2 o'clock, and nothing to drink throughout the long hot day, as it was Ramadan. Moreover, he was much addicted to the smoking of *kif*, a mixture of native tobacco and hashish. The sale and use of this drug by the Moors was, in accordance with the spirit of Koranic laws, declared illicit some years ago, but the Government evidently thinks it would be a pity to let religious scruples stand in the way of increasing the revenues of the treasury, so it is made a Government monopoly. Every year the monopoly is put up for sale to the highest bidder among the Jews, and in Tangier last year was disposed of for 5,000 dollars. The Moors, however, are the best customers of the drug, though to be seen smoking it is considered as disreputable as to smoke a briar on the way to church in England. The *kif* pipe is composed of a long wooden stem, ornamented with quaint coloured designs, on to which a small red clay bowl is fitted. The bowl only contains enough *kif* for about a dozen draws, and the smoke is inhaled into the lungs. The effect produced is soothing to the nerves, and a feeling of drowsiness soon overtakes the smoker. Constant addiction to the drug brings about loss of appetite and flesh, and weakens the mental, if not the physical, powers. Like opium, it does not arouse the evil or violent passions, but, on the contrary, lulls them into a lethargic calm, though the smoker is always irritable after a debauch. For those who do not smoke, *kif* is made up into a condiment, by the admixture of honey or some other sweet, and swallowed.

The Moors stood round this fellow as he lay upon

the ground, none knowing what to do with him. There was no water near, and I doubt that the fanatics would have allowed me to give it to him if there had been, but I succeeded in restoring him to consciousness in about five minutes. He was, however, unable to resume the march for some time, so two or three men were left behind to look after him, and he turned up in camp the same evening.

We had been told that we were only going to have a short day's march that day, but it was nearly sunset when we arrived at El Arba Sidi Ali dead tired. It was an exceedingly pretty spot that had been chosen for camping—right in a natural hollow in the hills. Late in the afternoon we had met a flight of locusts—that plague of Morocco that is sometimes more devastating than even the army of the Sultan—and also smelt the fresh salt-laden breezes that blew over the hills from the ocean. We could not see the sea, but we could not have been very far off, for during the silence of the night, when the camp had gone to sleep, and the fires were burning low in the moonlight, the gentle murmur of the breakers as they beat upon the Atlantic shore was wafted on our ears. It is marvellous how sound travels in that clear and silent atmosphere. On another occasion when the wind was blowing in from the sea, we all distinctly heard the thunder of the surf like the distant roar of a busy city, and we afterwards found that we were five miles from the nearest spot on the coast.

In the hush of night there is something sublime yet soothing in the sound of the waves as they roll in upon the shore—unhasting, unresting—and as I lay awake that night and hearkened to the faint echo of Nature's lullaby, I almost forgot my miseries in the pure delight of listening. Then on a sudden there burst upon the quiet air the blare of the brazen trumpet that woke the sleeping Moslems, and warned them to eat while the mantle of night was yet upon the earth, and fortify themselves for the struggle with another long weary day of Ramadan.

CHAPTER XXI.

TISNIT.

An early start—A fairy picture—Fragmentary humanity—A jeering crowd—Welcome home to the raiders—*Lab el barud*—We arrive at Tisnit—How their houses are built—Description of the town—A vile den—Embarak, the faithful—Concerning *mona*—Kaid Hassan's mission—A saddening sight—Treatment of prisoners in Morocco—Lord Salisbury's opinions and his acts—Recruiting the chain-gang—Al-al prophesies—Unsubstantial diet.

IT must have been at least half an hour before dawn when we were roused up next morning by the soldiers who were taking the tents down. The moon was shining brightly, and the embers of some of the camp-fires still glowed red. The night dews still lay heavy on the ground, and we hastily wrapped ourselves in our mackintoshes, and shivered in the early morning air. Tisnit was understood to be distant only four or five hours' march, and I wondered what could be the reason of this early start; but no explanation was given except that the Kaid wished to arrive there before mid-day. The first part of our route lay through a miniature forest of argan-trees, and perched on the top of a camel, one had to be careful of the overhanging branches if one wished to avoid the fate of Absalom. No regular food was given to the camels, which were simply turned loose to crop what vegetation they could find about the camping-grounds, and every now and then the brutes would stop short to munch the sharp, prickly foliage of the argan-trees, to which they seemed very partial.

After about three hours' marching we climbed the last range of hills before reaching the plain of Tisnit, from the summit of which a vast panorama lay stretched out below us. At first sight its fairy-like beauty resembled a mirage in the desert, but on closer examination one could see a great level plain, on which the morning mist was spread like a cloth, and in the hazy distance to the west could be seen Aglu and the sapphire sea beyond. A very steep descent soon brought us to the level, and then we made quick progress through the fields of growing barley, which these soldiers of 'the Slave of God'* heedlessly and needlessly trampled under their horses' hoofs. Beggars lined the roadside, some with little flags to attract attention, others content merely to spread a cloth on the ground to catch the *fluss*† that the more generous might throw, and call unceasingly upon Allah.

As we came nearer to the town we were met by 'the lame, the halt and the blind'—living witnesses of Sherifian tyranny and barbarism. One man, whose hands had both been chopped off, stretched out his stumps and called aloud for charity. Another, whose eyes had both been blinded by the red-hot iron, strained his sightless orbs to heaven in a mute appeal for pity. Another was minus a foot; and so on—

---

* Abd-el-Aziz (lit., the Slave of God) is the name of the present Sultan.

† Coins made of iron with a small admixture of copper, and worth a very fractional portion of a penny.

poor, wretched, lopped and mutilated specimens of humanity! It was indeed a moving spectacle.

They seem to be chary of bestowing names upon their *duars** in Sus—Tisnit, Massa and many other places standing not only for the town itself, but also for the country round about, and a number of smaller towns or *duars* in the vicinity. Before one of these outlying towns a halt was called. It was not necessary to pass through the town at all; in fact, a détour had been made to get to it, but it was part of Giluli's programme to parade and display his captives as much as possible, especially the Christians, whom he regarded as the greatest of his trophies. Moslem prisoners on the march in Morocco are a common enough sight, God knows, but few Moorish Kaids can boast of having dragged a party of Christians, in chains and on camel-back, over several hundred miles of country; and no opportunity was neglected of showing us off to the jeering, ignorant and fanatical natives.

All the women of the town were assembled on the tops of the houses, or the walls which encircled the place, and *lu-lu-ed* lustily as the procession approached. Some of the soldiers wished us to go close under the walls in order to afford the spectators the more amusement, but some of our friends spared us this humiliation, and interposed themselves between us and the wall. The Kaid, however, noticing this, ordered all the prisoners forward by themselves without any flanking cavalry, and the gates of the town being thrown open, we passed in with the jeers and insults of the populace ringing in our ears. Spitting was freely indulged in, but on our lofty seats we were

* Villages.

untouched by the more offensive part of this indignity. For once we heard no more the irritating *zìt, zìt** of our drivers hurrying us along, but were compelled to go as slowly as possible through the narrow streets in order to prolong the show. A halt was made in the centre of the town, and again before the exit gate, which was shut, and insults, curses, threats, and even stones, were hurled at our unoffending heads.

Once outside the town, we resumed our usual jog-trot, and presently came in sight of what looked like the advance guard of another army. It was the Khalifa of Kaid Giluli for this district, who had come out with a large escort to meet the victorious raiders returning home. A great deal of salaaming and saluting took place when the two detachments met, and from that point until our arrival before the gate of Tisnit the troops went through their favourite performance of *lab el barud*, or powder-play. It is indulged in on all festive occasions, and is a necessary accompaniment to the welcome of a distinguished visitor. It is a wild and bizarre display, but a short description will suffice.

About twenty horsemen, with long flint-lock guns loaded with blank charge, line up abreast and advance at a walking pace. Gradually this develops into a canter, which at a given signal from the leader breaks out into a furious gallop, the horses' unshorn tails streaming in the wind. Away they go at a breakneck pace, the men brandishing their guns over their heads and, suddenly, in the midst of their mad charge, a furious yell bursts out, the guns are brought to the shoulder, and a loud crackle of musketry, which should be simultaneous, rings on the air. The

* Go on.

phalanx parts in the middle, one half wheeling round to the left, and the other to the right, to make way for another line behind them, which goes through the same manœuvres. Sometimes the whole line wheels bodily round to form up again in the rear, or turns to face the advancing cavalry. On they come like a whirlwind, and it looks as if nothing but a stone wall or a line of serried bayonets would stop that impetuous avalanche of men and horses, but when within about a dozen yards the guns are fired at their imaginary foe, and in an almost incredibly short space the horses are reined up and the men whirl aloft their guns, flushed and exultant. Occasionally pantomimic performances are indulged in, such as turning round and firing behind them while at full gallop, throwing their guns into the air and catching them, standing up in the stirrups or on the saddles, and otherwise displaying their dexterity and horsemanship. The Moor is very proud of his horsemanship, and thinks that no nation in the world can rival his feats in the saddle; but, then, he also has a very high opinion of his shooting, which in comparison with that of most civilized nations is beneath contempt. In fact, in most things the modern Moor, who has not been brought much into contact with civilization, is a most amazing mass of conceit and self-sufficiency, the offspring of ironclad ignorance and fanatical prejudice.

To the accompaniment of this din of firing and the war-songs of the soldiers we entered Tisnit, the whole populace of the town having turned out and ranged themselves outside the gateway to witness the procession. We were almost in the van, with the Moorish prisoners, barefoot and in chains, immediately behind; but the reception was very different from that we had experienced at the last town. The crowd was quite well behaved, none spitting or insulting us in any way as we rode into the open square in the centre of the town.

Tisnit, like most Oriental and Mohammedan towns, looks better at a distance. Under that enchantment the mean mud houses look as if they were built of red sandstone, but a nearer view destroys the illusion. In Morocco nearly all the houses are whitewashed, inside and out, but in Sus the original mud of their habitations is usually left unadorned. The manner of building these *tabbia* structures is simple in the extreme. After the foundations have been laid, a wooden framework like a long deep box without a bottom is placed on the ground and filled to the top with this mixture of lime, rubble, sand, and water, and then beaten down with heavy wooden 'drivers' until it is a tight and compact mass. The framework is then lifted up, like the mould off a brick, and the operation repeated on another length. When the walls have reached the required height, and the requisite holes have been left for light and the escape of smoke, thick rough-hewn branches of trees are laid across as closely as they will fit, and mud put on the top to the height of 2 or 3 feet to form the roof, and the whole left to dry in the hot sun. Needless to say, these are frequently not waterproof, as we had afterwards the misfortune to discover. Little or no attempt is made towards architectural beauty, or external or internal ornamentation, their one solitary recommendation being the thickness of their walls, which makes them warm in winter and cool in summer.

Tisnit is composed entirely of these structures, most of them furnished with the customary courtyard for the animals, and the intersecting streets, or, rather, lanes, are narrow, dirty, and uneven. A great wall, perhaps a mile and a half or two miles in circumference, and pierced by several gates, surrounds the place; but the enclosed space is by no means entirely built over. A great open space near the western gate is capable of camping 20,000 men, whereas the normal population of the place is only about 2,000 or 3,000. There is another large square, in front of the house that Kaid Giluli had selected as his residence until the *kasbah* which he is building there should be completed, so that the question of 'open spaces' is not one that is likely to exercise the minds of the Tisnitites for many years to come. One or two lonely palm-trees raised their tufted heads above the dull monochrome of dirty red, but they only served to accentuate the monotony by the contrast. No city of lovely gardens here, like Marrakesh, where the date-palm, the pomegranate, and the fig-tree vie with each other in luxuriance and profusion, and the orange blossom sheds its lovely perfume on the air; no city of ruined mosques and palaces to tell the story of a once magnificent nation's faded glories, but only a mean inchoate mass of mud and squalor, silent yet eloquent testimony to the degeneracy of the people that raised it. And to think that five centuries ago Morocco was the pioneer of the civilization, the arts and sciences, of the West, and people sent their sons from Spain and other parts of Western Europe to her to receive their education!

After dismounting in the central square, we were shown into the garden of the Kaid's house, and began to think that we were going to be humanly treated at last, and given a tent in the garden more fitted for our accommodation than the bundle of rags and ropes that had served as such on the march so far. Vain hope! After a wait of half an hour or so, we were led outside again, and taken a few steps away to another house of the usual hovel description. If anything, our den—it could not by the grossest flattery be called a room—was worse than anything we had hitherto seen. It was about 8 feet square, and had at one time been used as a kitchen, as the walls, blackened by the smoke of many wood fires, plainly testified. There was no door; only a hole in the wall, large enough to admit of a man going in and out without stooping. A smaller hole above this was evidently made to allow the escape of smoke. No window illumined this dark and dismal hole, and a grass mat spread upon the cement floor comprised the furniture of the place.

To this wretched hovel some bread and honey was brought for us. The honey was mixed with argan oil, a process which in the opinion of any but a Moor ruins both ingredients. Al-al came not, nor was there any sign of the eggs, chickens, and other dainties with which we were to be regaled when we reached Tisnit. We were, however, allowed to sit outside in the stable-yard and enjoy the fresh air and sunshine, watching the clouds of locusts as they drove by overhead, and dreaming what fate might be in store for us. When night came, we rejoiced to find that, for once, we were freed from the gall of those accursed chains, but two armed soldiers guarded the narrow doorway as we slept. Across the yard, right opposite our den, and in a hovel similar to ours, but larger, the captured Susi were lodged. During the daytime they were chained together by the feet, while night, which should have brought the poor wretches rest, meant to them the added misery of a heavy iron collar round the neck.

Kaid Jaah had been to see us, but only for a few minutes, in the afternoon, and he had been the only one of our 'friendlies' to pay us a visit. We began to think that, stowed away in that rat-hole, we were lost trace of, but Embarak, the faithful, surprised us with his cheery voice and a dish of meat just as we were struggling to forget our troubles in sleep. He brought a friend, too, laden with a pot of tea, and we passed away half an hour of the time that crawled so lazily along in chatting and listening to stories of Embarak's rascality recounted by himself. The young scoundrel was cross-eyed and passing ugly, but as the hungry animals in the Zoo listen with joyful eagerness for the footsteps of their keeper at feeding-time, so we welcomed Embarak's daily coming, and thought his voice the sweetest music in the camp. From him we learned that we were to start on Monday morning for the Sultan's camp under the escort of Kaid Hassan, who had asked to be allowed to go.

On certain occasions during the year, of which the fast of Ramadan is one, it is the custom in Morocco for the various Kaids and Governors to send their *mona*, or 'present,' to the Sultan, which is understood to represent the taxes gathered from the tribes or townsmen. It is always an anxious time for the officials in question, fearing that the Sultan may consider the *mona* to be insufficient; and, if possible, they contrive not to visit the Court in person, but send a Khalifa or other emissary, in case his Sherifian Majesty should press them to stay indefinitely—not in his palace, but his prison.

A story is told of a Kaid who, by his rapacity and extortion, had accumulated a very considerable fortune at the expense of the unfortunate tribesmen he governed (!). On one occasion his *mona* was considered inadequate, and a letter was sent 'inviting' him to Court. On his arrival he was summoned to the presence of his imperial master.

'You have sent me 20,000 dollars,' said the Commander of the Faithful; 'that is not enough. You should have sent me 30,000 at least. Methinks a prison will suit you better than a *kasbah*.'

The Kaid was terrified, and pleaded to be allowed to return home to get the other 10,000 dollars, but he only thereby assured his fate.

'Oh, you have got another 10,000 dollars, have you, and you dare to rob me thus, and keep for your own use what belongs to your Sultan? Away with him to prison, and there let him stay until we learn the secret of where his ill-gotten treasure lies hid.'

And to prison he went, where he had ample leisure to repent, and to reflect upon the eternal truth of 'how wretched is that poor man that hangs on princes' favours.'

For this mission Kaid Hassan had been selected by Giluli, and he had promised his friend Bel F'kuk to look after us well on the road and treat us kindly, and we were all cheered by the news. Our treatment couldn't well be worse than it was under Giluli, and there was every prospect of it being considerably better.

The next day was gloriously fine and hot. Not a drop of rain had fallen since our capture, which was fortunate for us, considering the porous state of our ragged tent. In the morning Sabbah was sent for to go to the Khalifa's house. We thought this summons might portend fresh news for us, but it was only to amuse the Khalifa and his friends, and to ask him to explain the uses of some of the instruments belonging to the expedition which had been seized in our camp at Arksis. Before he left, however, Sabbah improved the occasion by getting from the Khalifa two pesetas wherewith to buy a pair of slippers. On being captured he had been deprived of his boots, and the slippers that had been lent him to enable him to march to Arksis had been taken away from him on arrival there. In this extremity de Reya had lent him a pair of 'Arctic' socks that he was wearing, while he himself was content with a pair of rubber sea-boots without socks of any sort.

In the afternoon we witnessed an operation that I never wish to see again. The blacksmith came into the yard with an anvil and hammer and a heap of ankle-bars and rivets. These fetters consisted of a flat bar of iron 9 or 10 inches in length, with a hole at each end. Through these holes were passed iron rings with the ends open, and the native prisoners were brought out one by one to have these infernal fetters fastened on their feet. The rings were put round their ankles, the ends brought together and riveted cold. Sometimes the hammer struck the foot as well as the iron, but not a moan or a murmur escaped the victim's lips. As soon as the operation was completed, the prisoner would hobble away, and seizing any old rags he could get, even tearing strips from his own clothes for the purpose, would wrap them round the iron to lessen the chafing on his already bleeding legs. In this manner are all the Sultan's prisoners riveted, and on arrival at the prison destined for their reception, some of the 'worst offenders' are further condemned to have heavy weights or cannon-balls attached to their chains, so that they

A BLACKSMITH AT WORK.

can only with the greatest difficulty drag themselves along at all. Age and youth, feebleness and strength, innocence and guilt, alike are disregarded. No trial takes place. A prisoner's arrest is proof sufficient of his guilt, and once immured within those living tombs, only one key can unlock the prison doors, and that is the key of gold. It is not an unusual thing for a poor wretch to lose the use of his lower limbs entirely in consequence of these heavy chains. Only last year a gentleman, whose veracity cannot for a moment be impeached,[*] revisited Morocco, and recorded that he 'saw a shocking sight of a man in Larache prison, unable to speak and dying. His legs were paralyzed owing to chains, and he was left in a condition too disgusting for description.'

In this connection I cannot refrain from quoting the account furnished to *Al Moghreb al Aksa*, a weekly newspaper published at Tangier in English, by their Mazagan correspondent last August, of an event that is of such frequent occurrence in Morocco as scarcely to excite more than passing notice or remark. 'Again,' he writes, ' we have had the sad experience of a most barbarous spectacle offered by the native authorities in the act of preparing the unfortunate prisoners who were brought some time ago from the Riff coast for transportation to Marrakesh.

'These poor Bocoya people, numbering nearly 250, including a large proportion of aged and decrepit persons, and even boys, in company with another batch of about 150 prisoners who were sent here from the neighbouring province of Abda, and others from different districts, making a total of about 500, had

[*] Mr. Henry Gurney, one of the executive committee of the Howard Association.

been lodged in a dungeon which, humanly speaking, could barely hold 100 persons. The only air inlet of this den of death being a small iron grated skylight in the centre, the suffering of the poor inmates, particularly in the present hot season, must have been horrible. There was no room for them to lie down, and they had necessarily to keep standing for many days. A roar of voices that could be heard from the surroundings from time to time, and three or four dead that had been taken out almost daily from this dungeon for interment during the summer, testify to the amount of torture that these poor people have had to endure.

'This week those belonging to the Bocoya tribe were taken out to be heavily fettered and removed to the southern capital. The sight was one of horror, as they appeared to be simply a procession of spectres half covered with dirty rags; many of them falling, as, owing to their miserable state of weakness, they could not stand, and most of them had to close their eyes, unable as they were to bear the glare of daylight. The stench emanating from their bodies and rags was unbearable, and no doubt this is one of the causes that have contributed to develop the typhoid fever now so prevalent.

'Two heaps of pieces of iron chain, with two collars each, were there near the town gate, ready for the prisoners, who repeatedly called out in anguish for water and bread. The barbarous operation of fettering these martyrs was then performed by several soldiers, and links were pinned by hammer, causing severe and unnecessary torture to the unfortunate creatures, who cried and trembled in agony. Many were wounded on the ankles and feet through badly-aimed hammering, and this barbarous treatment, which lasted three days, and raised considerable indignation among the European residents, did not move in the least the feelings of the native authorities. At last the wretched creatures were placed on camels and, escorted by a number of soldiers, commenced the still more painful experience of the road to Morocco City, in which they have to suffer from heat, thirst, hunger, the unbearable shaking of camel, their iron fastenings, and, above all, the merciless treatment of the Moorish soldiers, to which a large number of these unfortunate beings will succumb.

'These Bocoya prisoners are composed of the aged and infirm, as well as of a number of lads and boys, and even women, all helpless people who were unable to escape the snare prepared for them by the Sherifian troops on the Riff coast. Those that were responsible for the piratical acts, whom the Sultan pretended to punish, were able-bodied men, and, lacking no means of defence, fled to the mountains, where they defy the Government's authority.

'The prisoners remaining at Mazagan Gaol, mostly proceeding from Abda, are innocent people, well-to-do agriculturists, who, after having been squeezed of all that the Kaids could lay their hands on, are to be kept in prison until any further property they may have concealed is found.

'Such is the Moorish administration and its principles of justice! And yet this Government is frequently visited and invariably shown all respect and consideration by the representatives of the Great Christian Powers; but we never hear of any serious remonstrance against the barbarous outrages which are a matter of daily occurrence in this so-called empire, and which may be considered as a disgrace to humanity and civilization.'

Well might Lord Salisbury say, as he did at Glasgow on May 22, 1891 : 'Morocco still remains the home of the worst abuses, of the greatest cruelty, of the greatest ignorance and backwardness in all that conduces to prosperity and humanity. It is there that we hear of the most terrible cruelties, and we have no power to prevent them.' Yet seven years later we find this same politician, when Foreign Secretary and Prime Minister of the most powerful British Government of modern times, allowing British subjects to remain in the hands and at the mercy of Moorish Kaids for 100 days in flagrant defiance of all treaty rights, and humiliating his country by making a compact with 'our friend and ally, the Sultan of Morocco,' promising to punish these British subjects if his Sherifian Majesty would graciously condescend to hand them over, and having them tried in a Moorish town by a colonial judge without a jury, to be condemned on the evidence of negro slaves and Berbers, who were brought from the prison at Marrakesh for the purpose of identification, and who arrived in Tangier with their feet riveted together in the manner I have described above. Shade of Burleigh, that we should have come to this!

In addition to the prisoners that Giluli had picked up on the way, several men were brought out from the local prison to join the gang, which now numbered twenty, not counting ourselves. These Tisnit prisoners had evidently been confined for some months in a subterranean dungeon, where the light of the sun never penetrated, for their complexions were of an unhealthy, bilious yellow, and the bright daylight seemed to dazzle their eyes. Two of the slaves that had been taken were released, and found new masters among the officers, and an old Sherif who had been brought from El Arba Sidi Ali, accused of sheltering a fugitive Sbooya, was detained at Tisnit without being chained. In all probability he would be soon released, and meanwhile he was allowed to have his own servant to wait on him and bring his food, etc.

Al-al, who had not been near us since we had arrived, came in during the riveting process to tell us that we were going to Marrakesh. I asked him sarcastically if we should be fettered like the native prisoners, and he replied with a dull, far-away look in his eyes, begotten of *kif* and weak intellect, 'Perhaps, yes.' The fellow angered me, and I told him bluntly he was a liar; that we were going to Mogador without chains, and that if he only came to tell us false news, I should be glad if he kept away.

'All right,' he said; 'you will see. If you see Agadir, you will go to Mogador; if you don't, you will go over the Atlas to Marrakesh.' In any case, I was glad to hear that he was not coming with us, but going to stay at Tisnit awhile.

Slowly the day wore on to evening, and still no food was brought. A dry barley bannock had been given to each of us in the morning, and that was all we had had that day. The cares of office doubtless drove all thought of starving prisoners from the Kaid's mind, and even some of the soldiers pitied us. From their wallets they produced handfuls of roasted locusts—not the bean, but the locust of the air—which they offered to us. The insects did not look very tempting food, with their legs and wings still attached to their roasted bodies, but we were not in the mood to be over-dainty.

The soldiers assured us they were very good eating, and plucking off the heads, legs, and wings of a few, they pressed us to try them. I shut my eyes, thought of the first man who ate an oyster, and put one in my mouth. It had a flavour not altogether unlike that of a shrimp, and on this testimonial Beyerle was persuaded to follow my example. Then the others joined in, and if it was not a satisfying meal, it at any rate allayed somewhat the pangs of hunger that gnawed our stomachs, and added one more to our strange experiences in that strange land.

CHAPTER XXII.

GOOD-BYE TO GILULI.

I give a lesson on the uses of instruments—A penitent gaoler—Preparations for leaving Tisnit—Kaid Bel F'kuk's last act of kindness—A Moslem gem—Harangue from camel-back—Our new escort—Arrival at Massa—A 'square' meal—A woman in the party—Description of Massa—Highway robbery—The treelessness of Morocco—Dar el Kaid Hadj Hamed Ksim—Fording the river—We sight Agadir and the Atlas.

IN several respects we were worse off in this den at Tisnit than we were in our tent upon the march, not the least of which was that we could not even get stones for our pillows. It is not surprising, therefore, that we found sleep but a shy visitant, and that long before the dawn we were lying awake impatiently waiting for the day to break, and the hour to come when we should once more be reducing the distance that lay between us and Mogador. The sun, that never hastes and never rests, rose at last, but several hours passed by without a sign of our moving.

About ten o'clock a message was brought for me to go with Sabbah to the Khalifa. Kaid Jaah conducted us to a house at the other side of the town where we found Hadj Ali and several old friends with the Khalifa. On the floor of the room were displayed several instruments belonging to the expedition, the use of which the Khalifa wished to have explained to him. It was rather a hopeless task endeavouring to explain the workings of such a technical instrument as the telemeter, for example, to a man who had but a dim conception of the uses of a mariner's compass, but he listened with grave and polite attention, and apparent interest, to what I told him. At the conclusion he offered to sell us the things for 10 dollars *en bloc*, but I pointed out to him that in the first place we had been robbed of all our money, as well as the instruments which he was then showing to us, and that as the latter, at any rate, were of no use to him, he ought to hand them over to us. He didn't, however, fall in with my suggestion, and the things would probably find their way into the hands of some coast Jews in exchange for a few pesetas. He kept us chatting on trivial matters for about half an hour, whilst we consumed some bread and honey and tea that he ordered his servant to bring us, and then Kaid Jaah escorted us back the way we had come. At the corner of one of the streets, squatting in the shade against the wall, we came across one of the old soldiers that had been on special guard over us since our capture, and whom we had nicknamed 'Gaoler.' This was the individual who had shown a penchant for stealing our food on several occasions, but as he was going to stay behind at Tisnit, we thought we had seen the last of him. Seeing us approach, he got up on his feet and came towards us. Whether any vague apprehension had seized him that at some future time someone might be called to account for our unjustifiable treatment, and he was anxious to make his peace with us I can't say; but he was profuse in his apologies, and hoped we would forgive him for any ill he had done us, and wound up by calling upon God to 'put a blessing in our houses,' and, with a final 'Allah salaama,' the old scoundrel squatted down, and resumed his interrupted occupation of propping up the wall.

On returning to our quarters, we found that no breakfast had been sent by the Kaid, but Bel F'kuk had been faithful as ever, and the others, feeling sure that we should have had something to eat, had had an extra share. The Khalifa followed us soon afterwards, and made us a present of two pesetas each, and about 11 o'clock the order was given to *zit*. The native prisoners were the first to go, and a pitiable spectacle they presented as they hobbled out one by one in their fetters, their clothes filthy and in rags, their faces drawn by famine, and their spirits crushed by the hopelessness of their doom. When the miserable procession of spectres in dirty graveclothes had filed out, our turn came. We were taken first of all to the Kaid's house again, and waited in the garden while the mules were being got ready in the great square outside. At Tisnit it seemed we were to bid good-bye to camels, and be promoted to the dignity of mules, whilst the native prisoners were to ride the hated camels in pairs.

At length all was ready: the pack animals were loaded, the native prisoners were mounted, and we were led outside again. A great crowd thronged the square to see the cavalcade depart, and sticks were freely used by the Moors in authority to keep back the press of people. Quite a number of people came to bid us farewell—Hadj Ali, 'the Spaniard,' Embarak and others; and Kaid Hassan himself rode up to say that he was in command of the escort, and would treat us well. Embarak had told us the night before that his master would say good-bye to us before we left, and presently we saw Kaid Bel F'kuk making his way towards us on horseback, his kindly face beaming with good-nature. He shook hands with each of us in turn, and expressed the hope that we should soon see our own country again, and he left in Beyerle's palm a handful of silver, which, on being counted out, represented a dollar for each of us. I noticed, too, that poor Muley Abdallah was not forgotten. It was the last parting kindness of a man who had been kind to us throughout, and that almost alone of all that company. He had been to us the friend in need who is a friend indeed, and had shown towards us a constant and unfailing generosity, that we could hardly have expected had he been of the same creed and country as ourselves. He had probably never heard the words of the Founder of a faith older than that of Islam, 'I was an hungred, and ye gave Me meat: I was thirsty, and ye gave Me drink: . . . naked, and ye clothed Me. . . . I was in prison, and ye came unto Me;' but no man could have more faithfully carried out the spirit of that teaching, had he been taught the lesson daily from his earliest youth. And when one remembers that the objects of his charity were of a creed the professors of which his religion teaches him to look upon and hate as cursed infidels, his behaviour was the more remarkable. I have said some hard things about Mohammedanism and its followers, and I think a great many more; so it is with the greater pleasure, therefore, that I dwell upon this particular and striking exception to a general rule. Without fee, or even hope or expectation of reward—on this earth, at least—and even in spite of the known disapproval of his superior officer, he had done these things. Surely in that day that the Lord of Hosts shall make up His jewels, this Moslem gem, whose radiance had sparkled the more brilliantly for being found in one of the dark places of the earth, will receive a worthy setting!

Kaid Giluli himself at length appeared on horseback in the square, and the procession started, the crowd shouting and following to see the last of a spectacle they had never before beheld, and which, for the sake of the prestige of Europe, it is to be hoped they may never have the opportunity of witnessing again; and even the Jews in the little shops for a moment ceased haggling with their customers while the caravan rode by. The limits of the town were quickly reached, and from the top of the gateway looked down three ghastly severed heads that but a short time before had moved on the shoulders of men whose crime had been that they had failed to recognise that a Sultan's so-called government was a blessing to be fervently desired, and not resisted by every means that lay in their power. When about 100 yards outside the walls, one of the prisoners, a man originally a Sbooya, but who had left his tribe long ago for Ait Bubka, and had been seized there as a Sbooya, commenced an impassioned harangue to Kaid Giluli from the back of his camel. The caravan halted while he proclaimed his innocence, and, strange to say, the Kaid listened patiently but stolidly to what he had to say, but as soon as he had finished he ordered the march to be resumed. What mattered an innocent man or two—or hundreds of them, for that matter? The fetters were riveted on him, and it would take a great deal more than passionate pleas for justice or for mercy to loosen those iron bonds. About half a mile farther on, the Kaid and his contingent turned back to Tisnit, while the prisoners with their escort proceeded on their way.

We found our party to consist of about a score of horsemen, with the usual accompaniment of drivers for the mules and camels, of which there were a dozen of the former and fifteen of the latter for the transport of the captives and baggage. Of the natives, Muley Abdallah, El F'kir Embarak, and another old man, rode on mules, while the others were perched up in couples on the backs of camels. The forty or fifty rifles which had been surrendered by the Sbooyas and the Imstis were brought along with us. Kaid Hassan was very sociable, often riding alongside us, chatting and joking. Certainly it was less oppressive than being dragged at the tail of a half-civilized rabble that called itself an army, and being made the butt of brutal and callous Moorish soldiery, and our spirits began to rise somewhat at the immediate prospect of somewhat better treatment, and the hope that we cherished of seeing our own countrymen again in Mogador at no distant date. How long it was to be before our hopes were realized we little guessed.

The plain of Tisnit stretched for a long way northward, and for several miles we made good progress along fairly smooth roads. The day's march was without incident except that for the first time on the road the sun had set before we reached our camping-ground. The stars were out, and the full moon was just rising, when we arrived at Massa, a big, straggling town—or, rather, number of towns—built on the bank of a stream that in the rainy season must be quite a respectable river. It was the first *wad* worthy of the name that we had seen in Sus, and it looked quite dignified and placid as it flowed past the foot of the hill on which we camped, and reflected the red glow of the rising moon.

It was not long before the few tents were pitched. The Moorish prisoners had a large native camel-hair tent, while we were given our own white canvas soldiers' tent, instead of the ragged thing which had been allotted to us for the past fortnight. The two were pitched close together, the entrances facing one another. Kaid Hassan came to see us as soon as we were settled, and sent us tea and sugar, promising food as soon as it could be got ready. The latter was supplied, as is customary throughout Morocco whenever a caravan of any importance halts for the night, by the tribespeople. There are no inns, not even *posadas* such as are common in the country districts in Spain, and as all caravans are supposed to be travelling on the Sultan's business or under his protection, the tribespeople in the neighbourhood of the camp are required to provide *mona*, *i.e.*, food, including tea, sugar, candles, etc. If it should be a party of Christians travelling for their pleasure, and accompanied, as they generally are, by several Moorish soldiers, it is convenient, for many reasons, to camp under the protecting ægis of the Kaid's *kasbah*, and the *mona* in that case is provided by the Kaid himself. No remuneration is paid to the tribespeople, on the principle, I suppose, that they only enjoy the good things of life, and even existence itself, by the pleasure of the Sultan. A big bowl of meat and a liberal supply of corn bread fell to our share, which we eagerly devoured. It was the first 'square' meal that we had had for many a day, and we enjoyed it accordingly. After that came a dish of chicken *kuss*,

kuss, which we passed on to our more unfortunate fellow-captives. What was more to our liking was a box of cigars that Kaid Hassan brought us, and the whiff of a *flor de stinkadores*—made in Germany—coupled with the novel sensation of a full stomach, made us feel quite cheerful and optimistic.

We soon got a damper, however, as Kaid Hassan told us that he had received orders from Giluli to put the chains on us at night-time. Protestations and arguments were in vain. He himself, he said, would have liked to have let us enjoy as much freedom as possible, but if he failed to carry out Giluli's orders someone might report him, and he would get into trouble. Ultimately he agreed that only two of us each night should be chained together by the leg, well knowing that if we meditated any attempt at escape, we could not get far in chains, and we should, moreover, not be likely to leave two of our comrades behind. Another act of kindness on the part of Kaid Hassan was the present to Beyerle and myself of a new undervest each, and we only needed a rug to make us feel in clover. The Kaid had none to spare, but the tribespeople were again put under requisition, and a fine large rug, big enough to cover us all from top to toe, was borrowed, and thus the first night under our new custodian was a decided improvement all round.

Daylight, as usual, saw us astir next morning. There was not nearly so much delay in getting on the move as there had always been with Kaid Giluli's undisciplined mob, and far less noise, as Kaid Hassan himself monopolized all the shouting there was to be done. To our astonishment, we observed for the first time that we had a woman in the party. She was closely veiled, but, from what was visible of her, she seemed to be quite passably comely—for a lady of colour. From inquiries we made, we learned that Kaid Hassan had purchased her in Tisnit for 120 dollars, and was taking her with him on his journey to the Sultan. She and 'the Spaniard' were the first to start on the road, the cook being in charge of her and the Kaid's other impedimenta—tent, gear, etc.—so that all might be ready at the next camping-ground when the Kaid should arrive with the main body.

At the foot of the hill we forded the river without accident, though one of the soldiers got his mule somewhat out of its depth, and his own clothes wet in consequence. On the other side of the stream we had a fine level road for some considerable distance, and a good view of the conglomerations of houses that share, with the river and the district, the name of Massa. Built on the slope of the hill rising from the river, the place could easily be defended against an attacking force unprovided with artillery, and it was, in fact, this place that marked the southern limit of the Sultan's ravages in Sus in recent times, until Giluli achieved a certain notoriety by penetrating into the Sbooya country, with the aid of the M'tooga tribe, that live south of Agadir, whom he first subdued and then pressed into his service.

The camel-drivers and muleteers were in a sportive mood that morning, and amused themselves by relieving every man they met of his staff, without let or hindrance from the Kaid or any of his subordinates. One simple traveller, who perhaps harboured some antiquated notions concerning the rights of property, was foolish enough to resist this process of spoliation. I think he afterwards regretted it. Might is right in the land of 'the Slave of God,' and the soldiers of the 'Commander of the Faithful' are the licensed exponents of the gentle art of highway robbery. From walking-sticks they turned their attention to other 'unconsidered trifles,' in the way of portable property, and helped themselves to carrots growing in the fields by the wayside. The latter, I am not ashamed to say, we helped them to eat, as our breakfast had consisted of a dry barley-bannock each. Some women drawing water from a well fled at our approach, but were intercepted by one of the horsemen, and ordered to fill their water-bottles for our benefit. One of the men, after quenching his thirst, hung the bottle on his saddle-bow, but the woman pleading hard, the man was actually moved to give her half a peseta for it.

To look at this fair country, no one would imagine that the shadow of a curse was over the land. Field after field of growing corn we passed, and gardens of beans, olives, figs, and almonds innumerable, until we came to another stream, easily forded, and, crossing this and climbing the steep bank on the opposite side, entered what the inhabitants are pleased to call the 'port' of Massa. There were not many outward and visible signs of a port about the place—even the sea itself was not visible from where we were—but perhaps the origin of the designation is to be found in an ancient tradition, or was conferred in hopeful anticipation of the time when the Sultan, with the friendly assistance of the British Government, will no longer shut out Sus from the commerce of the world. As it was, the only signs of industry we met with were some women making grass mats on large frames. Soon we were out in the open again, and mile after mile we travelled over large sandy tracts which suggested our proximity to the sea.

What must strike every visitor to Morocco is its treelessness. Of course, the palmetto and the olive are ubiquitous, and the argan flourishes amazingly in certain districts; but they are not *timber*. Only the Forest of Mamora, in the neighbourhood of Rabat, is left to show what Morocco may once have been before the ruthless cutting down of trees, which has been going on the last thousand years, made naked its hills and valleys, and in no slight degree affected its climate. This stretch of country was the barest that we had yet traversed, and, though travelling was rather smoother and easier over these sandy dunes, I would rather have had the rougher roads of the more varied landscape. At length we came to a river, and the rolling dunes gave place once more to winding valley and rugged slope. Before us on a hill-top was the Dar el Kaid Hadj Hamed Ksim, which marked the limit of our day's journey. The river was the deepest we had so far come across, and in fording it one of the donkeys got out of its depth into a hole. All efforts to haul it out utterly failed, and the lopping off of a portion of the poor beast's tail with the dagger-knife of his enraged driver only gave unnecessary pain without achieving the desired result. What became of the unfortunate animal ultimately I don't know, but I was told that its pack was unloaded, and that it was left to drown or perish miserably as it stood with its feet embedded in the river's sandy bottom.

One other accident happened before we camped, one of the native prisoners falling from his camel. He was, however, not hurt, although his feet were chained together, and he was soon remounted.

The Kaid who had given his name to the *dar*, or house, on the hill, had once governed the district for some distance round; but after his death the tribe had come under the more powerful sway of Kaid Giluli, who now exercised undisputed jurisdiction under the Sultan from Mogador to Tisnit. With his son as principal Khalifa in his *kasbah* in the province of Haha, near Mogador, and other Khalifas or lieutenants scattered about the borders of Sus, Kaid Giluli had by fire and sword dragooned the Kabilas into submission, making his own headquarters at Tisnit, whence he could the more conveniently direct raiding operations against the stubborn and unbeaten tribes of Western Sus. This house at Ksima, which was a huge pile of *tabbia*, with more pretensions to architecture than most of such buildings possess, had not been taken over as one of his residences, but was occupied by the tribesmen of the village like a barracks.

Here, on the slope of the hill, between the *kasbah* and the market stalls, our tents were pitched for the night. As before, our tent and that of the native prisoners were pitched close together, so that one man sitting between could mount guard over both. Under Kaid Hassan we were allowed a little more freedom of movement, which made obedience to the calls of nature somewhat easier for us, though, of course, under the supervision of an escort.

From this spot we had a fine view of Agadir on the summit of a distant hill overlooking the sea, like some great white bird resting on the final peak before taking wing again across the blue ocean which lay below it. From Agadir the great range of the mighty Atlas Mountains rises and stretches away as far as the eye can reach, the peaks gradually becoming more and more majestic and imposing, until at length their summits are crowned with the eternal snows. And as I looked I remembered the words of Al-al, and knew that our road lay, not through the difficult and dangerous passes of those rugged mountains to Marrakesh, but by the sea-coast to Mogador.

CHAPTER XXIII.

ACROSS THE BORDER.

The 'irritability of Africa'—Collapse of the mules—We arrive at Agadir—Its history and present appearance—Our last look at Sus—Reflections thereon—The Governor of Agadir—An impromptu entertainment — Taga-zoost — Disappearance of my diary — I recover it by stratagem — Our supposed swimming powers—A companionable Kaid—The music of the Moors—Scandalous robbery—The Sultan's letters wetted—Misti has a narrow escape—Arrival at Eda Gilul—Last has an attack of fever—No more chains.

OFF again at sunrise! I think it is Henry Seton Merriman that speaks in one of his books of 'the irritability of Africa.' I suppose something of the sort was upon us that morning, for everyone seemed to be as touchy as tinder. One of the Moorish officers had objected to carry out some order of Kaid Hassan's, and the latter very quickly convinced him as to who was in command of the escort. It was a piece of ill-luck when, immediately after this, poor old El F'kir Embarak fell foul of the Kaid, for Hassan silenced the old man's complaints by giving him a savage prod in the chest with a long stick that he carried, which sent the Susi saint staggering backwards. Sabbah, too, who had not so far been a pattern of either good spirits, good temper, or good behaviour, had rather more to say to Beyerle concerning the loading of his mule than the ex-cavalry officer cared about, and when from grumbling he lapsed into blasphemy and personal abuse, his flow of language was promptly arrested by a back-hander across his mouth. Altogether it was a relief when we got under way, and the wrangling of the camp gave place to the light-hearted carolling of the Moorish soldiers with their cracked and unmusical voices. Truly the song of the modern Moor is a fearsome thing, being considerably inferior in point of harmony and rhythm even to that of the Spanish gipsy.

Our long forced marches were already beginning to tell upon the mules, mine particularly showing signs of giving out; and when the poor brute finally dropped on his knees and shot me over his head, I thought it would be a pleasant change to stretch my legs and walk. Kaid Hassan, however, thought it looked too 'free and easy,' so, meeting a man driving three unloaded camels, he stopped him in the name of the Sultan, and, calmly appropriating one of these travelling instruments of torture, ordered me to mount it. The man, of course, argued and protested against this arbitrary levy of transport, with many appeals and references to Allah, but he was eventually appeased on the Kaid promising to return him his beast as soon as we should meet on the road a man with a mule, as that was the animal he really wanted, though a camel would serve his purpose meanwhile. Fearing lest worse evil should befall him if he offered further opposition, the unfortunate camel-driver turned his three animals back, and retraced his steps with our caravan, fervently praying, no doubt, that the man with the mules would not be long in putting in an appearance.

After marching about three hours we came upon a fine sandy beach, and the broad blue sea which broke in creamy foam upon the shore cheered us like the meeting with an old friend. It was the Bay of Agadir. Not a sail was in sight; only two or three native rowing-boats were idly plying about for fish a mile or so from shore. The beach ends abruptly in a high hill, where the first of the Atlas summits—here of modest proportions—rises from the sea. This hill, on which the town of Agadir is built, rises almost perpendicularly from the shore, and the houses seem to be clinging to the steep cliff like limpets to a rock. The extreme summit is crowned by what appears to be a fort of Portuguese construction, from the battlements of which old-fashioned cannon are pointed in all directions.

Little more than a century ago the town of Agadir was a prosperous and populous seaport town, and the river Sus which flows into the sea below then bore upon its bosom the trading vessels of adventurous Bristol merchants to Tarudant, the famous capital of Sus, twenty or thirty miles up the stream. But now the mouth of the Wad Sus is nearly silted up with sand, and Agadir, with only a few hundred population, looks as if it had gone to sleep a couple of hundred years ago, and not yet wakened up. A revolution in 1770 largely contributed to its downfall, but the final blow was given when the late Sultan closed it as a seaport, and ordered all the Europeans resident there to transfer themselves and their trade to Mogador. Without a doubt it is the best landing-place, and the freest from surf, of any spot in the Sultan's dominions, and, with a little expenditure, Agadir could be transformed into a harbour far safer than Tangier or

Mogador. The reasons for closing it, therefore, would seem to be a little obscure. But the workings of the Moslem mind are subtle. Agadir is—or, rather, was—the nearest port to Sus, standing as it does just within the borders of Morocco proper, and by keeping it open the Susi, whom the Sultan has not yet tamed into the habit of paying taxes to the Governors whom he may set over them, could get their goods from Europe on payment of the ordinary Customs duties. But with Agadir closed, those goods must be landed at one of the more northern ports, and crossing the line of the Atlas range into and out of Sus, not only the goods can be taxed, but the very beasts that carry them, and communication between the Susi and the Christian, who will one day deliver him from the thraldom of the Moor, is rendered more difficult.

Half-way up the town we were ordered to dismount, as we were approaching the gateway of a saint-house, and it was considered profanation for a Christian or Jew to pass through except on foot. At this place, also, a poll-tax of a penny a head is levied on every traveller, which, however, also purchases the privilege of a night's shelter if so desired. As this is the main highway from Mogador to Western Sus and the South, a very fair income is doubtless derived from this toll-gate; but our party, being 'on his Majesty's service,' passed through untaxed. For the first time since we had landed at Arksis we saw a window of glass—evidence of former European occupation—and turning round before we passed through the gateway, we took our last look upon Sus, the unknown, the beautiful, the 'natural Garden of Eden,' 'the new El Dorado,' out of which the fanatical ignorance of the Moor, aided by the barriers of Nature, has striven for centuries to keep the hated Christian, that he might batten unhindered on the latent riches of its generous soil, wrung from an oppressed and downtrodden people—a land for which God has done so much, and man so little. What a shame it seemed! A shame crying aloud to unanswering Heaven and civilization for remedy! A land flowing with milk and honey, yet shut in from the outside world because the jealousy of the Powers of Europe keeps alive a realm that is tottering to ruin from its own inherent rottenness and decay. America has stepped in in the name of civilization to save the wretched Cubans from the cruel misrule of the Spaniard; England, in the same sacred cause, has rescued the Sudan and its people from the blighting curse of Mahdism. Who will cry 'halt' to the rapacious tyranny of the Moor, and deliver his land and peoples from a fanatical, ignorant, and barbarous despotism, which by fire and sword lays waste fair provinces, and eats up whole tribes, amid scenes of horror and bloodshed that might be torn from the darkest pages in the history of the Sudan or Armenia?

A little way past the town we saw a group of soldiers mounted and on foot, apparently going in the opposite direction. They were higher up the hillside than we were, but halted on seeing us, and made towards us. They proved to be the Governor of Agadir and his escort, who had been out for an early morning ride. Formal salutations were exchanged, and the Governor and his party turned back to accompany us a little on our way. In a minute or two, Kaid Hassan called me to his side to imitate, for the delectation of the Governor, the whistling of a bullet, and show him my false teeth, which were a never-failing source of wonder to these people. The Governor seemed sceptical as to my being able to eat with them, and on my offering to give him ocular demonstration, he produced a bag full of dates, biscuits, and almonds, which he divided amongst us. The end of it was that both we and the Governor were satisfied. Had he known we were coming, he said he would have had breakfast prepared for us. What appreciative audiences a ventriloquist would have in Morocco!

After accompanying us for about a couple of miles as a sort of guard of honour, the Governor and his escort turned and rode back to Agadir while we continued our journey. As that day's stage was about twenty-five miles, and camels over such roads (!) as are generally met with in Morocco do not travel more than about three miles an hour, we had to hurry along. All day long we followed the coast-line pretty closely, and about four in the afternoon we reached Taga-zoost, the spot chosen for our camping-ground. It was a pretty little hollow by the sea, completely shut in by hills which protected it from every wind except the west, and, strange to say, there was a well of excellent fresh-water scarce 100 yards from the sea-line. Immediately on arrival I jumped down from my mule—'annexed' on the way—and made for this well to get a drink. In my hurry I left my mackintosh in the *shwarri*, or pannier. As my diary was in one of the pockets, I hurried back to get it, as soon as I remembered my omission. The coat was there, but *the book was gone!* The driver told me that one of the soldiers had taken it, and I was in despair. I reported the matter to Kaid Hassan, and begged him to get it for me. This he promised to do, especially when I told him it contained the names of all the people who had treated us well, and his was writ large therein; but the promises of the Moor are like the proverbial pie-crust, and I began to fear that the note-book I had so jealously guarded so far was gone for ever. However, the Kaid had a small English clock that wanted repairing, and sent for me. Seeing my opportunity, I boldly undertook to mend it for him, as requested, if he would return me my book. No book, no clock; but at the same time I was very uneasy lest the clock should be damaged beyond my powers of remedy, with only an old knife for a tool. The book was produced, and I set to work on the clock. *It only wanted winding!*

The Kaid had been in rather a good humour all that day, and on the road had said he would let us have a swim in the sea when we should get into camp, but he afterwards repented, giving as excuse for his refusal that he feared we might swim away to Mogador! The power over and in the sea that the Moors credit the Christians with possessing is really astonishing.

There was no meat supper from the tribes for us that night, as the houses were too far away, but the Kaid's cook prepared some *kuss-kuss*, which Al-al used to tell us would fill up if it didn't fatten. As usual, the night was very cold, and we were blanketless as well as hungry. However, we succeeded in borrowing a camel-hair rug from Kaid Shiekh, an officer of the Sultan's army who had made himself very friendly with us, and came every evening to our tent to chat and joke. The poor fellow had not been home for four years, being employed fighting in some part or other of the Sultan's dominions, and used to tell us that he treated us well because we were in an unfortunate position, and he never knew when he might find himself in a similar predicament.

It was the turn of Beyerle and Last to have the chains on that night—the long and the short of it, as de Reya whispered under his breath—and in spite of the discomfort of being fastened to each other by a short ankle-chain, they were both soon sound asleep. The rest of us could not get to sleep for a long while, and so amused ourselves with a native fiddle till after midnight. The *gimbri*, or Moorish fiddle, is made of a piece of wood hollowed out and covered with goatskin, to which a long neck is fixed. Tuning-pegs, two gut-strings, and a roughly-made bridge complete the instrument, which is played, after the manner of a mandoline, by twanging the strings with a small piece of palm fibre. The natives have only the crudest idea of music, but are quite happy strumming on this primitive instrument, or listening to monotonous and unmelodious songs droned out to its accompaniment.

The *gimbri* was our lullaby, and the music of the breakers on the beach was our waking-song, and our march was resumed soon after sunrise, still following the coast-line. Here and there the track left the beach and wound along the hillsides, but we kept the sea always in sight. At one place the route lay along the edge of a sandy hill overhanging the sea. One false step of the mule or the camel, and the rider would have been precipitated 100 feet into the water below. Several times during the day we met caravans going south, and scarcely one was allowed to pass scot-free, Kaid Hassan appropriating a camel or a mule in the name of the Sultan as the spirit moved him. Sometimes this daylight robbery was indulged in out of pure love of the thing, and when more animals were not really wanted by our party. Once we met two men driving a couple of camels, one animal loaded and the other light. Seeing our party approaching, they endeavoured to get out of the way, but were unsuccessful. Both animals were seized, but the owner pleaded hard with Kaid Hassan to be allowed to go on his way unmolested, prayers and blessings falling from his lips in a passionate jumble of language. Eventually he was allowed to buy back one of his own beasts and go free, but the other, with its driver, was retained. The poor owner, however, had scarcely handed over the money demanded of him, when some of the soldiers, seeing that he had still some coins left, snatched his purse from his hand, and sent him penniless away, the Kaid not only not interfering, but laughingly encouraging his subordinates in their dirty work. With such an example as this set by those in authority, the predatory habits of the lower classes in Morocco are scarcely to be wondered at.

Shortly after this incident we met a couple of men on foot who looked like couriers. The Kaid stopped them, and, in reply to his questions, they told him that they were on their way to Kaid Giluli with a letter from the Sultan. We wondered if it concerned us, but there was no means of satisfying our anxiety, and we proceeded on our march, the couriers hurrying on towards Tisnit.

The mules that we had brought from Tisnit were by this time in a sorry condition, and continually breaking down under the strain of the journey. Sabbah was riding a mule that had been stolen *en route*, while his former mount had been given to de Reya, who was a lighter weight. Others had been lightened of their loads, which had been transferred to the camels that had been appropriated on the road, but none the less we had great difficulty at times to get the poor beasts along. Last's animal had only just managed to stagger into camp the day before, under the goad of continued prodding and whacking, and in the early afternoon my own mule showed such signs of fatigue that I had to dismount and walk.

On passing a fresh-water lake close to the shore, a halt was called to water the animals. We also took advantage of the opportunity to wash our feet, hands, and faces, which had not known water for several days. One of the mules, in drinking, stumbled, and fell into the water with its load. Among the things it carried was a bag containing letters for the Sultan and Giluli's son. These all got wet, and had to be laid out in the sun to dry.

An hour before sunset we reached camp, but half an hour before that Last had been compelled to dismount. His poor mule had struggled on until it could go no further, and had just lain down by the roadside to die. Twenty-four hours later it would be a clean-picked skeleton.

We had not expected *mona* at this camp, as scarcely any houses were visible, but we were agreeably surprised at receiving a very good dish of both meat and *kuss-kuss* with chickens. The latter we gave to the native prisoners.

From our camp next morning we struck inland, turning our backs on the sea. The road for some distance was easy travelling, and we made good progress, the monotony being varied only by the robbing of occasional caravans. Old Misti had a narrow escape of breaking his neck during the afternoon, as he fell backwards off his camel. I expected to find that he was at any rate seriously injured, but the old man was reserved for a less merciful fate. With the agility of a cat, he turned a somersault as he fell, and, chained though he was, alighted on his feet, none the worse except for a little shaking. Better for him had he died then, for he would thus have been spared an agonizing march of several hundred miles more, and a brutal thrashing administered to him at the Sultan's camp, under the torture of which the old and enfeebled fellow succumbed.

We arrived at Eda Gilul, Kaid Giluli's *kasbah*, about 4.30. His son, the Khalifa, no doubt expected us, but we dismounted in the adjacent market-place, and waited whilst Kaid Hassan had an interview with him in the *inzella*, or outbuildings for the accommodation of travellers and their animals. Presently Kaid Hassan returned, and conducted us into a square courtyard surrounded by rooms built of *tabbia*. At the door of one of these sat the Khalifa, awaiting our arrival, and we had just time to observe that he was a young man of barely thirty years of age, extremely stout, and with a pallid, unhealthy complexion, and small pigs' eyes that were almost hidden by welts of fat. His face was destitute of hair, with the exception of about half a dozen black bristles that had forced their way through his chin, and which he cherished as an incipient beard. His eyes had a shifty expression, and altogether he was by no means a prepossessing-looking individual.

By his orders we were installed in one of the rooms, adjoining the one occupied by Kaid Hassan, while the native prisoners were herded together in one on the other side of the quadrangle. It was not long before a tray was sent in to us with teapot, glasses, stove and all accessories necessary for the decoction of the Moors' favourite beverage, and early in the evening we were regaled with a great dish of meat stewed in argan oil, and garnished with raisins. Good grass mats, fairly new, covered the cement floor, but for covering for the night we had to have recourse to our own mackintoshes. And a very uncomfortable night we spent, for to the fleas and lice, with which we had by this time become only too painfully familiar, this room added the terror of bugs, the walls simply swarming with them.

On the top of his other miseries Last was seized with an attack of low fever, the symptoms of which were hot hands and headache, cold feet, aching limbs, drowsiness and a disinclination for food. Kaid Hassan went through the farce of asking us whether we would prefer to resume the march on the following morning, or rest for a day. Under the circumstances, we said we should prefer to rest, but we had no doubt that it was out of consideration for the mules, and not us, that we stayed a day at Eda Gilul. Moreover, there were the presents for the Sultan to be got ready, and letters to be written.

The next day the Khalifa came to pay us a visit, as did also a Jew who knew Sabbah's father in Mogador. To the latter our interpreter gave a pencil note to take to Mogador, but whether the missive was ever delivered I do not know. Here for the first time we were entirely free from chains. Whence the orders came I know not, but on arrival at Giluli's *kasbah* we said good-bye for ever to those hated fetters.

CHAPTER XXIV.

AN UNWELCOME INVITATION.

To the Sultan or Mogador?—An incident without a parallel—
The Khalifa congratulates us—Halt!—Sabbah is exultant—
Letters from the Sultan—We are invited to stay at Giluli's
Kasbah—Improved lodgings—A spider and his flies—A
musical evening.

ALL along the road we had been told by everybody that we were being taken to the Sultan, who was understood to be encamped with his army near Casablanca, busily occupied in 'eating up' the Shawia tribe. Knowing, as I did, that the treaties between Great Britain and Morocco provide that no British subject is to be detained, tried, or punished by the Moorish authorities for any alleged offence whatever, but that he shall be handed over to the nearest British Consul without delay, I could not help thinking that this story of 'going to the Sultan' was a little pleasant deception on the part of our captors, and that we were in reality on our way to Mogador. Of course, if this was our intended destination, Giluli could easily have put us on board the *Hassani* when we were captured at Arksis, and we should have been in Mogador in a couple of days; but at the same time the temptation to drag us round the country at the tail of his camp, and glorify himself by exhibiting to the natives a party of Christians ignominiously chained together, must have been strong to an ignorant and fanatical semi-savage like Kaid Said el Giluli. So far as I am aware, the history of Europeans in Morocco can show no parallel to such a scandalous outrage, and the fact that a Moorish Governor, ambitious and powerful though he may be in his own country, should be found daring enough to do so at the end of the nineteenth century is proof sufficient of how sadly British prestige and influence have declined of late years in Morocco.

However, whatever our destination might be, nine o'clock on Sunday morning, February 13, found us once more *en route*. The brief rest had done us all good; Last's fever had left him; and our spirits were buoyant at the prospect of that day's sunset seeing us within a day's journey of a civilized centre. That night, we were informed, we were to camp at the house of Sidi Ahmed, one of the officers in our escort, and the following night near the Palm Tree Hotel outside Mogador. Many were the speculations we indulged in on receipt of this piece of news, and finally came to the conclusion that the British Consul of Mogador would be at the Palm Tree Hotel to formally take us over; and possibly we might see the four Susi that had been left aboard the *Tourmaline* when Sabbah had come ashore. The Major would be sure to have gone to Mogador as soon as he had sent off his cable messages from the Canaries reporting our capture, and perhaps was still there waiting to take us aboard.

The Khalifa had come out with a small escort, to see us a short distance on our way, and chatted quite affably and confidentially with our interpreter. Among other things, he told him it was lucky for us that we had been captured by his father, Kaid Said, and not himself, as he would have killed us all on the spot, and not troubled to send us on to the Sultan. It was probably only braggadocio on the young Khalifa's part, but Sabbah thought the moment opportune to flatter him on his warlike prowess, and cadge a couple of pesetas from him, which he did successfully.

We had had nothing to eat or drink before starting, and after an hour or two on the march began to feel somewhat thirsty. We passed one or two pools, but the water was stagnant and unfit for drinking. Presently we came upon a man working in his field, and one of the soldiers shouted out to him to bring a jar of water from his well, with which request he promptly complied. While we were thus engaged, the Khalifa and Kaid Hassan being a little way behind us, a horseman galloped up in hot haste, and, after salaaming, entered into conversation with the two officials. We had by this time resumed our march, but had not gone many paces, when Kaid Hassan called out to us to stop. The native prisoners and their guards were by this time a long way ahead, but we turned back, wondering what was in the wind. On nearing the spot where Kaid Hassan was still talking to the Khalifa and the mounted messenger, he told us that instructions had just been received to send us to Mogador; and, without a word of farewell, he put spurs to his horse, and rode off with black looks to catch up the main body of the caravan.

On hearing the news, Sabbah gave vent to a wild yell of exultation, and would probably have executed a *pas seul* of joy if he had not been restrained, and told to try and not make himself ridiculous. The news was no less welcome to us all, but it was neither dignified nor desirable to make a display of our real feelings. The Khalifa, Sidi Embarak, asked us if we would rather go to Mogador straight away, or stay at his house and rest for a day. We replied that we would prefer to go on without delay, but he said he must first send back to his house for some letters which had come for him. The man who had ridden up in such haste had brought word that a courier had arrived with important news, after we had left the *kasbah* that morning, and he was now despatched to go back and fetch the letters, while we waited under the shade of a wide-spreading argan-tree, with what patience we could command.

He went off at a great pace, and it seemed little more than an hour before he was back and handed two letters to the Khalifa. One was from his father, Kaid Said, at Tisnit, and accompanied the other, which had been sent by the Sultan from the camp in Shawia. The latter instructed Giluli to deliver us to the Governor of Agadir pending further orders, and the couriers we had met near Agadir were the bearers of that message. On receiving this order, Giluli knew that we should have gone some distance past Agadir before the message could reach Kaid Hassan, so he despatched a fast courier with a letter to his son at Eda Gilul, telling him to detain us and lodge us at his own *kasbah* until the Sultan should signify his decision as to what he intended to do with us. Nothing of this was told us at the time, the Khalifa simply saying that we were free, and were welcome to his house, where he said we must stay a day or two before going on to Mogador. We could scarcely believe that we were free, but nevertheless rode back to the *kasbah* in a happier state of mind than we had known for many days. The proceeding seemed a little curious to us, but we concluded that the Khalifa was undesirous that we should make our appearance in Mogador in the wretched, ragged and woe-begone condition that we then found ourselves in, and was anxious that we should first get a change of clothing, a wash, and a little grooming-up generally. As far as external appearance went, we were not very creditable testimonials to the generous and hospitable care that Kaid Giluli was reported by certain ill-informed persons to have bestowed upon us.

On reaching the *kasbah* we were offered the choice of the room Kaid Hassan had occupied, or the one which had already been our lodging. As both were full of bugs and fleas, we asked if they hadn't got one that was not already inhabited. We were told to wait whilst the Khalifa was consulted, and in about half an hour we were conducted from the outbuildings to the *kasbah* itself, and there shown into a room that was at least better than anything we had yet seen. In the first place, one could enter it without being obliged to stoop for fear of cracking one's skull against the lintel, and the apartment boasted some slight attempt at decoration. A double niche was built into one of the *tabbia* walls, while the other three sides were so constructed as to form a projecting shelf about 4 feet from the ground. A great rudely-shaped roof-tree ran from one side to the other, supported by a hollow stone pillar in the centre of the room; and the ceiling was formed in the usual manner, smaller logs being laid athwart, and covered by a thick layer of mud to the height of 2 or 3 feet. On the cement floor were spread not only the familiar grass mats, but a large clean drugget carpet, which stretched from end to end, covering nearly half the room. Here some tea and food was brought to us, and we were in several ways made to feel that, if we were not free to move about as and where we liked, our circumstances were, at any rate, much improved.

In the afternoon we were permitted to go out for a walk in the neighbourhood of the *kasbah*—a privilege of which we readily availed ourselves. We were, of course, escorted by some of the Khalifa's retainers, but there was no more of that everlasting '*zìt, zìt*,' which had so often irritated us on the march.

After sunset, the Khalifa himself paid us a visit, and again impressed upon us that we were 'welcome' to his house. That is probably what the spider of the allegory said to the fly, and I was by no means certain that there was not some sinister meaning in the man's professions of hospitality. He brought with him a whistler to entertain us. He was a performer on a weird sort of reed instrument, which gave forth the most discordant and soul-harrowing sounds, but which seemed to be much admired by the Moors themselves. The Khalifa asked if any of us could play it, and Sabbah expressing confidence in being able to do so, the musician (!) was ordered to hand over his instrument to our interpreter. The thought of his treasured pipe being defiled by the lips of a Christian or a Jew was utterly revolting to his fanatical ideas, and while not daring openly to disobey the Khalifa's orders, he made a very wry face at the prospect. The Khalifa no doubt divined what was passing through the man's mind, but took great pleasure in exercising little petty tyrannies, and threatened him with punishment if he did not at once hand it over. The man hesitated no longer. Incidentally, I may remark that I never wish to hear a Moorish reed-pipe again. The Khalifa, being in a sportive humour, next asked Sabbah to take off a seaman's jersey that he was wearing, that he might examine it more closely. Sabbah did so, and the Khalifa then ordered his tame flautist to put it on. The poor fellow's horror-struck expression was really comical to witness, but the Khalifa was obdurate, and thoroughly enjoyed the spectacle of the man's mortification and disgust.

That concluded the entertainment, and we were then left to our own devices. A large blanket was brought us, sufficiently large to cover us all five, and with four of the *kasbah* hangers-on to act as guard, we made pillows of our coats, and stretched ourselves out to sleep.

CHAPTER XXV.

LIFE IN THE KASBAH.

Letter received from Consul Johnston—A parcel of good things—Moorish superstition—We manufacture *djinns*—The end of Ramadan—A gorging orgie—Ba-Hamed's policy—Description of the *kasbah*—Its internal economy—The prison and its occupants—Arab the slave-boy—Moorish etiquette in eating—Market-day at Eda Gilul—A courier arrives from the Sultan—A deluge of rain—A change of quarters.

THE Khalifa had said we should stay 'a day or two' at the *kasbah*, but day after day went by without any signs of our moving, and we began to be impatient. The Khalifa came to see us no more, and our guards would not, or could not, tell us anything. Other people about the place that we asked, such as the *taleb*, or scribe, said 'after the holidays,' and that was all the satisfaction we could get. The holidays were the three days following the fast of Ramadan, but they were a week hence. On the afternoon of Sunday, the 20th, we were cheered by the receipt of a letter from Mr. Johnston, the British Consul at Mogador, accompanied by a parcel of clothing, and other articles of which we stood much in need, such as soap and towels, and some bottles of comfort for the inner man. The messenger, who had come on mule-back from Mogador, had arrived on the previous Thursday, but it had taken the Khalifa three days to make up his mind whether he would let us have either the Consul's letter or his parcel. Finally he decided to do so, but sent his major-domo to tell us he was afraid he ought not to let us have anything from outside, and with instructions to see that the Consul's letter was given up to him after we had read it. We were, however, allowed to retain the newspapers which Mr. Johnston had thoughtfully included in his bag of good things, and never, I think, had any of us before read our morning journals so diligently as we did those treasured sheets at Eda Gilul. In them we read the first report of our capture, and were relieved to know that steps were being taken to secure our release. Then we devoured the other items of news, and finally fell back upon reading the advertisements, beginning with the 'Agony Column,' and ending with 'Situations Vacant.'

A curious thing happened in connection with these clothes. They were not delivered to us till late in the afternoon, and by the time we had scanned all the papers for news more directly concerning ourselves, the sun was on the point of setting. It being too dark to read any more, we were desirous of changing our clothes then and there, and having a thorough good wash. Clean clothes, soap and towels, were things with which we were anxious to renew acquaintance as soon as possible. We accordingly began preparations with a view to having an *al-fresco* bath; but the Moors, divining our object, protested with frantic vehemence. If we undressed and washed our bodies after sunset, they said, all the *djinns* in the neighbourhood would be attracted. The risk of becoming infested by evil spirits seemed to us worth running, considering how infested we already were by evil things of a more tangible character; and right glad we were to have, at any rate, a preliminary scouring, and feel clean and wholesome, if only for a day or so. The Moors, brave as they are in the presence of physical danger, are utter cowards where the invisible or occult is concerned, and our guards were horribly scared.

They prophesied all sorts of terrible things as a consequence of our imprudence, and when we laughed at their fears, they said, 'It's all very well for you Christians: you are in league with *djinns*, and suchlike, but we don't like them.' By the time they were ready to blow out the candle and go to sleep, they had worked themselves into a pretty tolerable state of nervous apprehension. In my pocket I found a few phosphorus matches, and an old schoolboy trick came back to my mind. When all was in darkness, I wetted the inside of one of my hands, and, drawing a weird face thereon with the match-head, soon had a *djinn* in good working order. The fraud was only detected after some time, when one of them suddenly and unexpectedly struck a match.

On Monday, the 21st, everyone was on the watch about sunset in the hope of observing the new moon, the appearance of which would mark the close of the great Mohammedan fast. The Khalifa went up on to the roof of one of the houses in the *kasbah* to get a better view; and the sun had scarcely descended behind the hills, when a succession of shots from his rifle betokened that the silver sickle of the moon was visible in the heavens, and the faithful need mortify the flesh no more for another year. We listened for the boom of the distant guns of Mogador to proclaim that the long and tedious fast was at an end, but they were not fired till the following morning, and even then many of the more devout followers of the Prophet would not touch food until they had made sure that the moon *had* really been seen. The sound of those guns must bring relief, not only to the Mohammedans themselves, but also to those Europeans who have Moorish servants; for the poorer Moors, at any rate, become not only ill-tempered, but positively stupid, towards the end of the fast in consequence of their long days of abstinence.

The day after the fast was one of positive gorging at the *kasbah*. From sunrise to sunset dishes of food followed one another at intervals of only a couple of hours or so. About seven o'clock in the morning great bowls of thin porridge—that we irreverently called 'skilly'—emerged from the kitchen; then came dishes of bread and oil, and cakes like Berlin pancakes with honey; *kuss-kuss*, chicken, goat, mutton, stewed in water and stewed in oil, succeeded one another in a scarcely interrupted procession all day long. There was no stint, even for the Christian; while the Moors simply stuffed themselves with food till one marvelled how they could possibly stow it away. And so the 'holidays' came and went, and still we stayed. Had we only been waiting for presentable clothes, as we had at first imagined, we could have started when Consul Johnston's consignment arrived, for now we were arrayed in all the glory of white cotton trousers and clean shirts. But the excuse now was that we were waiting for a letter from Tisnit, and gradually the whole story came out that was contained in the letters received by the Khalifa when we were stopped on the march; and we knew that the Sultan did not intend to give us up until he was compelled. Indeed, as we afterwards learned, Ba-Hamed, the Sultan's Grand Vizier, counselled by intriguers against Great Britain at the Moorish Court, of whom Dr. Linares, the French political agent, was foremost—meant to keep us as hostages, to use us, as the *Kölnische Zeitung* expressed it, 'as a means of putting pressure upon England when occasion should offer.' He also had the effrontery, when the Government's first application for our extradition was made, to demand an indemnity from Great Britain, to compensate for the expenses to which the Moorish Government had been put in connection with Giluli's expedition. Considering that this raid into Sus was determined upon before the *Tourmaline* was ever heard of in connection with Morocco, and was for the express purpose of punishing the Sbooya tribe for past sins, it is not surprising that Ba-Hamed's request was not complied with. Moreover, it would be interesting to know what expenses the Moorish Government had incurred in connection therewith, seeing that the necessary provisions for both men and animals were stolen from the tribes through whose lands they passed, and that the 'soldiers' were provided by Kaid Giluli, and not by the Government, their pay being the plunder they could lay their hands upon; and that Giluli recouped himself for any disbursements that he may have found necessary to make by exacting a monetary indemnity from all those tribes that he considered 'refractory,' and that he was able to subdue.

But of these negotiations we knew nothing at the time, and were simply encouraged and buoyed up by that blind, implicit faith in the protecting ægis of the Government, which most Britons cherish who have not been unfortunate enough to have to put it to the test. And so the days passed into weeks, and weeks into months. It would be tedious if I were to recount in detail all the incidents of our weary confinement in that country Moorish *kasbah*, but some idea of the place and the life that is led there with such appalling sameness and monotony week in, week out, the year through, may not be without interest.

The *kasbah* itself was a huge, rambling building, or conglomeration of buildings, erected on the slope of a hill in the form of a rough square. It comprised the residential quarters of the Kaid himself, though he was seldom there, and the Khalifa; a harem, stable-yard, storehouse, a prison, and any number of rooms for the accommodation of the household officials, slaves, and retinue generally. The material used was, of course, *tabbia*, but the walls were of imposing thickness. The approach was through a large gateway—closed and guarded at night-time—through which three mounted men could easily pass abreast. This led into a courtyard, surrounded on all sides by small buildings, except in one corner where there was a well. The Kaid's quarters and the harem were beyond this, so that altogether it was a place easily defensible in case of a siege —unless, of course, artillery were employed. It was in the room next to the well that we were installed, and the room contiguous with ours was the lodging of the *taleb*, or scribe, who filled up his spare time by tailoring, a small hand sewing-machine, made in Germany, being one of his most treasured possessions. These two rooms were approached through a miniature courtyard of their own, in which there was perhaps just sufficient room to swing a cat; and to this room and yard we were confined all the time, except during half an hour in the morning and afternoon, when we were escorted

KAID GILULI'S KASBAH.

out for a walk. Seen from the outside, the *kasbah* was strongly suggestive of what one imagines the castles of the Saxons to have been like, and the view from the top of the hill embraced a stretch of landscape that would have sent an artist into raptures. On all sides were rolling hills and verdant valleys, here a field of growing corn, yonder a garden of fig-trees, almonds, oranges and roses, and beyond, towards the north, a range of majestic hills raised their purple peaks, and lent an air of solemn grandeur to the scene. Though nearly half a day's journey away, they seemed to be quite close, so clear is the atmosphere, and when the wind blew in from the west, the low rumble of the sea, five miles away, could be distinctly heard.

The internal arrangements of the *kasbah* also, were not altogether unlike those of a European castle in feudal times. The Kaid—or in his absence the Khalifa—was the arbiter of all disputes between individual tribesmen. Assisted sometimes by a Kadi, or professional judge, he performed the dual function of police and county court. Court of Appeal there was none. The verdict of the Kaid was final. Underneath the room we occupied was the prison—a vile, poisonous, underground den of death, lighted only by a grated hole near the roof, which admitted what air found its way into the place. The wretched inmates of this dreary place, besides being fettered with an iron bar riveted round their ankles, were all chained together on one long chain, and led out for a few minutes once a day, just before sunset. Gaunt, miserable objects of pity they were, in their filthy clothes, hobbling along, scarce able to walk, for all the world as if they had just risen, foul and feeble, from an uncoffined grave. Their living tomb was lighted always by a primitive oil-lamp of the gravy-dish pattern, with the roughly-twisted cotton wick limply hanging from the spout. By the dim rays of this lamp the poor wretches worked from sunrise to sunset making mats, baskets, ropes and such-like of palm-fibre, grass, etc., the dull, sepulchral sound of the beating of the palm-leaves to separate the fibres being generally the first noise in the early morning to wake us to the consciousness that another weary day was dawning.

We ourselves were unrestricted as to when we should rise in the morning or turn in at night. At about seven in the morning a bowl of 'skilly' was brought, and a couple of wooden soup-ladles, which had to do duty for us five. A little negro slave-boy named Arab, who had been deputed by the Khalifa to attend to our few material wants, such as fetching water, charcoal for the stove, etc., seldom made his appearance except when food was about, and then he was most punctual in his attendance, in anticipation of some being left over for him. He could never complain that he went short of 'skilly.' Any time between one and three the next meal might be expected, consisting generally of goat flesh or mutton, stewed in oil or water, and usually cooked to perfection. The oil used was the common argan oil, which is decidedly a taste that a European is not endowed with by Nature, though he may acquire it. For my part I learned to like it very much, long before I had ceased to be a guest in Kaid Giluli's country-house; and many a time I thought I had never in Europe tasted such succulent and savoury stews as some of those we ate from one common dish in that *kasbah*, using our fingers for knife and fork, and a dirty towel for serviette. Several pancakes of white or black bread were brought with this dish, and a similar meal was brought about seven or eight o'clock. Though it was rather a far cry from the evening of one day to, say, two o'clock the following afternoon, I cannot say that we ever suffered from hunger while we were at the *kasbah*, but we did early begin to feel the want of vegetables, the meat, if garnished at all, being only sprinkled with a few olives, raisins, beans or chopped pumpkin.

Among the Moors there is an etiquette to be observed in eating as in drinking, and a Christian visiting Morocco does well to post himself up on these little ceremonials. The dishes, whether they be meat, *kuss-kuss* or anything else, are brought into the room one at a time on a wooden tray with pedestal feet, and a rim several inches in height. Resting against this rim are the loaves of bread for the feast. The dish is provided with an earthenware lid, and over all is a large conical fibre 'cosy,' giving the whole thing somewhat the appearance of a beehive. The men squat all round in a circle, and the tray is set down in the midst of them. The covers being removed, each man, with a preliminary 'Bismillah!' proceeds to help himself. If you are a guest your host will probably pick out a tit-bit, and, skilfully removing the bone with his fingers, offer you the meat. You may not like this method of being fed, but it is best to pretend you do. Only the right hand—which is first washed—is used, and, eating being regarded as a serious business, it is conducted in silence. The time for conversation is when the tea is brought in afterwards. When the meal is finished, you suck off all the superfluous grease from your fingers, piously ejaculate 'Hamdulillah!'* and wash your

* Thank God!

hands in the water which in good society is brought to you. To eructate is the highest compliment that you can pay your host, and the food you often get renders this to most people not difficult of accomplishment.

On Sundays—market-day—they must have had a busy time of it in the kitchen, for apparently anyone who liked to apply at the *kasbah* could have a free meal. True, it usually only consisted of bread and oil, but even then the loaves had to be baked. On that day we were not allowed to take our favourite walk, which was through the market-place towards the little stream which ran at the foot of the hill. The Khalifa feared that we might take the opportunity of speaking to some of the Mogador Jews who frequented the place, and we were forbidden to have conversation with anyone outside the *kasbah*, as strangers coming there were warned not to give us any information as to what was going on in the outside world. In spite of this we used to hear scrappy rumours of *bashadors* going to the Sultan; of heavy ransom being demanded for our release; and many other items of news which proved afterwards to have had more or less foundation of truth. Several times I applied to the Khalifa for permission to send a letter to the British Consul at Mogador, but without success. Once he promised that he would send a message for us, but he failed to keep his word.

On February 27 a mounted courier arrived with a letter from the Sultan for Kaid Said. He was instructed, he said, to travel with all possible speed to Tisnit, and by the Sultan's orders to take with him a horseman from Eda Gilul in case any accident should befall him on the way. The courier was only delayed whilst a letter was written by the Khalifa to his father, which was entrusted to the Giluli messenger, and both men left for Tisnit the same afternoon about 4.30. This incident cheered us up considerably, as we had no doubt that his mission had reference to our expected release. Indeed, we were told that the letter did concern us, but that it had to go on to the Kaid at Tisnit. Fast couriers could go there and back, they said, in six days, and then, *inshallah*,* we should be free. A week passed by, but there was no message from Tisnit.

On March 9, the long spell of magnificent weather was broken by a deluge of rain. There are no half-measures about the climate of Southern Morocco. When it does rain there is no misunderstanding about it. A dried-up river-bed will be transformed in a few hours into a rushing, hurrying torrent, and a placid and formidable stream swollen into a broad and impassable river. On this occasion, with few intermissions, it rained for a week, until we began to fear that it had forgotten how to leave off. By about the third day of the rain, the water had thoroughly soaked through the mud roof of our lodging and, dripping through, formed in pools upon the cement floor. It was difficult to find 6 feet of dry space anywhere, and when we went to sleep, it had to be with Beyerle's mackintosh and mine spread over us as best we could. The place became utterly uninhabitable, but luckily for us four or five of the Moors had to sleep in the same place where we were stalled ; and a report of the condition of affairs being sent to the Khalifa, he ordered us all to move into the next room, which was occupied by the *taleb*, and comparatively rain-proof, while the latter sought shelter in another part of the *kasbah*.

* Please God.

And all this time there was no news of the courier. The Moors may be deficient in many things, but they are never lacking in excuses. They told us that the rains had swollen the rivers, and that the courier could not cross. Bridges are, to all intents and purposes, unknown in Morocco; and in the rainy season it is no uncommon thing for travellers to be delayed for days waiting for the subsidence of a swollen stream. The man who had been sent from the *kasbah* had to be back, at the latest, by the coming Monday. Those were the Khalifa's orders, they said, and if he were not back by Thursday, the news in the letter from the Sultan was not for us. But Thursday came and went, and still there was no word.

CHAPTER XXVI.

LIFE IN THE KASBAH—*continued*.

A well-used pack of cards—An overheard conversation—News of the *Tourmaline*—A 'Bashador Inglìz' at the Sultan's camp—Fate of the Moslem prisoners—A murder trial—The 'leather glove'—I make a sketch of the *kasbah*—A quarrel with our guards—We resort to strategy to obtain tobacco—Pigs, *djinns*, and devils—The Khalifa makes a bargain with Sabbah—A Moorish idea of England.

THE daily life at the *kasbah* pursued its dull, monotonous course, and we began to feel sick at heart. How often we blessed Tajer Johnston for the thoughtfulness which had led him to provide us with a pack of cards! But for them I think we should have gone crazy, through sheer ennui. We had listened to de Reya's wonderful répertoire of stories of the sea; had heard all Beyerle's tales of Cairo, Paris, and Berlin; and knew Sabbah's whole career of light and shade from A to Z; and the store of anecdote was exhausted. So, in our extremity, we fell back upon our cards, and played four-handed cribbage and whist until you could scarcely tell the ace of spades for dirt. True, we tried the experiment of scraping the dirt off with the edge of a can-opener, but it was not a success.

One night when we had 'turned in,' but were all still awake, we heard a whispered conversation being carried on amongst our guards, to which the repetition of the word 'Sultan' first attracted our attention. They were speaking in the Shl'ha dialect, which Sabbah only imperfectly understood; but he gathered enough of their talk to learn that it was the intention of the Sultan to keep us prisoners for three years. Nice prospect indeed! And visions of Slatin, Neufeld, and the other captives in the Sudan rose up in my mind. And then I thought of those British subjects taken prisoners by the King of Naples years ago, and Palmerston getting up in the House of Commons and making his four hours' speech, threatening to send the whole Mediterranean fleet if the men were not released; and of that other famous speech, made in the United States Congress, by a man whose name I could not then recall, extolling the protecting care of Great Britain for her subjects, exemplified in the fact that she went to war with the King of Abyssinia for a similar reason. And the train of my thoughts carried me at express speed to more modern times, and I remembered the murder of Stokes in the Congo, and the apathetic indifference of the Government in his case; and, not having arrived at comforting conclusions, I thought the best thing under the circumstances was to go to sleep, which I accordingly did. Poor Sabbah was not so fortunate, for dread and terror kept him awake all night, and it was a great relief to him when morning came and he could ease his mind by talking the prospect over with us.

Other little items of 'news' had filtered through to us in those last few days: The *Tourmaline* was in Mogador; the pilot had been aboard her, and in consequence had been put in prison (query, quarantine) for three days. As a matter of fact, we learned afterwards that the yacht had been to Mogador to try and get some news of us, and to take in water; and the Moorish authorities, on ascertaining that she was the vessel that had been down to the Sus coast, refused to allow any of her party to land, and ordered out all the available forces in the town. A small army of coast defence was encamped on the beach, and the whole town was in a ferment of apprehension until this terrible visitor left the port. Another report was that she had gone to Tangier; and, again, that she had been captured at the Canaries, and was going to be given up to the Sultan.

At length the monotony was broken by the arrival at the *kasbah* of some of the men who had formed our escort from Tisnit. They had been to the Sultan's camp near Casablanca, to hand over the prisoners who had survived the hardships of the march.* From them we learned that Ben Omar, one of Kaid Giluli's Khalifas, who had been entrusted with the delivery of the customary 'present' to the Sultan, was waiting there for his Majesty's notification of acceptance. It is invariably an anxious time with the Kaid, until his messenger returns, and he learns that his 'present'—supposed to represent the taxes of his district—has been accepted. The men further informed us that a 'Bashador Ingliz' had arrived at the camp the day they left, and Ben Omar had been instructed to wait, in order that he might bring back the Sultan's orders concerning us.

'Now we shan't be long,' said de Reya; but he

---

* I afterwards heard from one of the captives in Tangier that five of his fellow-prisoners had died on the march, and that one—poor old Misti—had succumbed to the thrashing administered to him in the Sultan's camp.

proved a false prophet, for the emissary of the British Government entrusted with the mission of securing our release from the hands of the Moors was dancing attendance on the Grand Vizier for more than a month. We saw this 'Bashador Inglìz' subsequently in the capacity of 'witness for the Crown' at Tangier, and we ceased to be surprised at the length of time the negotiations had occupied. A sallow, insignificant-looking youth in the twenties, without that presence and dignity of appearance that go so far towards impressing such people as the Moors, it was not astonishing that the Grand Vizier compelled him to trail along with the camp, from the vicinity of Casablanca to Marrakesh, before he would give this representative of her Britannic Majesty's Government any satisfactory answer to the demands the latter was instructed to make. As correspondence clerk and interpreter to a firm of merchant grocers in Morocco, he would no doubt be excellently fitted, but as a diplomatic envoy he left much to be desired. Small wonder the Government offers a premium to Civil Servants who acquire a knowledge of the Arabic language, if the diplomatic ranks have to be recruited from such material as this.

Meanwhile the Moslem prisoners had been despatched to Marrakesh, in the gaol there to drag out the rest of their miserable existence; and Kaid Hassan and his party, having seen them effectively immured—those that had survived, at least—had gone on to Tisnit to report himself to Giluli. And we waited for Ben Omar. Every morning when we woke we said to ourselves, if not to each other, 'I wonder if Ben Omar will come to-day'; and our last thought ere we went to sleep was, 'Will Ben Omar come to-morrow?'

And the days grew into weeks, and we heard no more news.

Every day the Khalifa would sit in the gate or in the courtyard to administer 'justice,' in that rough-and-ready fashion for which Moorish Kaids are notorious. 'The Khalifa is making a law,' Sabbah used to say, and from a small hole in the door of our little yard we could often watch the proceedings. On one occasion a man was brought in who had been long 'wanted' for the murder of one of the Giluli tribe. He was driving three camels along the road near the *kasbah* when he was recognised and stopped. A few of the murdered man's friends were soon on the spot, and the murderer was promptly haled as a prisoner before the Khalifa. It was the quickest murder trial that I ever witnessed. The accusers related their story with solemn, unimpassioned demeanour, and the accused was heard in his own defence. The whole thing only occupied, perhaps, twenty minutes, and it didn't take twenty seconds for the Khalifa to give his verdict and pass sentence. The prisoner's camels were handed over to the man who had hired them to carry his goods, and who was accompanying them on the march, and one camel-load of sugar was confiscated by the Khalifa by way of court fees. The prisoner himself was taken away to join the wretched band in the subterranean dungeon below us. 'More sugar for the Khalifa,' was de Reya's only comment.

The Moors seldom inflict capital punishment even for murder, except by accident, when a prisoner inconsiderately dies under an excessive number of lashes. They prefer something more lingering and humorous, like the gentleman in 'The Mikado.' Even the punishment of the 'leather glove' is not nearly so much in vogue in Morocco as formerly. The 'leather glove,' which was a favourite instrument of torture with Giluli's predecessor in the governorship of the province of Haha, is applied in the following manner: A lump of quicklime is placed in a man's hand, which is then closed up into a fist, and the fist is then tightly bound with leather thongs. The hand is then plunged into a tub of cold water, and the agonies the poor wretch endures can be better imagined than described. For nine days the fist is kept closed, and mortification and death are frequently the result. Sometimes, however, a victim is lucky enough to escape with nothing worse than the loss of his hand.

It was with Nero-like tortures such as this that the late Kaid of Haha goaded his desperate tribesmen into revolt, which led to the sack of his *kasbah*, and himself being driven from the province. And it is upon such men as these that the British Government suggests that a 'severe censure' should be passed by the Sultan, as sufficient atonement for an unwarrantable outrage upon British subjects.

One day I succeeded in making a rough sketch of the interior of the main courtyard, and the fact being reported to the Khalifa, he sent a request that I would do one for him. Of course, I readily complied, but was careful to avoid putting in any human figures. The Koranic law forbids the making of any graven image, or drawing of a living being, as on the Day of Judgment Allah will require the perpetrator to endow his handiwork with life, and failing to comply with the Divine command, the erring mortal will be denied participation in the joys of Paradise that await the faithful Moslem. The Khalifa professed himself pleased with this little effort in draughtsmanship, and presented me with a loaf of sugar. Thinking the moment propitious, I asked him to allow me to send a message to the Consul at Mogador, as we were in need of soap and other articles. What we really wanted was to provide the Consul with an opportunity of sending us some more newspapers, in order that we might glean what was going on in the outside world; but the little man refused, saying that he would buy us what things we wanted himself. I thereupon told him we were very much in want of tobacco, and he said he would buy us some from the market on the following Sunday. Sunday came, but no tobacco. An incident occurred, however, that hastened the fulfilment of the Khalifa's promise. For a perfectly legitimate reason, we had asked our guards to allow us to go out into the fields adjoining the *kasbah* for a little while. Very surlily they complied, and the head of the gang gave vent to remarks reflecting upon the purity of our parentage. Thereupon I promised to show him how such observations would be met in our own country if he indulged in such language again, and, meeting the major-domo of the *kasbah* on our return, the matter was duly laid before him, with a request that he would inform the Khalifa. A few days afterwards there was another angry dispute between us and our gaolers which nearly led to blows; and the Khalifa, being informed of what had taken place, came to the conclusion that we were drifting into a condition bordering on dangerous lunacy for want of tobacco. Accordingly he despatched a man in hot haste to Mogador, with instructions to purchase as much tobacco as he could carry. The messenger was away three days, and then returned with about a dozen half-pound packets of the cheapest description of French 'caporal,' and a number of packets of cigarette-papers. After tea-leaves, dried wild-thyme, and other such substitutes for the soothing weed, a whiff of even that inferior stuff was delightful in the extreme. I am sure that Last, at any rate, would cheerfully have foregone one of the two meals a day provided for us rather than be deprived of his smoke.

The topic of religion did not often come up for discussion between us and our captors. In the early days of our sojourn in the *kasbah* the Khalifa's brother had tackled Sabbah, and told him that if he and his companions would turn Moslem we should be presented with wives, cattle, a farm, and other things that go to make a Moor's earthly paradise; but the scorn and contempt with which the offer was rejected did not tempt him to repeat it. But I was considerably astonished one day to see one of the Khalifa's sons with a young boar in his arms. Knowing that the *haluf* is an abhorred beast in the sight of a Moslem, I made inquiries, and found that it is quite a common practice among the wealthier Moors to keep these young pigs about their houses, as it is the popular belief that the animals attract the *djinns*, or evil spirits, that would otherwise seek a repose in the bodies of mortals. When a young pig is considered to be as full of bad spirits as he can conveniently accommodate, it is turned out to run wild, and afford sport on some future occasion when he is old enough to be worth hunting and killing. It seems an absurd superstition, but I made no remark about it, remembering the story of the Englishman travelling in Morocco who did give expression to his opinion on the subject. The traveller in question was rather taken aback when the Moor to whom he was speaking said, 'I don't know why you should say so. Did not your prophet Aissa (Jesus) once cast the *djinns* out of the people, and send them into the *haluf*?'

Another amusing instance of credulity was furnished by the Khalifa himself. In conversation with Sabbah one day, he asked our interpreter if he would take the responsibility of all his (the Khalifa's) sins for a consideration. Sabbah, seeing a chance of doing a little business, promptly asked him how much he would pay. The Khalifa thought two pesetas should be sufficient, and after a little discussion Sabbah agreed, and the money was handed over. 'Now, remember,' he said, 'you are responsible for all the sins I have committed up to to-day, and Allah knows I have paid you two pesetas.'

When we had become more familiar with our guards, we endeavoured to cultivate better relations by judicious gifts of sugar—in which article we were not by any means stinted by the Khalifa—and cigarettes to Obila, the head of the gang, he being the only one that smoked. Our object in thus propitiating them was to gain greater freedom out of doors, and longer spells of exercise, and, secondly, to induce them to give us any information that might reach them concerning ourselves. In the latter, however, we were only partially successful, the boy Hamed, an 'attaché'* of Obila's, being the only one that brought to us the rumours and gossip he picked up in the *kasbah*. These were often conflicting and unsatisfactory, but anything was better than absolute silence. Conversation with these men was somewhat difficult to maintain, as their intelligence

* Those familiar with life in Morocco will understand the application of my term.

was small, their range of subjects less, and their knowledge of things outside their own sordid daily lives meagre in the extreme. They were very much interested in hearing about London—'Lundrìs' and England are synonymous terms to them—and listened open-eyed like children to stories of the railway train, and its speed as compared with that of the baggage-camel. Nothing, however, would convince them that Morocco was not the finest country in the world in every way. Lundrìs might be all very well in its way with all these wonderful things—the invention of the devil—but we had no barley, or cattle, or gardens such as they had in Morocco, as we *all lived in ships!*

CHAPTER XXVII.

NEWS AT LAST.

We discuss the possibilities of escape—But resolve to wait—Good news for Giluli—Arrival of Ben Omar—Obila is confidential—The major-domo's news—We prepare for our departure—A strange request—How the news came—An irritating delay—Arab is moved to tears—Sabbah indulges in a little light banter—A sample of the Khalifa's 'justice' —Departure from the *kasbah*.

SUCH was the life we lived for nine tedious weeks in that *kasbah* in Haha — within a day's journey of Mogador, and yet cut off from civilization and communication with the outside world as effectively, almost, as if we had been in the heart of the desert of Sahra. When the second month had nearly gone by, and we were still without news of our long-expected release, we began seriously to discuss the possibilities of escape. Money—the golden key which unlocks so many doors, especially in Morocco—was lacking with us. Horses, even, were not available, and we had no weapons. We were absolutely dependent upon our mother-wit. Escape at night-time was out of the question. In the first place, four or five guards slept in the same room with us, and always in front of the door, like watch-dogs on the mat. And if by any chance we could have succeeded in getting out of our room without arousing our Moslem gaolers, there was still the outer gate of the *kasbah* itself, and that was locked and guarded from early evening to sunrise.

Our only chance would be when we were out for exercise. On such occasions it often happened that we were accompanied by an escort of only two, or perhaps three, men, and it would not have been a difficult matter to have lured them into the valley where the stream ran, and, under shelter of the trees, fallen suddenly upon them and overpowered them. But even then our difficulties would only have been commencing. We had made carefully-guarded inquiries as to the direction in which Mogador lay, but none of us had more than a general notion of the right road to take. Our absence from the *kasbah* would soon be noticed, the hue and cry would be raised, and in a very short time horsemen would be scouring the country round in all directions. No place but Mogador offered any safety for us, and the Moors knew well enough in which direction we should bend our steps. A reward would be offered for our recapture, and every tribesman in the district would join in the hunt for the Christians. Travelling by day, therefore, would be out of the question, and thirty-five miles of rough and hilly country lay between us and our goal. The woods would afford us fairly good concealment, and under the shelter of some friendly boulders we might hide and rest by day. But all this time we should be without food, except such roots and nuts as we might find on the way; and taking everything into consideration, the odds were a thousand to one against us. Still, the love of liberty is strong and deep; and we were sickened of our long captivity, and becoming desperate enough to seize any opportunity of escape that might present itself. So we waited and watched.

One day in the early part of April, some soldiers arrived from Marrakesh. The Sultan, having laid waste some of the fairest provinces in his dominions, had returned to his southern capital for a time, and the army was resting from its ravages and slaughter. Ben Omar had accompanied them; the Sultan—Allah protect him—had accepted Kaid Giluli's 'present,' and Ben Omar himself would arrive at the *kasbah* about an hour or two after sunrise on the morrow. Whether he brought news from the Christians or not they could not say; but we hoped for the best, and were in a fever of impatience for his arrival. We had our 'skilly' as usual the next morning, and about nine o'clock Ben Omar and a small escort rode up to the *kasbah*. We knew that there was no chance of our hearing anything definite for an hour or so, for it takes a Moor about as long to read and digest the contents of a letter as it does a snake to digest a meal, but we drew a hopeful augury from the fact that shortly after his arrival a great dish of meat was brought to us. It was long before our usual dinner-time, and we were inclined to think that it indicated an immediate start for Mogador. But no such order came, and we were taken out for our morning constitutional as usual. Outside we met one of the men who had come with us from Tisnit, and had accompanied Ben Omar to the Sultan. He had not been by any means unfriendly to us, and when we asked him if they had brought any news from the Sultan about us, he did not take refuge in evasion, but answered us straightway. Unfortunately, his reply was in the negative, and our hopes came down with a run to zero. All these weeks we had been waiting for Ben Omar; our faith had been resting on him; he was sure to bring the Sultan's orders touching ourselves, as it was for that reason he had been detained. And now he had come, and there was not a rag of comfort or a shred of news. That the 'Bashador Ingliz' had left Morocco City, we had heard some days ago, and we could not imagine that he had returned unsuccessful from such a mission as that. But there was not a word of our going, and the next day Ben Omar left the *kasbah*, the soldiers dispersed to their homes or elsewhere, and we sank back again into the rut of our wretched routine at the *kasbah*.

A plentiful crop of rumours, however, sprang up after Ben Omar's departure, and Hamed brought them all to us, with an air of great secrecy and mystery, when no one was near. They were conflicting, as usual, but the general tenor of them seemed to point to an early move in some direction. Finally Obila—that silent, goat-faced gaoler of ours—blurted out to us, on our way back from an afternoon walk, that the order had come to send us to Morocco City. We should have welcomed even that as a change, but I didn't believe he had got the destination correct.

The next morning, before we had risen, a message was brought in that the Khalifa wished to speak to Sabbah. He had often sent for Sabbah on previous occasions, when he wished for a little light entertainment, but this time we thought the visit portended something more. He had hardly gone, when the major-domo of the *kasbah*, who had often promised to give us the first information, as soon as the order came for us to go, burst into the room where we were, with a small crowd of hangers-on at his heels, exclaiming, '*Tajer Pyely! Tajer Green! Emshi Suerah,* *culchi !'** and he commenced to shake hands cordially with us all, as if we had been the dearest friends of his lifetime.

'To Mogador?' we repeated. 'When? To-day?' '*Iyeh, inshallah*' (Yes, please God).

This pious proviso is a very useful formula to the Moors, and is frequently used in making promises that they have no intention whatever of keeping, as they can then take refuge behind the Almighty when taxed for their breach of faith.

There is a story told of a man who kept a shop in Gibraltar, and knew the ways of the Moor. To him one day came one of the Faithful, who was desirous of buying some cloth. On being informed that the price was two dollars a yard, payment in sixty days, he replied:

'All right, I will take so much, and pay you in sixty days, *inshallah*.'

'No,' said the vendor, 'the price is two dollars, payment in sixty days; for sixty days, *inshallah*, the price is two dollars and a half.'

In this case, however, as it was evident that our marching orders had come at last, we did not doubt that we should be *en route* in an hour or two, and therefore we commenced making what toilet we could for the journey, in order to present as decent an appearance as possible on arrival at Mogador. The Khalifa had some weeks before provided us all with a pair of Moorish slippers—those heel-less, yellow Morocco leather *babouches* that a European can with difficulty keep on his feet at first, but which are so comfortable when one is used to them—and we had become so accustomed to going about thus shod that boots and

* 'Mr. Beyerle, Mr. Grey, you are all to go to Mogador!'

socks seemed to us an unnecessary adjunct of civilization. In point of fact, Beyerle and myself were the only members of the party that were thus endowed. Sabbah had been despoiled of his boots the day he landed on the beach at Assaka; Last's had succumbed to the vicissitudes of the journey; while de Reya's indiarubber sea-boots, in which he had come ashore, had been used for other than their original purpose when we had been confined to one room for more hours than Nature deemed desirable, and they had been thrown away. As regards clothing, we could number four coats among the five of us, in a more or less ragged condition, Sabbah being reduced to a seaman's guernsey; and while Beyerle's cord riding-breeches and mine had stood the wear and tear pretty well, the white cotton trousers of the others were fearfully and wonderfully patched with old pocket-handkerchiefs, and other similar material that was to be had at the *kasbah*. I had had all the hair of my head shorn off some weeks previously, as a check to overpopulation, but, speaking generally, we stood very badly in need of a barber and a bath.

In the midst of these preparations, Sabbah returned from his visit to the Khalifa. He confirmed what the major-domo had told us, and was in a state of delirious excitement at the near prospect of his release from captivity. Our few belongings were soon collected and put into a sack, and we were ready to start. Amongst our portable property was a corkscrew that Consul Johnston had sent to us. One of our guards, named Yusod, had seen the ease with which this little instrument had extracted corks from beer-bottles, and came to me and begged me to give it to him. I asked him what he wanted it for, and the following was his reply : '*Whew-w-w, ptt! pfs, pfs, pfs, pfs, clck!*' Reduced to paper it seems unintelligible; but accompanied by pantomimic gestures as it was, there was no mistaking his meaning. An imaginary bullet as it whistles along, suddenly stops, and buries itself in his arm or leg. That is where the corkscrew would come in. Driving it into the lead, as he had seen us do it into the cork, he would have it out '*clck*' before the wound was closed, and Yusod would be himself again! I made no effort to smother the laugh which his quaint idea provoked, and handed over the coveted treasure to him. I wonder if he has since had an opportunity of putting it to a practical test!

We were not much in the humour for 'skilly' that morning, being too impatient to be on the road; but an hour or two went by, and then we were told we should not start till after dinner, as there were not enough mules for us yet. Was this another of the Khalifa's jokes, I wondered. We should soon see; but meanwhile there was nothing to do but possess our souls in patience. Before dinner came we learned that we were not going to start at all that day, as Kaid Giluli had said in his letter that we were not to stop anywhere for the night on the road to Mogador, but make one journey of it, and as it was about a twelve hours' march, it was useless starting that day.

It was in this way that we learned whence the order for our departure had come. A letter had come from the Sultan a week or ten days ago, they told us, but it had to be sent on to Kaid Giluli at Tisnit, as the letter was addressed to him. The people at the *kasbah* professed to be ignorant of its contents until the courier arrived from Tisnit, but there is no doubt in my mind that the letter was brought by Ben Omar from Morocco City, after all, and that its purport was perfectly well known. And so, for the sake of an absurd formality, in spite of the fact that the Sultan had ordered our *immediate* despatch to Mogador, we were detained a further eight or ten days at the *kasbah*, whilst a courier was going to Tisnit and back. I was glad then that we did not know it when Ben Omar came, for the time we had to wait would have seemed twice as long. As it was, the day the news was given to us seemed the very longest of all the days we had passed at the *kasbah*.

We were to start at sunrise the next day, we were told, and in anticipation of a long day's journey we lay down to sleep earlier than usual in order to get a good night's rest. But we were all too excited to sleep much, and long before the dawn we were awake, listening to the long-drawn cry of the *mueddin* as it tore through the silence of the night to proclaim to the sleeping Moslems in the *kasbah* that 'there is no God but God, and our lord Mohammed is His prophet.' Five times a day does this invocation to prayer ring out from the minarets of the public mosques, or the courtyards of the *kasbahs* throughout Morocco, viz., before sunrise, again at noon, in the afternoon, before sunset, then in the evening between sunset and dark, and lastly, for the vesper prayer, between twilight and the first watch of the night. But our gaolers snored on, and we waited for the first streaks of dawn to find their way through the narrow hole in the wall which did duty for a window. Shortly after six o'clock they bestirred themselves, shuffled into their slippers, and crept out one by one. We went out, too, to see if we could observe any signs of activity in the courtyard. A small escort of horsemen would probably be sent with us, but there was no lack of men for such a purpose. It then transpired that the first excuse for our delay was the true one. The Khalifa had sent out demands the previous day for the neighbouring tribesmen to supply mules, and the required number had not yet been delivered.

'Why cannot we use the Khalifa's own mules?' we asked; 'there are plenty in the yard there.'

'*Y'allah tif!*' (Good gracious!), was the astonished reply; 'do you think the Khalifa is going to allow his mules to be ridden by Christians?' The bare idea of such a thing almost took his breath away.

Since the order for our removal had been received, we had been allowed slightly more liberty of movement, being free to walk about the main courtyard if we chose. In consequence we had a better opportunity of ascertaining what was going on, and gleaning information; and we soon learnt that all the mules that were wanted had arrived but two. Everyone agreed that we were really going to Mogador, but this farce with the mules might be played for a week if nothing were done to hasten things on somewhat. The Khalifa was suddenly solicitous about our material comfort, and sent a message that he could not think of letting us start on such a journey hungry, and that we must have some dinner before setting out. We had seen nothing of the Khalifa himself all the morning, as he was occupied in another part of the *kasbah*, to which we could not gain access; and the suggestion was mooted that, if no start was made by mid-day, we should ourselves walk out of the *kasbah* and strike out for Mogador afoot. The plan found favour with all but Beyerle, who counselled a still further exercise of patience, but, for my part, I thought sufficient

21—2

demands of that virtue had been made upon us; and both the Sultan and Kaid Giluli having ordered our removal, it was not likely that undue force would be used to detain us. In any case such action would bring matters to a head, and anything was better than this intolerable suspense.

While we were still debating the question, a message was brought that the Khalifa was desirous of seeing Sabbah. Seizing my opportunity, I went with him, in spite of the protests of the messenger. We found the Khalifa and his 'suite' sitting near the side, or prison, entrance to the *kasbah*. On seeing me, he asked me what I wanted, and I told him. If he had had orders to send us to Mogador, I said, let us go. We didn't care about mules, but would walk barefoot if necessary. He smiled at my eagerness, and said he was sorry to part with us, as he was only just beginning to like us. However, he supposed we must go; and ordering us to go back to our room, and eat some dinner that he would send to us, he promised that we should set off immediately afterwards.

On our return we found that a dish of meat had already been sent in; and we had hardly tasted more than a mouthful or so, when another messenger came in to tell us all to follow him. Cramming into our pockets all the bread that they would hold, we took leave of our late guards, preparatory to turning our backs upon the dingy den which for sixty-three days had been our common quarters. To each of them we gave some little souvenir, such as a handkerchief—which would be used for cleaning brass trays or tying up lumps of sugar—a looking-glass, or a few empty bottles—which are much prized by country Moors—and we left with blessings instead of curses. Poor little Arab, the black slave—to whom de Reya had given an old pink cotton shirt—was much affected. Probably he had never been so well fed in all his little life before we came (and our scraps and leavings became his perquisites), and as he said his *salaamas*, he lifted his hand, the cuff of his pink shirt dangling over his finger-tips, and wiped away the tears that were rolling down his dusky cheeks.

Sabbah was in lighter vein, and considered that he might now safely venture to chaff his late guards. During our detention at the *kasbah* the Khalifa had had orders from headquarters to provide us with good food, and plenty of it. Not daring to disobey, and yet not liking Christian prisoners to be better fed than their Moslem guards, he had changed their daily diet from the customary bread and oil and *tshisha* to meat and *kuss-kuss*, such as we were provided with. So Sabbah jocularly remarked to our junior gaoler, ' Well, Said, no more meat for you; you'll have to go back to bread and oil now.' But Said indignantly repudiated the assertion, declaring with some warmth that he often had meat for his dinner; in fact, he had bought half a peseta's worth about a month before we came!* and vehemently called upon Allah to burn his tormentor's father, grandfather, and ancestors generally.

Outside, we found the Khalifa still in the same spot. He was interviewing tribesmen, selecting our escort, and giving instructions generally. Another mule had arrived in the meantime, and one poor fellow was explaining to the little tyrant that he did not possess a

---

* In Southern Morocco a whole sheep can be bought for about two pesetas, or half a dollar.

mule, but he had brought his donkey instead, which he hoped Sid' Embarak would accept.

'All right,' said the Khalifa in his cheeriest tones, 'don't distress yourself; it will only cost you 30 dollars, but I'll take your donkey, anyhow;' and he waved his hand to signify that the interview was concluded. The poor tribesman shrank back, and, squatting himself on a mud heap, probably endeavoured to comfort himself with the reflection that 'it was written.' Anyhow, the 30 dollars would have to be paid, and the donkey would be held as security until it was. The poor wretch did not look as if he possessed 30 pesetas, let alone 30 dollars, but the prison door is always half open for such as he.

At length the time for our departure came. Calling us to him, the Khalifa handed to each of us a couple of dollars, and telling a man standing by to give us two loaves of white bread apiece, he shook hands with us all in turn, and, mounting our mules, we turned our backs on the *kasbah* at Eda Gilul, and set our faces towards Mogador.

CHAPTER XXVIII.

DELIVERED UP.

A last look at the *kasbah*—On the road to Mogador—A halt at Eda Igirt—The journey resumed—I kill a snake—Hydrophobia unknown in Morocco—The legendary founder of Mogador—A tedious wait—Arrival at Mogador—Our reception—Popular indignation in the town—A civilized Governor—European visitors—Departure from Mogador—We embark on board the *Hassani*—Arrival at Tangier—Beyerle is set free—Arrest of the British subjects—Concerning the British Consulate at Tangier—Conclusion.

DESCENDING the hill, we quickly left behind the mean and dirty-looking *sôk** on our right, and the fields of fast-ripening barley on our left, and, crossing the little stream at the foot, found ourselves following the path up the other side of the valley to which our eyes had been so often turned in the weeks that had passed. A few goats were browsing amongst the argan-trees as we passed, and some of them were even to be seen among the upper branches, where they had climbed in search of the fruit they like so well. At the top of the hill we all turned to take a last look at the huge fortress-like *kasbah* that had held us so long, and from which was misgoverned a province the size of Yorkshire—the largest of all the Moorish kaidships. What

* Market.

a fair picture it made, with its background of purple hills, and, in the near distance, its fields of waving corn, on which the unclouded sun smiled, surely in satire! and yet what a world of tyranny and misery it emblemized and typified!

But I was too full of the thought of approaching freedom to indulge in speculations of this sort, and we were a light-hearted party that jogged along on our mules that afternoon.

Forest after forest of argan-trees we passed, and valley succeeded valley in one bewildering panorama of beauty; and while the sun was still high in heaven, from the crest of a ridge of hills—those same hills that we could see from Eda Gilul, and which seemed so close —we descried the distant mountains of the Atlas, miles and miles away, whose snow-clad peaks, that seemed vainly striving to reach the blue above that domed them, gleamed white and dazzling in the torrid sun.

Twice on the road a brief halt was called that man and beast might slake their thirst at some clear babbling brook, and it was all but dark ere we reached our appointed resting-place for the night—an apparently half-empty house at a place called Eda Igirt. If Kaid Giluli had ordered that we should make one march of it to Mogador, the mandate was not carried out. As it was, after six hours' riding, we were still six hours' journey from Mogador; and we were glad enough, after our enforced spell of idleness at the *kasbah*, to jump down from our animals and rest. It was a relief, too, to get into our slippers again, and when the meat and *kuss-kuss* came along we were ready to do ample justice to it.

The stars were still bright in the sky when we were in the saddle again, and we had been on the road a good half-hour before the sun had risen. As we came nearer to Mogador, the country became more flat and sandy, and our progress was thereby somewhat accelerated. About eleven o'clock we arrived at the Palm Tree Hotel, one of Mr. Ratto's numerous ventures, so named after the tall solitary palm-tree that raises its head high above the two-storied building, and forms a conspicuous landmark for miles round. Having had no breakfast before starting, we had succeeded in raising a very respectable appetite, and persuaded our Moorish escort to allow us to go in and get some food, whilst they smoked a pipe of *kif* in the courtyard below. Our hunger, however, was greater than their patience, and almost before our eggs were boiled they were urging us to get into the saddle again. Under any circumstances we should not have been disposed to unduly hurry ourselves, but when the attendant Hebe produced some excellent bottles of lager-beer, our reluctance to tear ourselves away from such enjoyable surroundings may easily be understood. We certainly found the Khalifa's two dollars useful.

The animals were none the worse for their short rest, and we made rapid progress on the resumption of our march. One little incident occurred which showed the wholesome dread that the Moors in general have for snakes. Right in the middle of our path lay a snake coiled up in the hot sand, warming himself in the sun. There are only two kinds of poisonous snakes in Morocco, and this proved to be one of the species —the *lefah*, whose bite is fatal in a quarter of an hour. The Moors gave him a wide berth, but, being desirous of securing a specimen, and having riding-boots on, I borrowed a stick from one of the men and gave the reptile two blows on the back, which I calculated would be sufficient for any ordinarily constituted snake. Not wishing to unnecessarily delay the march, I picked up the reptile, intending to tie it up in my handkerchief, and remounted my mule. What was my horror, however, to see it wriggle convulsively! I was unwilling, though, to abandon my prize, so, seizing it deftly close to the head, I bent its backbone between my finger and thumb until I heard it snap, and then I knew that its powers of mischief were at an end.

It is said that hydrophobia is unknown in Morocco. Whether this is so or not, I cannot say; but certain it is that the treatment adopted in the case of snake-bite is the same as that advocated in Europe by the Buisson system. At least, the principle is the same, that of getting the patient into a thorough perspiration, though the methods employed are of course different. The virtue of this remedy is said to have been accidentally discovered by a man being bitten by a poisonous snake some miles from his home. Knowing that the bite was reputed to be fatal, and wishing to die among his own people, he ran as hard as he could —a veritable race with death. He reached his home streaming with perspiration, but the fatal issue he had apprehended had been unwittingly warded off. The virus of the snake had been carried out of his system with the perspiration. And now, when an Arab or a Moor is bitten, he hastens to his house or his tent with all speed, smothers himself in blankets, and waits for the result. If the efficacy of this remedy is only equal to its simplicity the necessity of Pasteur Institutes seems open to serious question.

After about an hour's more riding we came to the Wad Kseb, the old sand-swept, half-buried palace of the Sultan, and the saint-house to the memory of Sidi

Mogodul, the patron saint of Mogador. Tradition says that Mogodul is a corruption of McDougall, a Scotsman who in the bygone days was wrecked on that part of the coast and taken care of by the natives. Adopting the religion of his salvors, he acquired distinction on account of his manifest superiority in many respects, founded the town of Mogador, and died in the odour of Moslem sanctity, being to this day venerated as a saint. It is a pretty legend, but hardly squares with the stories that were most commonly circulated concerning Sali rovers, and the inhabitants of Barbary generally, two or three hundred years ago. To the Moors to-day Mogador is more commonly known as Suerah (the Beautiful), and certainly, as it first appeared to us rising like a mirage from the sandy desert by which it is surrounded, it is not entirely undeserving of the appellation. It is too well known to Europeans to need any detailed description from me here, but suffice it to say that it is the cleanest and best-paved town in all the sultanate. The port, too, although it has earned for itself among sailors the name of the 'Rat-trap,' is one of the most accessible on the Moorish coast; but it would not be able to hold a candle to Agadir if that place were reopened to commerce, and developed as it ought to be.

As we approached, the horseman who had been sent on in advance to notify the Governor of our coming, returned, and said that the latter required to see a letter from Kaid Giluli or his Khalifa before he could receive us. The leader of the escort therefore rode on into the town, and we were compelled to lie perdu, under the shelter of some gardens outside the town, for nearly two hours whilst these formalities were being gone through—doubtless to the accompaniment of a considerable amount of green-tea drinking. What would have happened had our arrival got wind among the Europeans of the town I hardly like to say, but it is more than likely that an impromptu rescue-party would have been formed to relieve the Moors of their troublesome charge—as was done on a certain former occasion—for there was great indignation, among the English and German residents particularly, at the unwarrantable length of time we had been kept prisoners by the Moors, in violation of all treaty, stipulations, and in defiance of all the rights of Europeans in Morocco.

However, our proximity was unsuspected, and when the Moorish officials came out from the town to receive us, they lost no time in getting us inside the gates, entering by a different one from that by which they had left. Once within sight of the town, the news soon spread, and as we rode through the streets, two by two, flanked by armed soldiers on each side, so that none could approach, windows were thrown open, and small knots of Jews and Christians gathered at the street corners and welcomed us by raising their hats and crying, 'God bless you, my boys!' 'Glad to see you safe!' and such-like greetings. Such a reception, after the rough and tumble of the last three months, was gratifying in the extreme, but served to aggravate the deep humiliation I felt, as a British subject, in being led through the streets in broad daylight under a guard of Moorish soldiers, as though there were no such officials as British Consuls, and no dignity left in a British Government to make such a parade impossible. For the first time on record were British subjects dragooned through the streets of a Moorish town, the butt and scorn of the ignorant Moslem population, while the more enlightened of them asked, 'Are they assassins, or what?' And when, instead of being delivered to our own Consul, as every treaty with Europe provides, we were marched to the house of the Basha, or Governor, there, in close confinement, to wait the arrival of the *Hassani*, which should take us on to Tangier, it is not to be wondered at that popular indignation ran high among the European residents in the town, without regard to nationality, and people asked each other, 'Is British power in Morocco so weak as to bear such an unwarranted imposition on the part of the Moorish officials?' 'Is this contemptuous treatment to be endured without remonstrance?' 'Are there no more treaty rights for us in Morocco?'*

At the house of the Basha we found very different accommodation from what we had been accustomed to. European chairs and a table were there, and mattresses to lie down upon—things we had not known for three months and more—and, moreover, there was Abdallah to wait on us, and cook us what food we cared to eat in the good old English way. Abdallah was somewhat of a character in his way, having been a ship's fireman, in following which interesting employment he had been shipwrecked, and taken to the Sailors' Home in London, where he had picked up a little pigeon English and sundry other accomplishments. As a steward, or valet, or bargainer with Jew pedlars, he was alike excellent, and his contempt for country Moors, as distinguished from town-bred, travelled Moslems like himself, was supreme.

Certainly Hadj Ali Ben-el-Hadj, the Basha of

* *Al Moghreb al Aksa*, April 30, 1898.

Mogador,* was as great a contrast to Kaid Giluli as one Moorish Governor could well be to another, and, as far as his orders would allow, he treated us more as guests than as prisoners, which we still were. We had hardly been installed in our new quarters half an hour, when Herr von Maur, the German Vice-Consul, came to pay a visit to Mr. Beyerle, and to express his satisfaction at seeing us safe in a civilized place once more after our unpleasant experiences, and a clerk from the British Consulate followed shortly after. A supply of new clothes was soon provided, and being now separated from Moors, niggers, etc., as far as actual contact was concerned, we could indulge in a thorough change of raiment without the fear of being infested with vermin again in a couple of days' time. This operation was carried out in the courtyard, and the old clothes put into a sack and sent off to the nearest laundry to be boiled.

Mr. Johnston himself called the next day, and told us that he had applied to the Basha for us to be handed over to him, in accordance with treaty stipulations, but the latter had refused to do so, saying that he had strict orders from the Sultan to keep us in his own house until the steamer *Hassani* was ready to embark us and take us to Tangier. For his own part, he said, he would like to give us up to our own countrymen, but he must carry out his instructions. At the same time, both the English and German Consuls were allowed to visit us as often as they

---

* To the great regret of all the residents of Mogador, this enlightened official died on October 15 last year. Besides speaking French and Spanish with fluency, he had the cultured manners of a European gentleman, and was an exceedingly able and popular Governor.

wished, and several other Mogador residents were granted similar permission. The *Daily Mail* correspondent, however, was not so successful, but if he was balked of a personal interview, he was determined to get his news somehow, and managed by a little judicious bribery to get a string of written questions smuggled in to me, which I answered as far as was politic under the circumstances. By that means, the news of our scandalous treatment—for which Lord Salisbury considers 'an expression of regret on the part of the Moorish Government, and a severe censure of Kaid Giluli,' sufficient reparation—was first made known to the public at home.

For rather more than a week we remained at Mogador, and then one morning we were told to prepare for going on board the *Hassani*. To avoid a demonstration, it had been given out in the town that we should leave at mid-day, when it was really intended that we should embark early in the morning. As a matter of fact, however, it was not until sundown that we really got marching orders, and the entire European population of the town was in the streets to see us off. They gathered in small knots here and there, at street corners and in the squares, and as we passed, closely guarded by soldiers, as when we arrived, hats were raised, and a cheery word or two of salutation greeted our ears. It was only when we got to Tangier that we learnt what desperate criminals we were—it had not occurred to us before.

Over our uneventful voyage up the Moorish coast I need not linger. We were free to walk about up and down the deck as we liked. The officers' mess saloon was reserved for us, the settees doing duty for seats at meal-time and berths at night. For my own part, I found the floor more comfortable. The lumbering old transport put into Saffi the morning after leaving Mogador, to land a present for the Sultan from the French Government, whose mission was then on the way to Morocco City. This consisted of a house of mirrors in sections, which was to be put up in the Sultan's palace or grounds, and was expected to be a source of wonder and delight to His Imperial Majesty; but unfortunately some of the sections were broken *en route*, and whether the house was ever erected I cannot say.

On the morning of April 29—after having been just 100 days in the hands of the Moors — we arrived at Tangier, and were taken to the British Consulate and handed over to Mr. Herbert White, the Vice-Consul. Beyerle, being a German, was passed on to his own Legation, and immediately set free; while the rest of us, being Britishers—or under the British flag, by reason of having signed articles on an English ship, as was Sabbah's case—were lodged in the cells attached to the Consulate, on a charge of 'illegally importing arms and ammunition into Moroquine territory.'

It seems to be the custom for writers of books of travel to bestow encomiums on all the officials of their country abroad with whom they come in contact; and to the kind-hearted consideration of Sir Arthur Nicolson, Her Majesty's Minister at Tangier, I have ample reason gratefully to testify. I wish I could say the same of his subordinates at the Consulate. Had I visited Tangier as a tourist, and been armed with introductions from people of consequence at home, I should—especially if I possessed a handle to my name —have been received in a manner of which I should doubtless now preserve a pleasant recollection. But I arrived there in a different capacity. I was a prisoner waiting trial, and as such had opportunities of becoming acquainted with the workings of the Consulate that are afforded to few strangers. One instance will suffice. The Attorney-General of Gibraltar as prosecuting counsel had some difficulty in bringing evidence to prove that we had all come from the *Tourmaline*. A month after our arrest, however, the six months for which the crew had signed articles expired, and in order to entitle those members who were detained at Tangier to their wages until arrival in England, it was necessary for them to notify the Vice-Consul as representing the Board of Trade. That was done, and the gentleman acting as Vice-Consul in the absence of his Chief requested a notification in writing. The innocent sailors, suspecting nothing, complied, and at the next hearing of the case the Attorney-General was in possession of a signed admission from them that they belonged to the *Tourmaline*. Mr. Fawkes, however, was too much of a gentleman to make a point of evidence thus obtained.

British Vice-Consuls are too often inclined to imagine that diplomacy, and not commerce, is their proper sphere. They should remember the words of the passport which enjoins them to render 'aid and assistance' to British subjects abroad; it says nothing about placing unnecessary obstacles and annoyances in their way. Even a visitor for such a sordid purpose as trade is entitled to some consideration, and a subject of the Queen does not forfeit all right and title to consideration at their hands because he has taken up his residence in a foreign country. And it may even happen that, in case of a dispute between a British subject and a native, the former may occasionally be in the right.

And here my story finishes. Of how we were detained for two months waiting trial whilst the court was finding out whether Sus was part of the Moorish dominions or not, and the Crown was getting its witnesses together, the principal of them being drafted from the prison at Morocco City, and arriving at Tangier with the fetters still riveted on their ankles; of how the two sailors who signed articles on a yacht, which they were told in the shipping office carried no cargo, were sentenced to three weeks' imprisonment as first-class misdemeanants for 'illegally importing arms and ammunition into Moroquine territory'; and how the writer was awarded four months on the same charge, on the ground that (to use the words of the judge) he was 'evidently a man of intelligence, and must have known what was going on'—all this was set forth in the newspapers of the time.

In conclusion, I think I cannot do better than quote the following remarks from the *Morning Post* of May 6, 1898: 'Let it be granted that the conduct of the Foreign Office was quite right up to the time of the landing from the *Tourmaline;* from that point it has been quite wrong, because it has been more occupied with abstract views of justice than with the varied interests and the precarious prestige of Great Britain in Morocco. Kaid Giluli should not have been permitted to keep his prisoners a day longer than was necessary to bring them to Mogador, and the four Englishmen should have been sent from Tangier to the home authorities at the same time as the German left. And at the very least the trial in Tangier should have been gone through with all possible speed. As it is, no more disastrous blow has been struck for fifty years at the reputation of Britain and the British than our conduct of the issue of the *Tourmaline* adventure. The Moors, in their barbarous ignorance of us, and in their preoccupation with themselves, will only understand our conduct as a confession of weakness—a weakness out of which Germany has cleverly scored a point of strength.'

APPENDIX.

As a comparative object-lesson in British justice abroad, and its administration, I append reports of the trial of the leader of the expedition, Major Spilsbury, and his subordinates, the former being tried before a jury at Gibraltar, and acquitted; the latter before Mr. Justice Gatty, sitting at Tangier as Judge and jury, and found guilty. These reports have been compiled principally from the London *Daily News* and the Tangier *Moghreb-al-Aksa*. The obvious conclusion to be drawn from the anomaly thus arrived at is that the sooner the 'Morocco Order in Council' is revised, the better. Especially is it desirable that all British subjects charged with offences in Morocco should be allowed the 'first constitutional privilege of an accused Englishman'—a trial by jury.

THE TRIAL OF THE 'TOURMALINE' CAPTIVES.

The British community in Tangier would have never dreamt a few months ago that their Consular Court was to become for several weeks one of the world centres of legal intelligence. Yet within a week the Consulate has been the scene of two trials, each of which is of unusual interest to the British public—viz., the preliminary hearing of the charge of murder against Callan, and the trial of the *Tourmaline* case, the main facts of which have already been reported.

Neither of these two cases is yet closed. The second one opened on June 14 before Judge Gatty, who came over from Gibraltar, the Crown being represented by Attorney-General Fawkes, Q.C., of Gibraltar. Mr. Ellis Griffith, M.P., who came from London, appeared for the prisoners Last, de Reya, and Sabbah. Grey, who had only that morning come out of hospital, defended himself.

Much interest is felt in the case in Gibraltar and Tangier. The fact that the prisoners were badly and, it appears, barbarously handled by the Moors does not release the British Government from its duty to the Moorish Government—viz., to try the prisoners for alleged offences against the latter.

A preliminary argument before the opening of the case took place between the Judge and the Attorney-General and Counsel.

The last-mentioned raised the question whether the offence had been committed in Moorish territory. He did not think the Secretary of State's letter (in reply to Judge Gatty's questions) could be given as evidence.

The Judge: Section 4 of the Foreign Jurisdiction Act states that the Secretary of State's decision is final. How do you get over that? The letter has been received through official channels. You will not dispute the signature, I suppose?

Mr. Griffith (jokingly): I don't know Lord Salisbury's signature (laughter).

Judge: I think the British Minister, who is in court, could prove it.

Mr. Griffith said he would ask for proof that the letter had been sent to the Secretary of State, that an answer had been received, and that this letter was the answer.

The Judge: I could go into the witness-box and prove that (laughter).

The Clerk of the Gibraltar Court deposed that he saw the Judge sign and address a letter to the Secretary of State. He (witness) wrote it out, and saw the reply. That letter was the reply.

Counsel: All that these documents prove is that your lordship has jurisdiction to try the case, but it does not show whether Arksis is in Moorish territory. I can show that the Moorish claims are of the most shadowy description.

Attorney-General Fawkes: I will have to ask for an adjournment. I have not enough witnesses.

Mr. Grey, addressing the Judge, said that the distance to Morocco was six days, and to Fez another six. The warrants were issued on February 10. Six weeks had elapsed since he arrived at Tangier.

Counsel applied under Order in Council 115 to issue subpœnas to Arthur Watling in Gibraltar. He took it the effect of the subpœna would be to give him safe conduct here. He was a very useful witness, having been on board the *Tourmaline*. Nobody would be guilty of contempt of court by interfering with him if he came on his lordship's subpœna.

The Judge: He would be protected if he went as a witness before a court of the Government of Morocco or a foreign court. If he were arrested, you could have the legality of his arrest tested. I refuse to give any opinion whether his arrest would be legal.

Counsel: In that case he will probably refuse to attend.

Mr. Grey: It is the interest of justice to seek truth rather than obtain a conviction. Our only witness (Beyerle) was allowed to leave the country because he was a German, and only the Englishmen have been arrested.

Counsel: I apply for a summons, and also for an order that Watling shall not be arrested here for any participation in the *Tourmaline* case, and that anybody arresting him shall be guilty of contempt of court.

Judge: Suppose the man had committed murder, would he be secure?—Counsel: I think so.

What authority?—I wouldn't make an application if we were in England, but there is a concurrent Moorish jurisdiction about which we don't know much, and what little we do know we don't like. (Laughter, in which prisoners joined.) In this country, where there is no law——

Judge (interrupting): You must not say law does not prevail here. —Counsel: But we can prove it. Counsel remarked that he was willing to leave Watling in his lordship's hands, adding that there was a risk of his arrest by another authority.

The Attorney General: I am not in a position to argue, but if he relies on English law, English law will be applied here.

The Judge granted a summons, but refused a safe conduct.

The Attorney-General said he was prepared to open the case on condition that he was not precluded from asking for an adjournment, because he had asked for witnesses who had not yet arrived. The release of these four prisoners was obtained with much trouble from the Moorish authorities, and within twenty-four hours they were charged. Now comes the question whether the length of time I am asking is reasonable.

The Judge: Well, you can go on, but I don't think it convenient.

CASE FOR THE PROSECUTION.

The Attorney-General, opening the case for the prosecution, said the proceedings were based on the Morocco Order in Council, sec. 107 and 108. Defendants were charged with attempting to smuggle into Morocco prohibited goods whereof the Moorish Government has a monopoly. The four prisoners, he continued, on the 10th of January landed on the coast of Sus—which, I put it, is within the territory of the Sultan; that I shall prove by the letter of the Secretary of State—and landed goods. Prisoners came by the *Tourmaline*, a vessel owned by the Globe Venture Syndicate (Limited), of 77, Palmerston Buildings, Old Broad Street, London. That ship was owned by A. G. Spilsbury, and was mortgaged to the Globe Syndicate, the debt being £1,300. The certificate of register is put in in evidence. The ship took on board arms at Antwerp and proceeded to Sus, the prisoners landing a portion of the arms. The *Tourmaline*, while the prisoners were ashore, remained near the coast until the *Hassani* arrived. The *Tourmaline* then slipped her anchor. The *Hassani* signalled that she wished to communicate with her, and lowered a boat. The *Tourmaline* then fired a shot from the quick-firing small gun they had on deck over the bows of the *Hassani*. As the boats from the *Hassani* approached they warned them off, and fired over them, and the *Tourmaline* then moved off. The captain of the *Hassani*, noticing there were tents on shore, and believing that Europeans were among the natives, landed soldiers. I shall call the captain of the *Hassani*, and he will tell that he saw some time after troops of the Sultan coming from inland and attacking the natives with whom the Europeans were. There was a fight, the natives fled, and the prisoners went with them. Soldiers from the *Hassani* patrolled up and down the beach. The first day after this the captain was with the Kaid of the Sultan who took the Europeans prisoners. Grey made a statement to the captain, and complained of his arrest, adding that British subjects were entitled by treaty to trade with Sus. I believe I shall be in a position (that depends on the witnesses) to produce one of the rifles landed by the *Tourmaline*, and shall ask your lordship on those facts to find that the prisoners were directly concerned in landing arms. The three prisoners, with the exception of Grey, belong to the *Tourmaline*. Grey admitted to the captain of the *Hassani* that he had landed from the *Tourmaline*. A letter was found among his papers. Prisoners were conveyed to the Sultan's camp, and subsequently handed over to the British authorities. The only way of proving that Sus is in Morocco is by the recognition of her Majesty.

FUNNY GERMAN WITNESS—HE WOULDN'T SWEAR.

The first witness, Captain Siebert, a German, and captain of the *Hassani*, was called, and one of the funniest scenes ever witnessed in any British law-court took place. The Bible was handed to witness, but instead of kissing it he drew back, and said, 'I won't swear.' Captain Siebert understands sailors' English, and speaks it fluently, albeit with a strong German accent; but the Judge's English was new to him, and as people did not always understand him on account of his strong German accent, he was made to repeat his answers. On his refusing to be sworn, the Counsel, Mr. Griffith, exclaimed sarcastically, 'We know a German criminal can get off, but not a witness!'

Attorney-General: Why do you object?—Witness: The German Minister sent for me, and said I must not swear. If they wanted me to swear, I should go to the German Legation.

While the captain was saying this, the German Chargé d'Affaires, who had been chatting in a friendly manner with the British Minister, Sir Arthur Nicolson, and who had just taken his seat on the Attorney-General of Gibraltar's bench, slipped out again into the next room. Apparently no one was prepared for this scene.

The Attorney-General: Oh, that's all! I propose we should adjourn to the German Legation—(laughter)—to have him sworn.

Counsel: I protest. Surely the court is not going to wander about into the German Legation.

The Judge: The German law prohibits the administration of oaths by any person whatever. For this reason commissions cannot go to Germany nor to Spain for the purpose of taking depositions.

Counsel: If he can't give evidence, we will dispense with him.

Attorney-General (to witness): Will you kindly step outside to consult the Chargé d'Affaires about the oath?

After a long consultation, the Attorney-General suggested that the German Chargé d'Affaires, being willing to administer the oath, all the parties should adjourn to the next room, prisoners included.

Counsel: If this is an English trial, let it be conducted according to English law; if not, according to German law. But what are we going to do in back-passages? This sort of thing is opera-bouffe. If your lordship adopts the suggestion—not that for a moment I believe you will—the statements made would not be evidence at all. I never heard of such a suggestion.

Judge: I do not take your friend's suggestion. To witness: Have you any religious belief?—Yes, Evangelical.

Can you conscientiously take an oath?—I don't know what you mean.

Does that religion allow you to swear?

'SOME DO, SOME DON'T.'

Witness (who clearly did not understand the question): People can believe what they like. Some swear, others don't. (Roars of laughter.)

Judge: Come, you mustn't answer like that. (An interpreter was sent for.)

Judge (to Attorney-General): You must find some means of swearing witness. The only way is to swear in open court.

Captain Siebert having remarked that he would swear if the oath were administered in court by the German Chargé d'Affaires, Counsel exclaimed: We take no instructions here from the German Embassy. He says he has a religious belief. He is entitled to no exception in this court.

Judge: Call the next witness.

Bensen, a Swede, chief engineer of the *Hassani*, on stepping into the witness-box, without even waiting to be questioned, exclaimed, 'You cannot force me to swear!' (Roars of laughter.)

Judge: On what grounds do you object?—Because I don't want to.

On what grounds?—I should like to know on what grounds I should swear. When the Consul says I shall, I shall; and if not, I shan't.

It must be explained here that Swedes in Morocco are under the protection of the German Legation. However, after a consultation in the next room, the German Chargé d'Affaires agreed that the objections of German law did not apply to the Swede, and Bensen took the oath. He deposed that he was chief engineer of the Sherifian steamer *Hassani*. When off the Sus coast he saw a steamer which was said to be the *Tourmaline;* he did not know whether she was at anchor or not. There was no other vessel in sight. Signals were made to her to which she replied; a boat was sent to the steamer. The *Tourmaline* fired a gun, then steamed off, and the boat returned to the *Hassani*. He heard the noise of the shot, but could not tell whether it passed over the ship or not. The *Hassani* had two boats lowered, which were kept patrolling between the *Hassani* and the land. He noticed some tents on shore, but could not see who were there. The *Tourmaline* was moving about, and had some persons on deck. Witness did not go on shore, but was in one of the boats. The *Hassani* remained there four or six days. The *Tourmaline* left for the southwest one day and a half before the *Hassani* left. Witness could not say how many armed men were in the boats, but estimated there were about twenty-five in each boat. The *Hassani*'s boats intended to board the *Tourmaline*. Witness had never been in Sus before. The men on the boats were Moorish soldiers.

Cross-examined by Mr. Grey, witness said he was surprised to see the *Tourmaline* there. There is no regular landing-place, and witness saw no white flag on shore.

Cross-examined by Counsel: We were never nearer than half a mile to the steamer.

One day you heard something whistling; you thought it was a bullet?—Yes.

At any rate it did no harm?—No, I had just awakened.

There were twenty-five men in each of your boats, and by accident they were armed?—Yes; we were armed because the steamer was a strange one, and the coast unsafe.

At this stage the case was adjourned until the following day.

At the continued trial Abderrahman Bel Hassen ben Said, whose evidence was translated by Mr. John Kirby Green, son of a former Minister to Morocco, said that he went down from Mogador to Sus coast in the *Hassani*.

IN THE KAID'S TENT.

He continued: We noticed a steamer about four or five months ago. When the steamer saw us it went away. The captain of the *Hassani* hoisted a flag, the steamer stopped, and we sent a boat with soldiers, whereupon the steamer went away, going backwards and forwards. Next day she got nearer, and we put boats to keep guard. Next day the steamer fired a shot, and from shore a shot was fired at the guard. Then the steamer left, going backwards and forwards for two or three days. From there she went to Assaka, and the *Hassani* followed her. About an hour after our arrival there the steamer left, and we went on shore to camp at Arksis, Kaid Giluli the Sultan's Governor's camp. We went to the Kaid, and remained about an hour in his tent, when they brought in the Europeans, led by a party consisting of natives and soldiers. The Kaid asked through an interpreter what they were doing there. A man like Grey replied: 'We have come to buy and sell in the country.' At least, it was a man like Grey, but I am not certain. There were four Europeans and an interpreter. He said: 'We have not come to do anything wrong, but to trade according to treaty between our Government and yours.' The man had a book in his hand, and said: 'Treaties are in it.' The Kaid answered, 'I do not know anything about these treaties. You must remain prisoners with me till I get orders from the Sultan.' We left the prisoners there in the tent. The Kaid had a European gun. One of the prisoners was speaking a European language. One of the party who spoke in Arabic appeared to be interpreting for them. The people in the dock are like the prisoners, but I am not certain.

Cross-examined by Mr. Griffith: Witness was an official of the Sultan at Mogador, and was paid for this expedition. There were about fifty soldiers on the *Hassani*, and the sailors were also given guns. They were sent to catch a boat. They went once or twice to the Sus coast, but did not know the country.

The steamer stopped, you sent two boats of armed men, and the little steamer went away?—Yes.

By Mr. Grey: One of the men was dressed exactly like you. I did not hear one ask the Kaid, 'Are we in Sus territory?'

Kaid Brahim el Udjuh, white-haired, with dark, piercing, yet sad eyes, and wearing a white burnous and a blue robe, told the same story as the preceding witness, describing the scene in the tent.

By Counsel: Did the steamer fire towards the land or towards the *Hassani*?—Up in the air.

Exactly. It was a signal shot, then?—It looked like it.

Well, that didn't frighten you very much?—No. The little steamer went behind at anchor. Nobody fired. We answered merely the shots that came from shore.

By the Attorney-General: I cannot write. I trust to memory.

Counsel: My friend suggests that people who cannot write have better memories.

Attorney-General: They have.

The court was then adjourned till two.

On the resumption Ahmed el Marakshi, a soldier, was called. He told almost word for word the same tale as to what occurred in the Kaid's tent.

Cross-examined: You're a Government employé?—Government sends me as an *amin*. An *amin* is a man who fetches treasure if he can find it.

Your duty is, when you see anything belonging to a European, to take it from him and bring it home?—Yes.

Hope you succeeded?—Yes.

Did you get much?—No, because the Kaid had taken things.

Oh, the Kaid wanted to be an *amin* himself? (Roars of laughter.) —Every Kaid is an *amin*, but every *amin* is not a Kaid. A Kaid can do the work of an *amin*.

The former Arab witness recalled, in reply to a question as to the nature of the treasure of which he was in search, said: We had to take food to the soldiers of the Sultan.

But what do you mean by treasure?—If I found anything belonging to Europeans, I was to bring it back to Mogador.

No particular thing?—No, anything.

By the Attorney-General: Is the Kaid Giluli an officer of the Sultan?—Yes. A Kaid means a man who has the Government power. Kaid Giluli is the Governor of Sus under the Sultan.

How do you know?—He catches and imprisons everything. He also takes taxes.

Has he ever taken taxes?—I don't know.

THE CHASE OF THE 'TOURMALINE.'

Captain Siebert of the *Hassani*, who refused to swear previously, now consented, permission by telegram having been received from Berlin. He said that the *Hassani* was a public vessel, belonging to the Sultan. He received orders to take the vessel to Arksis, on the coast of Sus, in January last. He had on board beside the crew fifty soldiers and some Moorish authorities. At Arksis he saw the little steamer not far off from the land.—My instructions were to bring up any steamer on the coast. We signalled to the little steamer to stop. We had something to tell. We were carrying the Moorish flag. We had also the Moorish pennant on the middle mast. We told the commander that he had to follow us to Mogador. I ordered forty soldiers to get on board the little steamer, and stay there until we arrived at the Moorish port. I told the soldiers to use arms only in self-defence. The boats were about 200 yards from the steamer when she steamed away. We followed her at full speed, but, our steamer being slower, she escaped. We had seen three tents on the shore, 200 metres from the place where the little steamer had been, and some natives. The tents were European. We returned to the place. The tents were broken down when I came.

After anchoring I saw Europeans ashore, and I told my boats to make them prisoners if they tried to go on board their own little steamer. I saw them through my glass. I made sure that there were Europeans among the natives. The boats patrolled that first day until it was dark. The little steamer came once so near that they called. But as they had refused to communicate when I sent the boat, I refused to do so now. I can't tell the story so plainly as I did five months ago. I saw people next on the beach, and ordered my people to go nearer and make sure what it was. When I was near, the natives on shore began to fire. Bullets dropped in the water. I called the boats back. They answered. The little steamer made one signal that the boat to the north should not come so near, or they would fire. Some shots were fired, but I cannot say whether by the little gun on board or from rifles, but at any rate they were fired from the vessel. I heard a shot fired from the *Hassani*, and went up on deck and asked the chief mate about it. He replied to my question. We then lifted our anchor, and she went away. She only went out of sight in the night. In the morning we saw her again. We signalled to the boats not to go too near when shot was fired. I sent a boat with a message to the Kaid Giluli to a place called Muley Abdallah. The Kaid was commander of the Sultan's troops. I saw the Kaid arrive at this place one afternoon preceded by lots of horsemen. The latter fired, had a fight with the natives, and pulled down tents. One horseman had a Moorish flag. Then all disappeared, natives and tents. Then the *Tourmaline* steamed to the south, and we followed her, but gave up the chase.

Witness went on to say that he landed at Arksis, went to the Kaid Giluli, and that natives arrived and made a report. On the following day these four prisoners and another were brought. He was quite certain about their identity. Witness identified the interpreter. 'Mr. Grey,' he continued, 'asked if I was captain of the *Hassani*. I said "Yes." He asked me questions, but I said it was better if he asked the Kaid.' Mr. Grey told the captain he did not understand being hunted and having to run away, and that their lives were in danger. He said to the Kaid that he came to do business with the natives, and that by treaty every British subject had the right to trade. He saw a gun like a quick-firing gun on board the steamer.'

By Counsel: My intention was to take the people.

Your instructions were to capture people there whether doing right or wrong?—My instructions were that no people had any business there.

And had Providence been favourable, you would have taken the vessel to Mogador?—Yes.

Did you say in the Kaid's tent that you would have sunk the vessel had you been able?—My instructions were to catch her. Nobody can tell what will happen in a row. It is a necessary precaution to have a rifle in going on land. Certainly I would not go myself.

By Mr. Grey: My instructions were to capture the boat, but not to sink her. I always told my men not to fire unless others fired on them. On Friday the natives waved a white robe. I thought it was a signal. The boats came near, and the natives fired. I took it they wanted to kill the men in my boat.

Would you be surprised to hear that a bullet from a boat went through the *jelaba* of a man?—I would never trust in a white flag when I am on the Sus coast.

'BEER FOR A FRIEND.'

How long have you been captain of the *Hassani*?—About three years.

Have you ever been suspended?—No.

Been accused of smuggling?—I took six cases of beer for a German friend at Tangier from a German steamer calling at Mogador. Then people said I had been engaged in contraband of war. Complaint was laid before Si' Mohammed Torres. A letter was sent from Mogador to Tangier, and Si' Mohammed Torres sent officers on board; but I was never suspended, and lived all the time on board. I never land goods without passing the Custom House.

Did you never land goods at Arksis?—Oh, you mean the twelve

bottles. I sent them for the prisoners because Beyerle told me they were suffering from thirst. It is not fair to bring up against me an act of kindness to you all.

But you sent Beyerle a bill for it all at Tangier?—Yes.

WAS IT THE 'TOURMALINE'?

Carl Sievers, chief officer of the *Hassani*, said the *Tourmaline* fired a shot which went over the bows of the *Hassani*.

Why do you call it the *Tourmaline*?—Because Beyerle wrote it down in my book.

Counsel: That's not evidence.

Attorney-General: Of course I will not take advantage of it.

Witness said he must suppose that the shot came from the vessel. He had served in the German army, and had experience.

But you did not see a shot fired from the land?—No, because I was looking at the *Tourmaline*.

You were looking the other way?—I could not look both ways at the same time.

No, of course not.

Cross-examined on the scene in the Kaid's tent, witness said he spoke to Beyerle in German. Counsel suggested that what was written in a book in the course of conversation in a language the other prisoners could not understand was not evidence.

Attorney-General: Is it conceivable the prisoners behind should not have seen it?

Counsel remarked that, the conversation being in a language the English prisoners did not understand, they could not be reasonably taken to have understood the object of the note in the book.

Judge: I am not inclined to let this document be put in. Surely you can find other means of proving the ship was the *Tourmaline*.

Attorney-General: You put me in a most difficult position.

Witness said he had been to Sus.

Would it be a reasonable precaution to have a gun?—At all events, one should have arms with one.

Would an escort of fifty or a hundred men be reasonable for a European?—I cannot tell.

If you went would you like an escort?—Yes.

The Attorney-General urged most strongly the objections of the Government to let out Mr. Grey on his own recognisances.

Counsel: If your lordship had been sitting in London, you would not even commit the prisoners on the evidence. There is not even a *primâ facie* case.

The Attorney-General applied to have the case adjourned for six weeks, as he had some more witnesses who were coming from Sus, and who, he understood, had not yet arrived. They might, he said, be here any day, but he would give a definite undertaking to go on, and complete the case whether they had arrived or not that day six weeks. Mr. Griffith opposed so long an adjournment, and the Attorney-General then agreed to accept a month. He, however, was instructed to oppose Mr. Grey's application to be released on his own recognisances, and the latter then argued that the Judge had no power to adjourn for a longer period than fourteen days, except in case of 'necessity,' which, he urged, had not been made out in this case. There had been ample time for the witnesses to have arrived from Sus, as the warrants under which the prisoners were arrested were issued on February 10 last.

Ultimately the Judge adjourned the case for a fortnight, expressing his opinion that he would not grant another adjournment if the Moorish Government witnesses still failed to appear, unless very strong reasons were shown.

At the renewed hearing, Acting Vice-Consul Madden gave evidence regarding the men signing articles. The Sbooya witnesses were then called. Some of them looked very frightened. They identified the prisoners as the men who formed part of the chain-gang which they saw on the way to the interior.

The first witness said: Guns were landed from a steamer by Europeans; they also landed cartridges. It is a sin to break oath. The prisoners gave their names to our tribe. We are in the hands of God. I am the Sultan's prisoner. I am only a chief of my own family. God alone knows; God sees all.

Each witness said he had not spoken previously about the case to anyone. On cross-examination all admitted having spoken with Mr. Irwin, the Drogman at the British Legation. They were kept without food for a long time at the commencement of their captivity, as Kaid Giluli was fighting. They all contradicted themselves when cross-examined. The last witness, a Moor, not a captive, refused to answer questions, saying he came to give evidence, not to quarrel; when pressed, said, 'I don't remember.' He told Grey he was afraid to give evidence for the defence because of the Kaid.

One of Kaid Giluli's men gave evidence that at the outset the prisoners had no food. He asked Giluli to remove their irons and treat them better.

Two Antwerp Customs officials gave evidence to the effect that it was within their knowledge that a quantity of guns and munitions of war were shipped at Antwerp on board a steamer flying the British flag. They could not identify any of the prisoners.

The proceedings terminated by his lordship declaring the prisoners guilty of illegally importing arms and ammunition.

The court sat again the following morning to pass sentences.

Asked whether he had anything to say why sentence should not be passed on him, Grey said that in the House of Commons Mr. Balfour admitted that British subjects had a right to travel in Morocco. He had come to Morocco with a camera and a diary. The camera was in the hands of the British Consul, the diary was safe in England. Beyond that he had committed no offence. He would read Lord Salisbury's opinion of the Moorish Government, as expressed in a public speech on May 22, 1891, but he was stopped by the Judge: 'You will do yourself no good by abusing the Moorish Government. I do not think it right or proper to listen to any abuse of this country.' Grey attempted to argue, remarking that he was merely quoting the words of a British Prime Minister, but the Judge again stopped him. Grey continued that he had suffered imprisonment since January. It was true that he had landed both powder and ball; but the powder was Vichy salts, and the balls were Beecham's pills. He urged that at any rate if he were found guilty the Judge would be of opinion that he had been punished enough.

Mr. Ellis Griffith, M.P., then, speaking in behalf of de Reya, Last, and Sabbah, said: Your lordship has chosen to disbelieve the statements of four Englishmen, and to take the statements of Moorish prisoners. In England no deposition of prisoners who turn Queen's evidence is worth anything unless corroborated. These Moors are practically witnesses of the Sultan—either in his pay or out of his prisons. I think it very unfortunate that trial by jury does not exist in this country, because I am certain that no English jury would have found these men guilty. I do not enter into the merits of the case, but I can bring circumstances which deserve your lordship's consideration. Does your lordship think these three men had any criminal intent? My friend says they came to Morocco for gain. What gain could they have? They were common sailors working for a miserable wage. Their crime has been obeying their orders. They are in prison because they have committed their duty. Would your lordship say it was a material circumstance that Beyerle went rejoicing home because he was a German while these men are tried because they are Englishmen? There are two theories of punishment in this case. The theory of the prosecution is that we are bound to please the Moorish Government. We know these prisoners have been handed up to the British Government on certain terms. (The Judge, interposing: I have no knowledge of any terms.) I could not abuse the Government of Morocco; I could not do it any harm, whatever I said. Your lordship has disbelieved these men's statement; the responsibility is upon your lordship. You have found them guilty; that ought to be sufficient satisfaction to the Moorish Government. But these men have never been convicted of any former offence; this present offence is of a purely technical character, and I ask your lordship not to send them to prison.

His eloquent speech was listened to in perfect silence, but many eyes were full. Mr. Griffith himself was much moved. It was expected that the Judge would interrupt him, but nothing of the kind happened. When Mr. Griffith sat down, the public, consisting chiefly of British subjects, broke out into applause.

The Judge was evidently much moved by the electricity in the air, and his voice quivered and his hand trembled as he addressed the prisoners. Addressing Grey, he said: You have set up the defence that you went to Sus in order to photograph. I have no doubt that you knew that this was an expedition for importing goods and material of war. I have no doubt you knew they were landed at Sus, and that you took part in it. You were intelligent enough not to let your intelligence outrun your zeal. This is a most serious case of smuggling. It is impossible to imagine a more serious one. It means that you were importing arms without the knowledge of the Moorish Government to slaughter human beings. This expedition was fitted out on a scale which showed what a serious offence was contemplated. You must take the consequences. You have been a long time in prison. I also take into consideration that you were unable to get bail. You still have to suffer. My sentence is that you be imprisoned as a first-class misdemeanant for four months.

The Judge, addressing Last and de Reya, said: I put you both in the same category. Your case is very different indeed. You are sailors on board a ship, and it is quite right of you to urge that you were in a subordinate position. At the same time you have been concerned in an illegal expedition, and you have to be punished. I take into account that you have been three months in custody, and that your offence is a technical one; but you acted foolishly, when you saw the arms taken on board at Antwerp and discovered that you had been taken from England on false pretences. Whatever the consequences were, you should have refused to remain with the ship. Had you suffered no imprisonment at all I should have made a difference between you and Grey. Your sentence is three weeks' imprisonment as first-class misdemeanants. Sabbah, your case is far more serious; you were the interpreter. You must have known what the *Tourmaline* was doing if anybody knew. I consider you to be in the forefront of this business, and let it be a lesson to you not to commit this offence again. There would be no such illegal expeditions if there were no interpreters. I pass upon you the same sentence as upon Grey.

A growl of disapproval ran through the crowded court, during which the Judge hurriedly left his seat on the bench.

THE CASE AGAINST MAJOR SPILSBURY.

Major Spilsbury was arrested in London in July, 1898, under the Fugitive Offenders Act, 'for that he, being a British subject, did, on or about January 13, 1898, on the Sus coast, within the territorial waters of the Empire of Morocco, in the steamship *Tourmaline*, with others to the number of three or more, unlawfully and riotously assemble and riotously make an assault upon certain soldiers of the Sultan of Morocco by firing on the Sultan's ship, named the *Hassani*, and participating in an assault on the boats belonging thereto, and at the time manned by such soldiers.'

He was brought up at Bow Street, and committed to take his trial at Tangier. On appeal to the Queen's Bench, the venue was changed to the Supreme Court at Gibraltar, the Lord Chief Justice expressing the opinion that he should be tried by a jury if possible. Mr. Justice

APPENDIX

Gatty maintained that he had no power to try the case except according to the Morocco Order in Council, which precluded a jury. A further appeal was therefore made—this time to the Privy Council—with the result that the case was returned to Judge Gatty to be tried before a jury at Gibraltar.

Many of the witnesses who gave evidence at Tangier appeared for the prosecution against Major Spilsbury, and gave similar testimony. For the defence, Captain Graham, of the *Tourmaline*, was called, and put in his log, which showed that the *Tourmaline* was five miles distant from shore when the signal-gun was fired.

Major Spilsbury, in his evidence, deposed that in June, 1897, he interviewed the Grand Vizier at the Moorish capital, and thence proceeded to Mogador, where he concluded a convention with the two principal Sus chiefs. This convention was also laid before Mr. Johnston, the British Vice-Consul at Mogador. Major Spilsbury returned to England in August, 1897, and communicated with the Globe Syndicate.—'The same warnings which were made to me,' said Major Spilsbury, 'were made to the directors of the syndicate, but none of them was arrested or deprived of his pension. Had I known that the territory belonged to the Sultan of Morocco, I would not have gone there.'

Mr. Ellis Griffith, for the defence, addressed the jury in an eloquent speech of two hours' duration. He stated that the witnesses for the prosecution were foreigners and Moorish subjects anxious to procure a conviction. He pointed to the discrepancies between the various witnesses, both here and in Tangier, especially in converting the *Tourmaline's* signal-gun into an assault, and he submitted that the prosecution was got up by the Foreign Office because Major Spilsbury had refused their advice. Major Spilsbury was amply justified in repelling the *Hassani*, whose objects were unlawful. On the evidence of the captain of the *Hassani*, Major Spilsbury was justified in taking reasonable defensive measures for himself and crew. No evidence in support of the alleged assault had been given.

The Attorney-General, addressing the jury for the Crown, contended that the defendant participated in a coast rebellion against the Sultan of Morocco, and was guilty of unlawful assembly on the Sus coast. The importation of arms and a cargo of quick-firing guns, and the ability to use them, coupled with his threats, amounted to an assault.

Chief Justice Gatty summed up strongly in favour of the Crown, pointing out that Major Spilsbury had practically admitted in correspondence the main issues of the case, but at the request of counsel for the defence he told the jury that the defendant had denied any participation in a land attack.

The jury then retired. They were absent for sixteen minutes, and on returning gave a verdict of 'Not guilty,' which was received with an unparalleled amount of applause for a court of justice. A large crowd followed Major Spilsbury to the Royal Hotel, cheering him all the way.

THE QUESTION OF MOROCCO.

THE 'TOURMALINE' 'RAID.'

(Special article which appeared in the London 'Daily News,' July 16, 1898, by the special correspondent at Tangier.)

Now that all the prisoners of the *Tourmaline* have been found guilty and sentenced, there is no harm in saying that an all-round acquittal would have inflicted the greatest injury on British influence in Morocco. On the other hand, the verdict of guilty has not heightened that influence, but has only prevented worse mischief. The *Tourmaline* expedition, like the Jameson raid, which it resembles on a smaller scale, placed England in the most false position with regard to 'her friend' the Sultan of Morocco. If Judge Gatty, who came over from Gibraltar, and under the Foreign Jurisdiction Act sat as judge and jury, acquitted the prisoners, all the rivals of British influence would have told the Sultan that Grey and the others had got off because they were only the agents of England, who was trying in an underhand way to break up Morocco. If the Judge found the prisoners guilty, the verdict would be attributed, not to a sense of justice, but to a fear of the Sultan. On leaving the court after the verdict, I was asked by Arabs, 'Has England won, or has the Sultan?' The Arabs have no idea that the judgment is based purely on points of law. They say: 'Allah i jal el baraka fy Sultan' ('God bless the Sultan'); 'Killifkûm bezzizminkum besh trabbu dekelnes del Compania Ingliz lemsha li Sùs' ('He has forced you against your will to punish the people of the Sus Company').

One of the chief branches of the import trade of Morocco is smuggling, done openly by means of bribery. Rifles are strictly prohibited, the Sultan fearing, with good reason, that his loyal subjects might become bad taxpayers as soon as they had arms in their hands. In fact, there is no case of any Moorish tribe ever paying the Sultan's taxes whenever they are able to resist payment. Arms are therefore prohibited, and yet they are imported wholesale in broad daylight at every Custom House. The *Tourmaline*, however, attempted the smuggling of arms on a larger scale than usual, and trusted not to the persuasiveness of bribes, but to the speed of her engines.

It was intended to sell them to the revolted tribes. The tribes, however, got the rifles without payment—in fact, stole them as they were lying on the shore. The Sultan's steamer *Hassani* then came on the scene, and chased the *Tourmaline*. The latter ran away, abandoning the men on shore to their fate. Grey, Last, de Reya, and Sabbah, and the German Beyerle, were taken by the tribes with whom they intended to trade. These tribes sold them to the Sultan, their enemy, for 400 dollars. The Sultan of Morocco claimed a right to punish the prisoners. He argued that the capitulations—*i.e.*, the rights of British courts to try British subjects for offences committed in Morocco—only applied to offences against individuals.

The *Tourmaline* prisoners had been guilty of an offence against his own sovereignty, and the treaty between the Queen and the Sultan did not apply. His case was a very plausible one. It was with the greatest difficulty he was persuaded to hand over the prisoners. The Dragoman of the British Legation in Tangier had to go all the way to Fez and see the Sultan. The latter said, 'If I give you the prisoners, the British Government must promise me that they shall be punished.'

Of course Lord Salisbury cannot undertake to say what a Judge will do; he could only promise to prosecute, and instruct the Attorney-General of Gibraltar to press upon the Judge the importance of the case. The prisoners were eventually surrendered, but with the utmost reluctance on the Sultan's part. Beyerle, being a German, was handed over to his Consul, who allowed him to escape. Escape is hardly the right word. Beyerle was told that he was a free man, and that he could ask heavy damages of the Sultan for false imprisonment and ill-treatment. One of the most remarkable features of the *Tourmaline* case is this difference of treatment between the Englishmen and the German. Mr. Ellis Griffith, M.P., counsel for the defence, made the most of it, but the point is one of sentiment. The German Government have refused to recognise the Sultan of Morocco's jurisdiction over the Sus coast; therefore Beyerle has committed no offence. There is something still more remarkable. While Grey, de Reya, Last, and Sabbah are imprisoned for selling arms to the Sus tribes, a German is now fitting out another expedition at Hamburg for the purpose of supplying these very tribes with rifles; and, according to common report at Tangier, we shall find a German protectorate over the Sus coast before many months are over. There is nothing to stop Germany; she has never recognised the Sultan's authority as we have done—apparently out of pure good-nature—and the Sultan can show no title founded on effective occupation. As Mr. Ellis Griffith showed, his sovereignty over the Sus coast is of the most shadowy and intermittent character, sometimes greater, sometimes less. No writer on Morocco has ever been able to draw the southern boundary of that empire.

How did we come to recognise the Sultan's misrule over this coast? Was it in return for some consideration, or is it another 'ignominious surrender'? Of course, pledged as we are, the British Government was unable to defend the *Tourmaline* prisoners, and, in fact, Sir Arthur Nicolson may be thought lucky to have obtained their surrender by the Sultan.

THE END.

October, 1899.

Mr. Edward Arnold's

New Books and Announcements.

Telegrams:
'Scholarly, London.'

37 Bedford Street,
Strand, London.

New and Forthcoming Books.

AUTOBIOGRAPHY OF DEAN MERIVALE,

With Selections from his Correspondence.
Edited by his Daughter, JUDITH ANNE MERIVALE.

One vol., with Photogravure Portrait, demy 8vo., 16s.

EXTRACT FROM THE PREFACE.

'My father's Autobiography and Letters were originally printed for private circulation among members of his own family and some of his more intimate friends. Many persons, however, beyond these limits having expressed an interest in the book, it is now offered to the public at large, with the addition of a few letters, addressed to Dean Lake, which have only recently come into my hands, and the omission of such others as seemed to possess more domestic than general interest.'

PASSAGES IN A WANDERING LIFE.

By THOMAS ARNOLD, M.A.

One vol., octavo.

The author of these reminiscences is the second son of the late Dr. Arnold of Rugby. His recollections of old school and college days refer to many well-known people. After leaving the University he emigrated to New Zealand, at the time when the country was first being settled, and his account of the early colonists and their life forms an interesting subject of comparison with more modern phases of development. Returning to England, he settled in Oxford, and his friendship with the late Cardinal Newman supplies materials for some valuable pages.

EASTERN ESSAYS.

By ——.

One vol., demy 8vo., 16s.

The work opens with an Introduction pointing out that Turkey is unlike any other country in Europe. Turks, Greeks, Servians, Bulgarians, etc., live side by side, quarrelling with one another, and each having their own language, religion, and customs, not in different districts as in Austria, but in the same district. The explanation of this is given only by history. The Turks in a way are a great Conservative force. They have preserved the strange medley which they found in Eastern Europe exactly as it was when they first appeared. The introduction is, therefore, followed by a historical sketch of the Balkan Peninsula before the capture of Constantinople. Then succeeds a chapter describing the Turk. What is the most important influence to which the Turk has been subjected?—Mohammedanism. An essay is devoted to this and another to the Eastern Orthodox Church. Further essays discuss Turkish Administration, and work out the details in chapters on the Greeks, the Slavs, the Albanians, etc. The whole work is extremely valuable and important, and will, it is hoped, be ready by Christmas.

TANGWEERA:

A Life among Gentle Savages.

By C. NAPIER BELL, M.I.C.E.

With numerous Illustrations from Sketches by the Author.
One vol., demy 8vo., cloth, 16s.

In this book are recounted the adventures of a youth passed among the Indians of the Mosquito Coast, and of the forests through which the rivers of that little-known region flow. The author was in childhood the playmate of the young Mosquito king, who at that time enjoyed British protection; and, speaking the language of the Indians like one of themselves, had every opportunity of observing their habits and dispositions, as well as those of the wild animals which he hunted in their company. The beautiful and curious birds of the Central American forests have been his favourite study. An introductory chapter gives some account of the manner in which the Mosquito region, destined perhaps to become better known to the rest of the world when the Nicaragua Canal is made, obtained and lost its position as a more or less fully recognised British dependency.

HUBERT HERVEY,
Student and Imperialist.
A Memoir.
By the Right Hon. EARL GREY,
LATE ADMINISTRATOR OF RHODESIA.

One vol., demy 8vo., with Photogravure Portrait and other Illustrations and a Map, 7s. 6d.

EXTRACT FROM THE PREFACE.

'My knowledge of Hubert Hervey during the last few years of his short career, when he was serving the British South Africa Chartered Company, first in their London offices, and subsequently in responsible administrative posts in Rhodesia, led me to regard him as one of the most chivalrous and high-minded men it has been my privilege to meet. Such was the wealth of Hervey's strong individuality that he left to all who were acquainted with him an abundant store of memories, varied, original and characteristic. But the attraction of his personality was rooted and grounded in the yet deeper strata of great principles and high ideals.'

CONTENTS.

Chap. I. Eton and Cambridge.—II. Dreams in London.—III. In the Chartered Company's Office.—IV. En route for the Frontier.—V. The Matabele War.—VI. At Work under Jameson.—VII. The Second Matabele War.—VIII. The Last Fight.

FINLAND AND THE TSARS.
By JOSEPH R. FISHER, B.A.,
BARRISTER-AT-LAW.

Demy 8vo., cloth.

The Tsar's Manifesto of February 15, 1899, and the New Military Law, are regarded in Finland as a virtual abolition of the constitutional liberties solemnly guaranteed to the Grand Duchy by the Tsar Alexander I., and confirmed by all his successors. Finland is one of the most interesting States in Europe, and one of the least known to Englishmen, and this book aims at giving such an account of the land and people as will enable readers to understand and to sympathize with the Finlanders in their present trouble. The author has had exceptional opportunities of becoming acquainted at first hand with the constitutional issues in dispute, and in 'Finland and the Tsars' English readers will for the first time have an authentic account of the origin and significance of the last stand for liberty under the Russian Crown.

IN MOORISH CAPTIVITY:

An Account of the 'Tourmaline' Expedition to Sus, 1897-1898.

By HENRY M. GREY,
A MEMBER OF THE EXPEDITION.

One vol., demy 8vo., Illustrated, 16s.

The author's 'hundred days in Morocco' formed probably as unpleasant an experience as has ever fallen to the lot of an Englishman. Trading in arms and ammunition with the subjects of a foreign potentate against his will is no sinecure, even if the potentate be only Sultan of Morocco. Deprived of the countenance of the British Government, the *Tourmaline* Expedition was unfortunate from the first. Mr. Grey graphically narrates the incidents of the voyage, the landing at Sus, and the treachery of the natives. Then followed the separation of the party by the Moorish cruiser *Hassani*, the author's capture and miserable march overland to Mogador, often in chains and subjected all the time to the grossest indignities.

CONTENTS.

Chap. I. An Ill-omened Start.—II. Across the Bay.—III. Island Nights' Entertainment.—IV. Dangerous Delay.—V. Arksis.—VI. The Indaba.—VII. The Council of the Forty.—VIII. Damp Days.—IX. Treachery at Work.—X. Naval Manœuvres.—XI. El Arabi to the Rescue.—XII. Attack on the Camp.—XIII. In the House of the Wolf.—XIV. El Arabi comes Ashore again.—XV. Before the Kaid.—XVI. The Beginning of the Raid.—XVII. Camp at Tlata.—XVIII. Giluli's Vow.—XIX. On the Road Northward.—XX. Still Northward.—XXI. Tisnit.—XXII. Good-bye to Giluli.—XXIII. Across the Border.—XXIV. An Unwelcome Invitation.—XXV. and XXVI. Life in the Kasbah.—XXVII. News at Last.—XXVIII. Delivered up.

ENGLAND IN EGYPT.

By SIR ALFRED MILNER, G.C.M.G.,
GOVERNOR OF THE CAPE COLONY.

With an additional chapter, bringing down the work to the end of 1898,

By CLINTON E. DAWKINS,
LATE FINANCIAL SECRETARY TO THE KHEDIVE, FINANCIAL MEMBER OF THE INDIAN COUNCIL, ETC.

Sixth Edition, revised, with Maps, 6s.

BRITISH MERCHANT SEAMEN IN SAN FRANCISCO.

By the REV. JAMES FELL.

Crown 8vo., cloth, 3s. 6d.

The author spent five years in San Francisco engaged in work connected with the Mission to Seamen, and during that period became thoroughly conversant at first hand with the dangers and difficulties that beset our sailors on the Pacific ports. His account of their troubles is extremely interesting, and written with a moderation that carries conviction.

SUMMARY OF CONTENTS.

San Francisco — The Bay — Discontent — Food — Ship's Tailors — Pocket Money — Crimping — Running Men Out — Allotment Notes — Paying off — Apprentices and Desertion — The Seamen's Institute — Sickness at Sea.

PEN AND PENCIL SKETCHES

OF

SHIPPING AND CRAFT

ALL ROUND THE WORLD.

By R. T. PRITCHETT,

MARINE PAINTER TO THE ROYAL THAMES YACHT CLUB.

With more than Fifty full-page Illustrations from Sketches by the Author, demy 8vo., 10s. 6d. net.

This beautiful volume is dedicated by permission to the Right Hon. Lord Brassey, K.C.B., 'in pleasant recollection of many thousand miles in the *Sunbeam*, R.Y.S.' Mr. Pritchett has, in fact, enjoyed unique opportunities of cruising all over the world, and his collection of sketches of shipping and craft of various types, made on the spot, in every latitude, cannot fail to interest all lovers of the sea. Among the craft sketched will be found an immense variety of vessels large and small, commencing with the Royal Yacht *Victoria and Albert*, and ending with Malay proas at the Murray Islands in the Antipodes. Mr. Pritchett's skill as a marine painter is well known, and great care has been taken to reproduce his exquisite drawings with fidelity. The descriptive letterpress is enriched with many an anecdote and yarn from the author's world-wide experiences.

ANIMAL LIFE AND INTELLIGENCE.

By C. LLOYD MORGAN, F.R.S.,
PRINCIPAL OF UNIVERSITY COLLEGE, BRISTOL; AUTHOR OF 'HABIT AND INSTINCT,' ETC.

A New Edition, entirely revised and largely rewritten, one vol., octavo.

In revising this work the author, besides bringing the discussion as far as possible abreast of the most recent work and thought on the subject with which it deals, introduces the results of his own later investigations. He also aims at increased unity of plan, by making the whole discussion subservient to his central theme—a consideration of the rôle which has been played by consciousness in organic evolution. With this end in view much of the treatment is recast, some of the sections which seemed too technical, too metaphysical, or too divergent from the central theme, have been cut out, while others having more direct bearing on that theme have been introduced. The author trusts that any delay in the reissue which may be occasioned by thorough revision may be held justifiable if the work be thus rendered more distinctive in plan and less inadequate in execution.

ENGLISH POLITICAL PHILOSOPHY:

An Exposition and Criticism of the Systems of Hobbes, Locke, Burke, Bentham, Mill and Maine.

By WILLIAM GRAHAM, M.A.,
PROFESSOR OF JURISPRUDENCE AND POLITICAL ECONOMY AT QUEEN'S COLLEGE, BELFAST.

One vol., octavo, 12s. net.

ESSENTIALS IN RELIGION:

Being Sermons delivered in Canterbury Cathedral.

By the REV. F. J. HOLLAND,
CANON OF CANTERBURY.

Crown 8vo, 3s. 6d.

CONTENTS.

I. Essentials and Non-essentials.—II. The Ever-blessed Trinity.—III. Faith which worketh by Love.—IV. The Divine Sacraments.—V. The Foundation of the Church.—VI. The Organization of the Church.

NEW WORKS OF FICTION.

RED POTTAGE.

By MARY CHOLMONDELEY,
AUTHOR OF 'DIANA TEMPEST,' ETC.

Crown 8vo., 6s.

THE COLOSSUS.

By MORLEY ROBERTS,
AUTHOR OF 'A SON OF EMPIRE,' ETC.

Crown 8vo., 6s.

A WINTER IN BERLIN.

By MARIE VON BUNSEN,
TRANSLATED BY MRS. STRATFORD DUGDALE.

Crown 8vo., 5s.

POEMS OF GEORGE CRABBE.

Selected and Edited by BERNARD HOLLAND, M.A.

With six Photogravure Illustrations elegantly printed and bound, one vol., crown 8vo., 6s.

POEMS AND SONGS OF DEGREES.

By ROBERT J. GLENCAIRN.

Crown 8vo., 5s. net.

Q'S TALES FROM SHAKESPEARE.

By A. J. QUILLER COUCH ('Q'),
AUTHOR OF 'DEAD MAN'S ROCK,' ETC.

One vol., crown 8vo., 6s.

It is hoped that this volume, which has been unfortunately delayed, will be ready this autumn. 'Q' proposes to treat the Historical Plays of Shakespeare as Lamb treated the Comedies, and Mr. Quiller Couch's charming pen will, it is believed, provide a worthy supplement to Lamb's classic volume.

REALLY AND TRULY!
Or, The Century for Babes.

Written by ERNEST AMES, and Illustrated by MRS. ERNEST AMES.

Fully and brilliantly coloured, price 3s. 6d.

This is the Christmas book for 1899, by the authors of 'The Patriot Baby,' which was so successful last year. Enlarged experience has helped them to make an even more attractive volume than the last. The rhymes and pictures deal each with some striking event of the century, from a comic standpoint.

A MORAL ALPHABET,
In Words of from One to Seven Syllables.

By H. B. and B. T. B.,
AUTHORS OF 'MORE BEASTS,' 'THE MODERN TRAVELLER,' ETC.

4to., fully Illustrated, with Cover in Colour, 3s. 6d.

We hardly know whether to describe this as a children's book. It is a return from the satire of 'The Modern Traveller' to the authors' original and simpler style, as exemplified in 'The Bad Child's Book of Beasts' and 'More Beasts,' and should be appreciated by all who enjoyed those volumes.

RUTHLESS RHYMES FOR HEARTLESS HOMES.

The Verses by COLONEL D. STREAMER; the Pictures by G—— H——.

One vol., oblong crown 4to., 3s. 6d.

This volume, which is dedicated by permission to Mrs. W. H. Grenfell, will, it is hoped, prove amusing to parents and others. To those who are not afraid of their children imitating the sad examples suggested by the Ruthless, Heartless Rhymes we would heartily recommend the book.

CONVERSATIONAL OPENINGS AND ENDINGS.

Some Hints for Playing the Game of Small Talk and other Society Pastimes.

By Mrs. HUGH BELL.

Square 8vo., with Cover designed by Mrs. Ames, 2s. 6d.

This little book was printed as a pamphlet some years ago, and the small edition was soon exhausted. Mrs. Bell has now entirely revised the original and enlarged it to its present size. The openings are constructed on the plan of Chess Openings. Among the earlier numbers are the Diner Out's Opening, the Aunt's Friend's Opening, the Returned Traveller's Opening, etc.

PARIS:

A History of the City from the Earliest Times to the Present Day.

By HILAIRE BELLOC,
AUTHOR OF 'DANTON,' ETC.

One vol., Illustrated.

ABSOLUTELY UNIQUE GIFTS FOR CHRISTMAS.

WILD FLOWERS FROM PALESTINE.
Gathered and Pressed in Palestine.
By HARVEY B. GREENE.

With an Introduction by the Very REV. S. REYNOLDS HOLE, DEAN OF ROCHESTER.

Cloth elegant, 16mo., 4s. 6d.

This unique volume contains seventeen specimens of pressed wild flowers from the Holy Land, with appropriate descriptive letterpress. Mr. Greene has made three journeys to Palestine, collecting its floral treasures with the willing assistance of a large number of native Arabs. 'The flowers,' says Mr. Greene, 'are richer and more precious than all others in the world. More precious not because more perfect, not because sweeter, but because the Lord Jesus Christ while here upon earth saw and loved these same flowers, and used them to illustrate eternal truths.'

PRESSED FLOWERS FROM THE HOLY LAND.
Gathered and Pressed in Palestine.
By HARVEY B. GREENE,
With an Introduction by DEAN HOLE.

Tastefully bound, 32mo., paper, 2s. 6d.

This is a smaller souvenir, with twelve pressed flowers, collected as already mentioned. The flowers are beautifully pressed, and the brief accounts of them are very interesting, giving references to passages in the Bible where they are mentioned.

A FLOWER FROM THE CHRIST LAND.
A lovely Christmas Card containing a Single Pressed Flower.
Price 6d.

'Consider the lilies of the field, how they grow.'

PUBLICATIONS OF THE ESSEX HOUSE PRESS.

The Guild of Handicraft has purchased from the trustees of the late Mr. William Morris the plant and presses of the Kelmscott Press, and has made arrangements with different members of Mr. Morris's staff for permanent employment at Essex House, with a view to their ultimate election into the Guild. It is the hope of the Guild by this means to continue in some measure the tradition of good printing and fine workmanship which William Morris revived.

The Kelmscott Press blocks being deposited at the British Museum, and the types not for sale, the books to be issued from the Essex House Press will be in a new type to be designed by Mr. C. R. Ashbee. As this type will not be ready for some time, one of the best of the eighteenth-century Caslon founts has been purchased, and in this the first two or three books are being produced.

THE TREATISES OF BENVENUTO CELLINI ON METAL WORK AND SCULPTURE.

Translated by C. R. ASHBEE.

Price 35s. net.

This volume is richly illustrated with reproductions of Cellini's works, and is the first translation from the original. To metal workers, students and artists it cannot fail to be of great value and interest.

THE HYMN OF BARDAISAN:

The First Christian Poem rendered into English Verse from the Original Syriac.

By F. CRAWFORD BURKITT, of Trinity College, Cambridge.

The edition is limited to 300 copies, of which 250 only are for sale at 7s. 6d. net, and 25 will be issued in special bindings, from £1 1s. to £3 3s. extra, executed by Mr. Douglas Cockerell, and designed some by him and some by Mr. C. R. Ashbee.

BUNYAN'S PILGRIM'S PROGRESS.

This will be the next volume from the Essex House Press. The edition will be limited to 750 copies, of which 50 will be in special binding as above, and the rest in white vellum, price £1 10s. net.

Among other works in preparation by the Essex House Press are: 'The Poems of Shakespeare,' 'The Book of Psalms,' 'The Vision of Piers Ploughman,' Sir Thomas Hoby's translation (Elizabethan) of Baldassare Castiglione's 'Courtier,' Froissart's 'Chronicles,' 'The Poems of Burns,' etc.

ENGLAND IN THE NINETEENTH CENTURY.

By C. W. OMAN,
FELLOW OF ALL SOULS' COLLEGE, OXFORD; AUTHOR OF 'A HISTORY OF ENGLAND'; 'THE ART OF WAR IN THE MIDDLE AGES,' ETC.

One volume, crown 8vo., 3s. 6d.

This volume supplies a much felt need in providing a lucid history of the events of our own time within a moderate compass, and brought down to the last year of the nineteenth century.

THE STORY OF ENGLAND.

By E. S. SYMES,
AUTHOR OF 'THE STORY OF LANCASHIRE'; 'THE STORY OF LONDON,' ETC.

Fully Illustrated, crown 8vo., 2s. 6d.

This is a short history for boys and girls, intended as an introduction to the chief events of 'our island story,' told in such a way as to attract rather than repel the young readers. Special attention is called to the fine series of portraits from Lodge's famous collection and other authentic sources.

A SERIES OF LOCAL HISTORIES.

The following volumes are now ready. They are intended to introduce young people to what is best worth knowing in connection with their own part of the kingdom, and give the history, geography, and industrial progress of the locality, together with many interesting legends, stories, and biographies of famous people. The illustrations have been very carefully selected, and help to make the volumes most attractive:

Price 1s. 6d. each.

THE STORY OF LONDON.	THE STORY OF LANCASHIRE.
THE STORY OF THE MIDLANDS.	THE STORY OF YORKSHIRE.
THE STORY OF WALES.	THE STORY OF THE WEST COUNTRY,
THE STORY OF SCOTLAND.	[*In the Press.*

AFRICA, AS SEEN BY ITS EXPLORERS.

Edited by E. J. WEBB, M.A.

Illustrated, crown 8vo., 2s.

This is a collection of extracts from the narratives of African exploration and discovery from Herodotus to Stanley, and gives an interesting record of the process of unfolding the Dark Continent to civilization.

PICTURES OF GEOGRAPHICAL SUBJECTS.

Edited by W. L. WYLLIE, A.R.A.

A magnificent and entirely new series in chromolithography, from original designs by Mr. W. L. Wyllie, Mr. C. W. Wyllie and Mr. G. C. Kerr.

The size of each picture is 30 × 20 inches; they are admirably adapted for framing, and will give constant pleasure on the walls.

Price 1s. 6d. each, net.

Portsmouth Harbour.	Mount Vesuvius.
The Land's End, Cornwall.	The Pyramids.
Mont Blanc.	Hong Kong.
The Rhone Glacier.	In the Arctic Regions.

It will be observed that each picture represents some typical feature in geography: thus the picture of Vesuvius shows a volcano, the Land's End a cape, etc.

LECTURES ON THEORETICAL AND PHYSICAL CHEMISTRY.

PART I.—CHEMICAL DYNAMICS.

By Dr. J. H. VAN 'T. HOFF,
Professor at the University of Berlin.

One vol., demy 8vo., 12s. net.

A MANUAL OF HUMAN PHYSIOLOGY.

By LEONARD HILL, M.B.,
Lecturer on Physiology at the London Hospital Medical School, and Hunterian Professor Royal College Surgeons; Author of 'Physiology and Pathology of the Cerebral Circulation.'

Nearly 500 pages and 170 Illustrations, 6s.

A MANUAL OF PHYSIOGRAPHY.

By ANDREW HERBERTSON, F.R.G.S.,
Assistant Reader in Geography at the University of Oxford.

Fully Illustrated.   [*In the Press.*

PHYSICAL CHEMISTRY.

By Dr. R. A. LEHFELDT,
Professor of Physics at the East London Technical College.

One vol., crown 8vo.   [*In the Press.*

BIOGRAPHY AND REMINISCENCES.

Alexander. RECOLLECTIONS OF A HIGHLAND SUBALTERN, during the Campaigns of the 93rd Highlanders in India, under Colin Campbell, Lord Clyde, in 1857-1859. By Lieutenant-Colonel W. GORDON ALEXANDER. Illustrations and Maps. Demy 8vo., cloth, 16s.

Arnold. PASSAGES IN A WANDERING LIFE. By THOMAS ARNOLD, M.A. (See page 1.)

Boyle. THE RECOLLECTIONS OF THE DEAN OF SALISBURY. By the Very Rev. G. D. BOYLE, Dean of Salisbury. With Photogravure Portrait. One vol., demy 8vo., cloth, 16s.

Clough. A MEMOIR OF ANNE J. CLOUGH, Principal of Newnham College, Cambridge. By her Niece, BLANCHE A. CLOUGH. With Portraits. 8vo., 12s. 6d.

De Vere. RECOLLECTIONS OF AUBREY DE VERE. Third Edition, with Portrait. Demy 8vo., 16s.

Hare. MARIA EDGEWORTH: her Life and Letters. Edited by AUGUSTUS J. C. HARE, Author of 'The Story of Two Noble Lives,' etc. With Portraits. Two vols., crown 8vo., 16s. net.

Hole. THE MEMORIES OF DEAN HOLE. By the Very Rev. S. REYNOLDS HOLE, Dean of Rochester. With Illustrations from Sketches by Leech and Thackeray. Popular Edition. Crown 8vo., 6s.

Hole. MORE MEMORIES: Being Thoughts about England spoken in America. By Dean HOLE. With Frontispiece. Demy 8vo., 16s.

Hole. A LITTLE TOUR IN AMERICA. By Dean HOLE. Illustrated. Demy 8vo., 16s.

Hole. A LITTLE TOUR IN IRELAND. By 'OXONIAN' (Dean HOLE). Illustrated by JOHN LEECH. Large crown 8vo., 6s.

Holland. LETTERS OF MARY SIBYLLA HOLLAND. Selected and edited by her Son, BERNARD HOLLAND. Second Edition. Crown 8vo., 7s. 6d. net.

Jowett. BENJAMIN JOWETT, MASTER OF BALLIOL. A Personal Memoir. By the Hon. L. A. TOLLEMACHE. Third Edition, with portrait. Cloth, 3s. 6d.

Le Fanu. SEVENTY YEARS OF IRISH LIFE. By the late W. R. LE FANU. Popular Edition. Crown 8vo., 6s.

Macdonald. THE MEMOIRS OF THE LATE SIR JOHN A. MACDONALD, G.C.B., First Prime Minister of Canada. Edited by JOSEPH POPE, his Private Secretary. With Portraits. Two vols., demy 8vo., 32s.

Merivale. THE AUTOBIOGRAPHY OF DEAN MERIVALE. With Selections from his Correspondence. (See page 1.)

Morley. THE LIFE OF HENRY MORLEY, LL.D., Professor of English Literature at University College, London. By the Rev. H. S. SOLLY, M.A. With two Portraits. 8vo., 12s. 6d.

Mott. A MINGLED YARN. The Autobiography of EDWARD SPENCER MOTT (NATHANIEL GUBBINS). Author of 'Cakes and Ale,' etc. Large crown 8vo., 12s. 6d.

Pigou. PHASES OF MY LIFE. By the Very Rev. FRANCIS PIGOU, Dean of Bristol. Fifth Edition. With Portrait. Demy 8vo., 16s.

Rochefort. THE ADVENTURES OF MY LIFE. By HENRI ROCHEFORT. Second Edition. Two vols., large crown 8vo., 25s.

Roebuck. THE AUTOBIOGRAPHY AND LETTERS of the Right Hon. JOHN ARTHUR ROEBUCK, Q.C., M.P. Edited by ROBERT EADON LEADER. With two Portraits. Demy 8vo., 16s.

Simpson. MANY MEMORIES OF MANY PEOPLE. By Mrs. M. C. SIMPSON (née Nassau Senior). Fourth Edition. Demy 8vo., 16s.

Stevenson. ROBERT LOUIS STEVENSON. By WALTER RALEIGH, Professor of English Literature at University College, Liverpool. Second Edition. Crown 8vo., cloth, 3s. 6d.

Tollemache. TALKS WITH MR. GLADSTONE. By the Hon. L. A. TOLLEMACHE. With Portrait. Cloth, 6s.

Toynbee. ARNOLD TOYNBEE: a Reminiscence. By SIR ALFRED MILNER, G.C.M.G. Crown 8vo., paper, 1s.

Twining. RECOLLECTIONS OF LIFE AND WORK. Being the Autobiography of LOUISA TWINING. One vol., 8vo., cloth, 15s.

THEOLOGY.

Bell. THE NAME ABOVE EVERY OTHER NAME; and other Sermons. By the late Canon BELL, D.D., formerly Rector of Cheltenham, and Hon. Canon of Carlisle. Crown 8vo., 5s.

Bell. THE GOSPEL AND THE POWER OF GOD. Sermons preached by Canon BELL. Crown 8vo., 3s. 6d.

Hole. ADDRESSES TO WORKING MEN from Pulpit and Platform. By Dean HOLE. Crown 8vo., 6s.

Hole. FAITH WHICH WORKETH BY LOVE. A Sermon preached after the funeral of the late Duchess of Teck. Vellum, 1s. net.

Holland. ESSENTIALS IN RELIGION. By Canon HOLLAND. (See page 6.)

Onyx. A REPORTED CHANGE IN RELIGION. By ONYX. Crown 8vo., 3s. 6d.

HISTORY.

Benson and Tatham. MEN OF MIGHT. Studies of Great Characters. By A. C. BENSON, M.A., and H. F. W. TATHAM, M.A., Assistant Masters at Eton College. Third Edition. Crown 8vo., cloth, 3s. 6d.

Gardner. FRIENDS OF THE OLDEN TIME. By ALICE GARDNER, Lecturer in History at Newnham College, Cambridge. Second Edition. Illustrated, 2s. 6d.

Gardner. ROME: THE MIDDLE OF THE WORLD. By ALICE GARDNER. Illustrated, 3s. 6d.

Lane. CHURCH AND REALM IN STUART TIMES. A Course of Ten Illustrated Lectures arranged to accompany a Series of 600 Lantern Illustrations. By the Rev. C. ARTHUR LANE, Author of 'Illustrated Notes on English Church History.' One vol., crown 8vo., 3s. 6d. net.

Milner. ENGLAND IN EGYPT. By Sir ALFRED MILNER. (See page 4.)

Oman. A HISTORY OF ENGLAND. By CHARLES OMAN, Fellow of All Souls' College, and Lecturer in History at New College, Oxford; Author of 'Warwick the Kingmaker,' 'A History of Greece,' etc. Crown 8vo., cloth, 5s.

Also in two parts, 3s. each. Part I., to A.D. 1603; Part II., from 1603 to present time. And in three Divisions: Div. I., to 1307, 2s.; Div. II., 1307-1688, 2s.; Div. III., 1688 to present time, 2s. 6d.

Oman. ENGLAND IN THE NINETEENTH CENTURY. By CHARLES OMAN. (See page 12.)

Ransome. THE BATTLES OF FREDERICK THE GREAT. Extracted from Carlyle's 'History of Frederick the Great,' and edited by the late CYRIL RANSOME, M.A., Professor of History at the Yorkshire College, Leeds. With numerous Illustrations by ADOLPH MENZEL. Square 8vo., 3s. 6d.

Rendel. NEWCASTLE-ON-TYNE: Its Municipal Origin and Growth. By the HON. DAPHNE RENDEL. Illustrated. Crown 8vo., 3s. 6d.

Symes. THE STORY OF ENGLAND. By E. S. SYMES. (See page 12.)

LITERATURE AND CRITICISM.

Bell. KLEINES HAUSTHEATER. Fifteen Little Plays in German for Children. By Mrs. HUGH BELL. Crown 8vo., cloth, 2s.

Butler. SELECT ESSAYS OF SAINTE BEUVE. Chiefly bearing on English Literature. Translated by A. J. BUTLER, Translator of 'The Memoirs of Baron Marbot.' One vol., 8vo., cloth, 5s. net.

Collingwood. THORSTEIN OF THE MERE: a Saga of the Northmen in Lakeland. By W. G. COLLINGWOOD, Author of 'Life of John Ruskin,' etc. With Illustrations. Price 10s. 6d.

Cook. THE DEFENSE OF POESY, otherwise known as AN APOLOGY FOR POETRY. By Sir PHILIP SIDNEY. Edited by A. S. COOK, Professor of English Literature in Yale University. Crown 8vo., cloth, 3s. 6d.

Cook. A DEFENCE OF POETRY. By PERCY BYSSHE SHELLEY. Edited, with Notes and Introduction, by Professor A. S. COOK. Crown 8vo., cloth, 2s. 6d.

Davidson. A HANDBOOK TO DANTE. By GIOVANNI A. SCARTAZZINI. Translated from the Italian, with Notes and Additions, by THOMAS DAVIDSON, M.A. Crown 8vo., cloth, 5s.

Ellacombe. THE PLANT-LORE AND GARDEN-CRAFT OF SHAKESPEARE. By HENRY N. ELLACOMBE, M.A., Vicar of Bitton. Illustrated by Major E. B. RICKETTS. Large crown 8vo., 10s. 6d.

Fleming. THE ART OF READING AND SPEAKING. By the Rev. Canon FLEMING, Vicar of St. Michael's, Chester Square. Third Edition. Cloth, 3s. 6d.

Garnett. SELECTIONS IN ENGLISH PROSE FROM ELIZABETH TO VICTORIA. Chosen and arranged by JAMES M. GARNETT, M.A., LL.D. 700 pages, large crown 8vo., cloth, 6s. 6d.

Goschen. THE CULTIVATION AND USE OF IMAGINATION. By the Right Hon. GEORGE JOACHIM GOSCHEN. Crown 8vo., cloth, 2s. 6d.

Harrison. STUDIES IN EARLY VICTORIAN LITERATURE. By FREDERIC HARRISON, M.A., Author of 'The Choice of Books,' etc. New and Cheaper Edition. Large crown 8vo., cloth, 3s. 6d.

Hudson. THE LIFE, ART AND CHARACTERS OF SHAKESPEARE. By H. N. HUDSON, LL.D. 2 vols., large crown 8vo., cloth, 17s.

Kuhns. THE TREATMENT OF NATURE IN DANTE'S 'DIVINA COMMEDIA.' By L. OSCAR KUHNS, Professor in Wesleyan University, Middleton, U.S.A. Crown 8vo., cloth, 5s.

Lang. LAMB'S ADVENTURES OF ULYSSES. With an Introduction by ANDREW LANG. Square 8vo., cloth, 1s. 6d. Also the Prize Edition, gilt edges, 2s.

Maud. WAGNER'S HEROES. By CONSTANCE MAUD. Illustrated by H. GRANVILLE FELL. Third Edition, crown 8vo., 5s.

Maud. WAGNER'S HEROINES. By Constance Maud. Illustrated by W. T. Maud. Crown 8vo., 5s.

Raleigh. STYLE. By Walter Raleigh, Professor of English Literature at University College, Liverpool. Third Edition, crown 8vo., 5s.

Reynolds. STUDIES ON MANY SUBJECTS. By the Rev. S. H. Reynolds. One vol., demy 8vo., 10s. 6d.

Rodd. THE CUSTOMS AND LORE OF MODERN GREECE. By Sir Rennel Rodd, K.C.M.G. With seven full-page Illustrations. 8vo., cloth, 8s. 6d.

Schelling. BEN JONSON'S TIMBER. Edited by Professor F. E. Schelling. Crown 8vo., cloth, 3s. 6d.

VARIOUS QUILLS. A Collection of Poems, Stories and Essays contributed by the Members of a Literary Club. Crown 8vo., 5s.

POETRY.

Bell. DIANA'S LOOKING-GLASS, AND OTHER POEMS. By the late Rev. Canon Bell, D.D., Rector of Cheltenham, and Hon. Canon of Carlisle. Crown 8vo., cloth, 5s. net.

Bell. POEMS OLD AND NEW. By Canon Bell, D.D. Cloth, 7s. 6d.

Collins. A TREASURY OF MINOR BRITISH POETRY. Selected and arranged, with Notes, by J. Churton Collins, M.A. Handsomely bound, crown 8vo., 7s. 6d.

Glencairn, R. J. POEMS AND SONGS OF DEGREES. (See page 7.)

Gummere. OLD ENGLISH BALLADS. Selected and Edited by Francis B. Gummere, Professor of English in Haverford College, U.S.A. Crown 8vo., cloth, 5s. 6d.

Holland. VERSES. By Maud Holland (Maud Walpole). Crown 8vo., 3s. 6d.

Rodd. BALLADS OF THE FLEET. By Sir Rennel Rodd, K.C.M.G. Crown 8vo., cloth, 6s.

BY THE SAME AUTHOR.

FEDA, AND OTHER POEMS, CHIEFLY LYRICAL. With etched Frontispiece. Crown 8vo., cloth, 6s.

THE UNKNOWN MADONNA, AND OTHER POEMS. With Frontispiece by Richmond. Crown 8vo., cloth, 5s.

THE VIOLET CROWN, AND SONGS OF ENGLAND. With Photogravure Frontispiece. Crown 8vo., cloth, 5s.

FICTION.

About. TRENTE ET QUARANTE. Translated by Lord NEWTON. Crown 8vo., 3s. 6d.

'Adalet.' HADJIRA: A Turkish Love Story. By 'ADALET.' One vol., crown 8vo., cloth, 6s.

Adderley. STEPHEN REMARX. The Story of a Venture in Ethics. By the Hon. and Rev. JAMES ADDERLEY, formerly Head of the Oxford House and Christ Church Mission, Bethnal Green. Twenty-second Thousand. Small 8vo., elegantly bound, 3s. 6d. Also, in paper cover, 1s.

Adderley. PAUL MERCER. A Tale of Repentance among Millions. By the Hon. and Rev. JAMES ADDERLEY. Third Edition. One vol., crown 8vo., cloth, 3s. 6d.

Bunsen. A WINTER IN BERLIN. By MARIE VON BUNSEN. (See page 7.)

Burneside. THE DELUSION OF DIANA. By MARGARET BURNESIDE. Second Edition, crown 8vo., 6s.

Charleton. NETHERDYKE. By R. J. CHARLETON. One vol., crown 8vo., 6s.

Cherbuliez. THE TUTOR'S SECRET. (Le Secret du Précepteur.) Translated from the French of VICTOR CHERBULIEZ. One vol., crown 8vo., cloth, 6s.

Cholmondeley. A DEVOTEE: An Episode in the Life of a Butterfly. By MARY CHOLMONDELEY, Author of 'Diana Tempest,' 'The Danvers Jewels,' etc. Crown 8vo., 3s. 6d.

Cholmondeley. RED POTTAGE. By MARY CHOLMONDELEY. (See page 7.)

Coleridge. THE KING WITH TWO FACES. By M. E. COLERIDGE. Eighth Edition, crown 8vo., 6s.

Collingwood. THE BONDWOMAN. A Story of the Northmen in Lakeland. By W. G. COLLINGWOOD, Author of 'Thorstein of the Mere,' 'The Life and Work of John Ruskin,' etc. Cloth, 16mo., 3s. 6d.

Crane. GEORGE'S MOTHER. By STEPHEN CRANE, Author of 'The Red Badge of Courage.' Cloth, 2s.

Dunmore. ORMISDAL. A Novel. By the EARL OF DUNMORE, F.R.G.S., Author of 'The Pamirs.' One vol., crown 8vo., cloth, 6s.

Edwards. THE MERMAID OF INISH-UIG. By R. W. K. EDWARDS. Crown 8vo., 3s. 6d.

Falkner. MOONFLEET. By J. Meade Falkner. Second Edition, crown 8vo., 6s.

Ford. ON THE THRESHOLD. By Isabella O. Ford, Author of 'Miss Blake of Monkshalton.' One vol., crown 8vo., 3s. 6d.

Gaunt. DAVE'S SWEETHEART. By Mary Gaunt. One vol., 8vo., cloth, 3s. 6d.

Hall. FISH TAILS AND SOME TRUE ONES. Crown 8vo., 6s.

Harrison. THE FOREST OF BOURG-MARIE. By S. Frances Harrison (Seranus). Crown 8vo., 6s.

Hutchinson. THAT FIDDLER FELLOW. A Tale of St. Andrews. By Horace G. Hutchinson, Author of 'My Wife's Politics,' 'Golf,' 'Creatures of Circumstance,' etc. Crown 8vo., cloth, 2s. 6d.

Knutsford. THE MYSTERY OF THE RUE SOLY. Translated by Lady Knutsford from the French of H. de Balzac. Crown 8vo., cloth, 3s. 6d.

Lighthall. THE FALSE CHEVALIER. By W. D. Lighthall. Crown 8vo., 6s.

McNulty. MISTHER O'RYAN. An Incident in the History of a Nation. By Edward McNulty. Small 8vo., elegantly bound, 3s. 6d.

McNulty. SON OF A PEASANT. By Edward McNulty. One vol., crown 8vo., 6s.

Montrésor. WORTH WHILE. By F. F. Montrésor, Author of 'Into the Highways and Hedges.' Crown 8vo., cloth, 2s. 6d.

Oxenden. A REPUTATION FOR A SONG. By Maud Oxenden. Crown 8vo., 6s.

Oxenden. INTERLUDES. By Maud Oxenden. Crown 8vo., 6s.

Pinsent. JOB HILDRED. By Ellen F. Pinsent, Author of 'Jenny's Case.' One vol., crown 8vo., 3s. 6d.

Roberts. THE COLOSSUS. By Morley Roberts. (See page 7.)

Spinner. A RELUCTANT EVANGELIST, and other Stories. By Alice Spinner, Author of 'Lucilla,' 'A Study in Colour,' etc. Crown 8vo., 6s.

Williams. THE BAYONET THAT CAME HOME. By N. Wynne Williams. Crown 8vo., 3s. 6d.

TRAVEL AND SPORT.

Bell. TANGWEERA. By C. N. BELL. (See page 2.)

Beynon. WITH KELLY TO CHITRAL. By Lieutenant W. G. L. BEYNON, D.S.O., 3rd Ghoorkha Rifles, Staff Officer to Colonel Kelly with the Relief Force. With Maps, Plans, and Illustrations. Second Edition. Demy 8vo., 7s. 6d.

Bottome. A SUNSHINE TRIP: GLIMPSES OF THE ORIENT. Extracts from Letters written by MARGARET BOTTOME. With Portrait, elegantly bound, 4s. 6d.

Bradley. HUNTING REMINISCENCES OF FRANK GILLARD WITH THE BELVOIR HOUNDS, 1860-1896. Recorded and Illustrated by CUTHBERT BRADLEY. 8vo., 15s.

Bull. THE CRUISE OF THE 'ANTARCTIC' TO THE SOUTH POLAR REGIONS. By H. J. BULL, a member of the Expedition. With Frontispiece by W. L. WYLLIE, A.R.A., and numerous full-page Illustrations by W. G. BURN-MURDOCH. Demy 8vo., 15s.

Burton. TROPICS AND SNOWS: a Record of Sport and Adventure in Many Lands. By CAPTAIN R. G. BURTON, Indian Staff Corps. Illustrated, demy 8vo., 16s.

Chapman. WILD NORWAY. By ABEL CHAPMAN, Author of 'Wild Spain.' With Illustrations by CHARLES WHYMPER. Demy 8vo., 16s.

Custance. RIDING RECOLLECTIONS AND TURF STORIES. By HENRY CUSTANCE, three times winner of the Derby. One vol., crown 8vo., cloth, 2s. 6d.

Freshfield. THE EXPLORATION OF THE CAUCASUS. By DOUGLAS W. FRESHFIELD, F.R.G.S., lately President of the Alpine Club. Illustrated with Photogravures and Maps, 2 vols., 4to., £3 3s. net.

Gleichen. WITH THE BRITISH MISSION TO MENELIK, 1897. By Count GLEICHEN, Grenadier Guards, Intelligence Officer to the Mission. Illustrated, demy 8vo., 16s.

Gordon. PERSIA REVISITED. With Remarks on H.I.M. Mozuffered-Din Shah, and the Present Situation in Persia (1896). By General Sir T. E. GORDON, K.C.I.E., C.B., C.S.I. Formerly Military Attaché and Oriental Secretary to the British Legation at Teheran, Author of 'The Roof of the World,' etc. Demy 8vo., with full-page Illustrations, 10s. 6d.

Grey. IN MOORISH CAPTIVITY. By H. M. GREY. (See page 4.)

Hall. FISH TAILS AND SOME TRUE ONES. By BRADNOCK HALL, Author of 'Rough Mischance.' With an original Etching by the Author, and twelve full-page Illustrations by T. H. McLACHLAN. Crown 8vo., 6s.

Macdonald. SOLDIERING AND SURVEYING IN BRITISH EAST AFRICA. By Major J. R. MACDONALD, R.E. Fully Illustrated. Demy 8vo., 16s.

McNab. ON VELDT AND FARM, IN CAPE COLONY, BECHUANALAND, NATAL, AND THE TRANSVAAL. By FRANCES MCNAB. With Map. Second Edition. Crown 8vo., 300 pages, 3s. 6d.

Pike. THROUGH THE SUB-ARCTIC FOREST. A Record of a Canoe Journey for 4,000 miles, from Fort Wrangel to the Pelly Lakes, and down the Yukon to the Behring Sea. By WARBURTON PIKE, Author of 'The Barren Grounds of Canada.' With Illustrations by CHARLES WHYMPER, from Photographs taken by the Author, and a Map. Demy 8vo., 16s.

Pollok. FIFTY YEARS' REMINISCENCES OF INDIA. By Lieut.-Colonel POLLOK, Author of 'Sport in Burmah.' Illustrated by A. C. CORBOULD. Demy 8vo., 16s.

Portal. THE BRITISH MISSION TO UGANDA. By the late Sir GERALD PORTAL, K.C.M.G. Edited by Sir RENNEL RODD, K.C.M.G. With an Introduction by the Right Honourable Lord CROMER, G.C.M.G. Illustrated from Photos taken during the Expedition by Colonel Rhodes. Demy 8vo., 21s.

Portal. MY MISSION TO ABYSSINIA. By the late Sir Gerald H. PORTAL, C.B. With Map and Illustrations. Demy 8vo., 15s.

Reid. FROM PEKING TO PETERSBURG. A Journey of Fifty Days in 1898. By ARNOT REID. With Portrait and Map. Large crown 8vo., 7s. 6d.

Slatin and **Wingate.** FIRE AND SWORD IN THE SUDAN. By Sir RUDOLF SLATIN PASHA, K.C.M.G. Translated and Edited by Colonel Sir F. R. WINGATE, K.C.M.G. Fully Illustrated. Popular Edition. 6s. Also a few copies of the Original Edition. Demy 8vo., 21s.

Smith. THROUGH UNKNOWN AFRICAN COUNTRIES. By A. DONALDSON SMITH, M.D., F.R.G.S. With Illustrations by A. D. MCCORMICK and CHARLES WHYMPER. Super royal 8vo., One Guinea net.

Stone. IN AND BEYOND THE HIMALAYAS: A RECORD OF SPORT AND TRAVEL. By S. J. STONE, late Deputy Inspector-General of the Punjab Police. With 16 full-page Illustrations by CHARLES WHYMPER. Demy 8vo., 16s.

Thompson. REMINISCENCES OF THE COURSE, THE CAMP, AND THE CHASE. By Colonel R. F. MEYSEY THOMPSON. Large crown 8vo., 10s. 6d.

Warkworth. NOTES FROM A DIARY IN ASIATIC TURKEY By EARL PERCY (then Lord Warkworth). With numerous Photogravures. Fcap. 4to., 21s. net.

THE SPORTSMAN'S LIBRARY.

Edited by the Right Hon. Sir HERBERT MAXWELL, Bart., M.P.

A Re-issue, in handsome volumes, of certain rare and entertaining books on Sport, carefully selected by the Editor, and Illustrated by the best Sporting Artists of the day, and with Reproductions of old Plates.

Library Edition, 15s. a Volume. Large-Paper Edition, limited to 200 copies, Two Guineas a volume. Also obtainable in Sets only, in fine leather bindings. Prices on application.

VOLUME I.

Smith. THE LIFE OF A FOX, AND THE DIARY OF A HUNTSMAN. By THOMAS SMITH, Master of the Hambledon and Pytchley Hounds. With Illustrations by the Author, and Coloured Plates by G. H. JALLAND.

Sir RALPH PAYNE-GALWEY, Bart., writes: 'It is excellent and beautifully produced.'
'Is sure to appeal to everyone who has had, or is about to have, a chance of a run with the hounds, and those to whom an unkindly fate denies this boon will enjoy it for the joyous music of the hounds which it brings to relieve the winter of our discontent amid London fogs.'—*Pall Mall Gazette.*
'It will be a classic of fox-hunting till the end of time.'—*Yorkshire Post.*
'No hunting men should be without this book in their libraries.'—*World.*

VOLUME II.

Thornton. A SPORTING TOUR THROUGH THE NORTHERN PARTS OF ENGLAND AND GREAT PART OF THE HIGHLANDS OF SCOTLAND. By Colonel T. THORNTON, of Thornville Royal, in Yorkshire. With the Original Illustrations by GARRARD, and other Illustrations and Coloured Plates by G. E. LODGE.

'Sportsmen of all descriptions will gladly welcome the sumptuous new edition issued by Mr. Edward Arnold of Colonel T. Thornton's "Sporting Tour," which has long been a scarce book.—*Daily News.*
'It is excellent reading for all interested in sport.'—*Black and White.*
'A handsome volume, effectively illustrated with coloured plates by G. E. Lodge, and with portraits and selections from the original illustrations, themselves characteristic of the art and sport of the time.'—*Times.*

VOLUME III.

Cosmopolite. THE SPORTSMAN IN IRELAND. By a COSMOPOLITE. With Coloured Plates and Black and White Drawings by P. CHENEVIX TRENCH, and reproductions of the original Illustrations drawn by R. ALLEN, and engraved by W. WESTALL, A.R.A.

'This is a most readable and entertaining book.'—*Pall Mall Gazette.*
'As to the "get up" of the book we can only repeat what we said on the appearance of the first of the set, that the series consists of the most tasteful and charming volumes at present being issued by the English Press, and collectors of handsome books should find them not only an ornament to their shelves, but also a sound investment.'

VOLUME IV.

Berkeley. REMINISCENCES OF A HUNTSMAN. By the Hon. GRANTLEY F. BERKELEY. With a Coloured Frontispiece and the original Illustrations by JOHN LEECH, and several Coloured Plates and other Illustrations by G. H. JALLAND.

'The latest addition to the sumptuous "Sportsman's Library" is here reproduced with all possible aid from the printer and binder, with illustrations from the pencils of Leech and G. H. Jalland.'—*Globe.*
'The Hon. Grantley F. Berkeley had one great quality of the *raconteur*. His self-revelations and displays of vanity are delightful.'—*Times.*

Volume V.

Scrope. THE ART OF DEERSTALKING. By WILLIAM SCROPE. With Frontispiece by EDWIN LANDSEER, and nine Photogravure Plates of the original Illustrations.

> 'With the fine illustrations by the Landseers and Scrope himself, this forms a most worthy number of a splendid series.'—*Pall Mall Gazette.*

> 'Among the works published in connection with field sports in Scotland, none probably have been more sought after than those of William Scrope, and although published more than fifty years ago, they are still as fresh as ever, full of pleasant anecdote, and valuable for the many practical hints which they convey to inexperienced sportsmen.'—*Field.*

Volume VI.

Nimrod. THE CHASE, THE TURF, AND THE ROAD. By NIMROD. With a Photogravure Portrait of the Author by D. MACLISE, R.A., and with Coloured Photogravure and other Plates from the original Illustrations by ALKEN, and several reproductions of old Portraits.

> 'Sir Herbert Maxwell has performed a real service for all who care for sport in republishing Nimrod's admirable papers. The book is admirably printed and produced both in the matter of illustrations and of binding.'—*St. James's Gazette.*

> 'A thoroughly well got-up book.'—*World.*

Volume VII.

Scrope. DAYS AND NIGHTS OF SALMON FISHING. By WILLIAM SCROPE. With coloured Lithographic and Photogravure reproductions of the original Plates.

> 'This great classic of sport has been reissued by Mr. Edward Arnold in charming form.'—*Literature.*

COUNTRY HOUSE.

Brown. POULTRY KEEPING AS AN INDUSTRY FOR FARMERS AND COTTAGERS. By EDWARD BROWN, F.L.S. Fully Illustrated by LUDLOW. Revised Edition, demy 4to., cloth, 6s.

BY THE SAME AUTHOR.

PLEASURABLE POULTRY-KEEPING. Fully Illustrated. One vol., crown 8vo., cloth, 2s. 6d.

INDUSTRIAL POULTRY-KEEPING. Illustrated. Paper boards, 1s. A small handbook chiefly intended for cottagers and allotment-holders.

POULTRY FATTENING. Fully Illustrated. New Edition. Crown 8vo., 1s. 6d.

Cunningham. THE DRAUGHTS POCKET MANUAL. By J. G. CUNNINGHAM. An introduction to the Game in all its branches. Small 8vo., with numerous diagrams, 2s. 6d.

Ellacombe. IN A GLOUCESTERSHIRE GARDEN. By the Rev. H. N. ELLACOMBE, Vicar of Bitton, and Honorary Canon of Bristol. Author of 'Plant Lore and Garden Craft of Shakespeare.' With new Illustrations by Major E. B. RICKETTS. Second Edition. Crown 8vo., cloth, 6s.

Gossip. THE CHESS POCKET MANUAL. By G. H. D. GOSSIP. A Pocket Guide, with numerous Specimen Games and Illustrations. Small 8vo., 2s. 6d.

Hole. A BOOK ABOUT ROSES. By the Very Rev. S. REYNOLDS HOLE, Dean of Rochester. Sixteenth Edition. Illustrated by H. G. MOON and G. S. ELGOOD, R.I. Presentation Edition, with Coloured Plates, 6s. Popular Edition, 3s. 6d.

Hole. A BOOK ABOUT THE GARDEN AND THE GARDENER. By Dean HOLE. Popular Edition, crown 8vo., 3s. 6d.

Holt. FANCY DRESSES DESCRIBED. By ARDERN HOLT. An Alphabetical Dictionary of Fancy Costumes. With full accounts of the Dresses. About 60 Illustrations by LILLIAN YOUNG. Many of them coloured. One vol., demy 8vo., 7s. 6d. net.

Holt. GENTLEMEN'S FANCY DRESS AND HOW TO CHOOSE IT. By ARDERN HOLT. New and Revised Edition. With Illustrations. Paper boards, 2s. 6d. ; cloth, 3s. 6d.

'WYVERN'S' COOKERY BOOKS.

Kenney-Herbert. COMMON-SENSE COOKERY : Based on Modern English and Continental Principles Worked out in Detail. Large crown 8vo., over 500 pages. 7s. 6d.

BY THE SAME AUTHOR.

FIFTY BREAKFASTS : containing a great variety of New and Simple Recipes for Breakfast Dishes. Small 8vo., 2s. 6d.

FIFTY DINNERS. Small 8vo., cloth, 2s. 6d.

FIFTY LUNCHES. Small 8vo., cloth, 2s. 6d.

Shorland. CYCLING FOR HEALTH AND PLEASURE. By L. H. PORTER, Author of 'Wheels and Wheeling,' etc. Revised and edited by F. W. SHORLAND, Amateur Champion 1892-93-94. With numerous Illustrations, small 8vo., 2s. 6d.

Smith. THE PRINCIPLES OF LANDED ESTATE MANAGEMENT. By HENRY HERBERT SMITH, Fellow of the Institute of Surveyors ; Agent to the Marquess of Lansdowne, K.G., the Earl of Crewe, Lord Methuen, etc. With Plans and Illustrations. Demy 8vo., 16s.

White. PLEASURABLE BEE-KEEPING. By C. N. WHITE, Lecturer to the County Councils of Huntingdon, Cambridgeshire, etc. Fully illustrated. One vol., crown 8vo., cloth, 2s. 6d.

MISCELLANEOUS.

Clouston. THE CHIPPENDALE PERIOD IN ENGLISH FURNITURE. By K. WARREN CLOUSTON. With 200 Illustrations by the Author. Demy 4to., handsomely bound, One Guinea net.

GREAT PUBLIC SCHOOLS. ETON — HARROW — WINCHESTER — RUGBY — WESTMINSTER — MARLBOROUGH — CHELTENHAM — HAILEYBURY — CLIFTON — CHARTERHOUSE. With nearly 100 Illustrations by the best artists. Popular Edition. One vol., large imperial 16mo., handsomely bound, 3s. 6d.

HARROW SCHOOL. Edited by E. W. HOWSON and G. TOWNSEND WARNER. With a Preface by EARL SPENCER, K.G., D.C.L., Chairman of the Governors of Harrow School. And Contributions by Old Harrovians and Harrow Masters. Illustrated with a large number of original full-page and other Pen-and-ink Drawings by Mr. HERBERT MARSHALL. With several Photogravure Portraits and reproductions of objects of interest. One vol., crown 4to., One Guinea net. A Large-Paper Edition, limited to 150 copies, Three Guineas net.

Hartshorne. OLD ENGLISH GLASSES. An Account of Glass Drinking-Vessels in England from Early Times to the end of the Eighteenth Century. With Introductory Notices of Continental Glasses during the same period, Original Documents, etc. Dedicated by special permission to Her Majesty the Queen. By ALBERT HARTSHORNE, Fellow of the Society of Antiquaries. Illustrated by nearly 70 full-page Tinted or Coloured Plates in the best style of Lithography, and several hundred outline Illustrations in the text. Super royal 4to., Three Guineas net.

Herschell. THE BEGGARS OF PARIS. Translated from the French of M. LOUIS PAULIAN by LADY HERSCHELL. Crown 8vo., 1s.

Pilkington. IN AN ETON PLAYING FIELD. The Adventures of some old Public School Boys in East London. By E. M. S. PILKINGTON. Fcap. 8vo., handsomely bound, 2s. 6d.

Ricketts. COMPOSITE BOOK-PLATES. A Reproduction of 60 Book-Plates by T. SIMSON, F. BRAMLEY, and the Editor, E. BENGOUGH RICKETTS. Boards, 6s. net.

ILLUSTRATED HUMOROUS BOOKS.

Ames. REALLY AND TRULY. By Mr. and Mrs. ERNEST AMES. (See page 8.)

H. B. and B. T. B. MORE BEASTS (FOR WORSE CHILDREN). New Edition. One vol., 4to., 3s. 6d.

BY THE SAME AUTHORS.

THE MODERN TRAVELLER. One vol., 4to., 3s. 6d.

A MORAL ALPHABET. (See page 8.)

Lockwood. THE FRANK LOCKWOOD SKETCH-BOOK. Being a Selection of Sketches by the late Sir FRANK LOCKWOOD, Q.C., M.P. Third Edition. Oblong royal 4to., 10s. 6d.

Reed. TAILS WITH A TWIST. An Animal Picture-Book by E. T. REED, Author of 'Pre-Historic Peeps,' etc. With Verses by 'A BELGIAN HARE.' Oblong demy 4to., 3s. 6d.

Streamer. RUTHLESS RHYMES FOR HEARTLESS HOMES. By Colonel D. STREAMER. (See page 9.)

SCIENCE AND PHILOSOPHY.

Arnold-Forster. ARMY LETTERS, 1897-98. By H. O. ARNOLD-FORSTER, M.P. Crown 8vo., 3s. 6d.

Burgess. POLITICAL SCIENCE AND COMPARATIVE CONSTITUTIONAL LAW. By JOHN W. BURGESS, Ph.D., LL.D., Dean of the University Faculty of Political Science in Columbia College, U.S.A. In two vols., demy 8vo., cloth, 21s.

Graham. ENGLISH POLITICAL PHILOSOPHY. By W. GRAHAM. (See page 6.)

Holland. SUGGESTIONS FOR A SCHEME OF OLD AGE PENSIONS. By the Hon. LIONEL HOLLAND, M.P. Crown 8vo., 1s. 6d.

Hopkins. THE RELIGIONS OF INDIA. By E. W. HOPKINS, Ph.D. (Leipzig), Professor of Sanskrit and Comparative Philology in Bryn Mawr College. One vol., demy 8vo., 8s. 6d. net.

Ladd. LOTZE'S PHILOSOPHICAL OUTLINES. Dictated Portions of the Latest Lectures (at Göttingen and Berlin) of Hermann Lotze. Translated and edited by GEORGE T. LADD, Professor of Philosophy in Yale College. About 180 pages in each volume. Crown 8vo., cloth, 3s. 6d. each. Vol. I. Metaphysics. Vol. II. Philosophy of Religion. Vol. III. Practical Philosophy. Vol. IV. Psychology. Vol. V. Æsthetics. Vol. VI. Logic.

Morgan. ANIMAL LIFE AND INTELLIGENCE. By Professor C. LLOYD MORGAN, F.R.S. (See page 6.)

BY THE SAME AUTHOR.

HABIT AND INSTINCT: A STUDY IN HEREDITY. Demy 8vo., 16s.

THE SPRINGS OF CONDUCT. Cheaper Edition. Large crown 8vo., 3s. 6d.

PSYCHOLOGY FOR TEACHERS. With a Preface by Sir JOSHUA FITCH, M.A., LL.D., late one of H.M. Chief Inspectors of Training Colleges. Third Edition. One vol., crown 8vo., cloth, 3s. 6d.

Paget. WASTED RECORDS OF DISEASE. By CHARLES E. PAGET, Lecturer on Public Health in Owens College, Medical Officer of Health for Salford, etc. Crown 8vo., 2s. 6d.

Pearson. THE CHANCES OF DEATH, and other Studies in Evolution. By KARL PEARSON, F.R.S., Author of 'The Ethic of Free Thought,' etc. 2 vols., demy 8vo., Illustrated, 21s. net.

Perry. CALCULUS FOR ENGINEERS. By Professor JOHN PERRY, F.R.S. Crown 8vo., 7s. 6d.

Shaw. A TEXT-BOOK OF NURSING FOR HOME AND HOSPITAL USE. By C. WEEKS SHAW. Revised and largely re-written by W. RADFORD, House Surgeon at the Poplar Hospital, under the supervision of Sir DYCE DUCKWORTH, M.D., F.R.C.P. Fully Illustrated, crown 8vo., 3s. 6d.

Taylor. THE ALPHABET. By ISAAC TAYLOR, M.A., LL.D., Canon of York. New Edition, 2 vols., demy 8vo., 21s.

THE JOURNAL OF MORPHOLOGY. Edited by C. O. WHITMAN, Professor of Biology in Clark University, U.S.A. Three numbers in a volume of 100 to 150 large 4to. pages, with numerous plates. Single numbers, 17s. 6d.; subscription to the volume of three numbers, 45s. Vols. I. to XIV. can now be obtained.

Van 'T. Hoff. LECTURES ON THEORETICAL AND PHYSICAL CHEMISTRY. Part I., Chemical Dynamics. (See page 15.)

Young. A GENERAL ASTRONOMY. By CHARLES A. YOUNG, Professor of Astronomy in the College of New Jersey, Associate of the Royal Astronomical Society, Author of 'The Sun,' etc. In one vol., 550 pages, with 250 Illustrations, and supplemented with the necessary tables. Royal 8vo., half morocco, 12s. 6d.

PRACTICAL SCIENCE MANUALS.

Dymond. CHEMISTRY FOR AGRICULTURAL STUDENTS. By T. S. DYMOND, of the County Technical Laboratories, Chelmsford. Crown 8vo., 2s. 6d.

Halliday. STEAM BOILERS. By G. HALLIDAY, late Demonstrator at the Finsbury Technical College. Fully Illustrated, crown 8vo., 5s.

Wilson. ELECTRICAL TRACTION. By ERNEST WILSON, M.I.E.E., Professor of Electrical Engineering at King's College, London. Illustrated. Crown 8vo., 5s.

THE NATIONAL REVIEW.

Edited by L. J. MAXSE.

Price Half a crown Monthly.

The 'National Review' is the leading Unionist and Conservative Review in Great Britain. Since it passed into the control and editorship of Mr. Leo Maxse, most of the leaders of the Unionist Party have contributed to its pages, including the Marquis of Salisbury, Mr. Arthur Balfour, Mr. J. Chamberlain, and Lord George Hamilton. The episodes of the month, which give a masterly review of the important events of the preceding month, form a valuable feature of the Review, which now occupies a unique position among monthly periodicals.

PUBLICATIONS OF THE INDIA OFFICE AND OF THE GOVERNMENT OF INDIA.

Mr. EDWARD ARNOLD, having been appointed Publisher to the Secretary of State for India in Council, has now on sale the above publications at 37 Bedford Street, Strand, and is prepared to supply full information concerning them on application.

INDIAN GOVERNMENT MAPS.

Any of the Maps in this magnificent series can now be obtained at the shortest notice from Mr. EDWARD ARNOLD, Publisher to the India Office.

The following Catalogues of Mr. Edward Arnold's Publications will be sent post free on application:
CATALOGUE OF WORKS OF GENERAL LITERATURE.
GENERAL CATALOGUE OF EDUCATIONAL WORKS, including the principal publications of Messrs. Ginn and Company, Educational Publishers, of Boston and New York.
CATALOGUE OF WORKS FOR USE IN ELEMENTARY SCHOOLS.
ILLUSTRATED LIST OF BOOKS FOR PRESENTS AND PRIZES.

BOOKS FOR THE YOUNG.

SIX SHILLINGS EACH.

FIRE AND SWORD IN THE SUDAN. By Sir RUDOLPH SLATIN and Sir F. R. WINGATE. (See page 23.)

MOONFLEET. By J. MEADE FALKNER. (See page 21.)

FIVE SHILLINGS EACH.

SNOW-SHOES AND SLEDGES. By KIRK MUNROE. Fully illustrated. Crown 8vo., cloth, 5s.

RICK DALE. By KIRK MUNROE. Fully illustrated. Crown 8vo., cloth, 5s.

THE FUR SEAL'S TOOTH. By KIRK MUNROE. Fully illustrated. Crown 8vo., cloth, 5s.

HOW DICK AND MOLLY SAW ENGLAND. By M. H. CORNWALL LEGH. With numerous Illustrations. Foolscap 4to., 5s.

DR. GILBERT'S DAUGHTERS. By MARGARET HARRIET MATHEWS. Illustrated by CHRIS. HAMMOND. Crown 8vo., cloth, 5s.

ERIC THE ARCHER. By MAURICE H. HERVEY. With 8 full-page Illustrations. Handsomely bound, crown 8vo., 5s.

THE REEF OF GOLD. By MAURICE H. HERVEY. With numerous full-page Illustrations, handsomely bound, gilt edges, 5s.

BAREROCK; or, The Island of Pearls. By HENRY NASH. With numerous Illustrations by LANCELOT SPEED. Large crown 8vo., handsomely bound, gilt edges, 5s.

WAGNER'S HEROES. By CONSTANCE MAUD. Illustrated by H. GRANVILLE FELL. Crown 8vo., 5s.

WAGNER'S HEROINES. By CONSTANCE MAUD. Illustrated by W. T. MAUD. Crown 8vo. 5s.

THREE SHILLINGS AND SIXPENCE EACH.

TALES FROM HANS ANDERSEN. With nearly 40 Original Illustrations by E. A. LEMANN. Small 4to., handsomely bound in cloth, 3s. 6d.

THE SNOW QUEEN, and other Tales. By HANS CHRISTIAN ANDERSEN. Beautifully illustrated by Miss E. A. LEMANN. Small 4to., handsomely bound, 3s. 6d.

HUNTERS THREE. By THOMAS W. KNOX, Author of 'The Boy Travellers,' etc. With numerous Illustrations. Crown 8vo., cloth, 3s. 6d.

THE SECRET OF THE DESERT. By E. D. FAWCETT. With numerous full-page Illustrations. Crown 8vo., cloth, 3s. 6d.

JOEL: A BOY OF GALILEE. By ANNIE FELLOWS JOHNSTON. With ten full-page Illustrations. Crown 8vo., cloth, 3s. 6d.

THE MUSHROOM CAVE. By EVELYN RAYMOND. With Illustrations. Crown 8vo., cloth, 3s. 6d.

THE DOUBLE EMPEROR. By W. LAIRD CLOWES, Author of 'The Great Peril,' etc. Illustrated. Crown 8vo., 3s. 6d.

SWALLOWED BY AN EARTHQUAKE. By E. D. FAWCETT. Illustrated. Crown 8vo., 3s. 6d.

HARTMANN THE ANARCHIST; or, The Doom of the Great City. By E. DOUGLAS FAWCETT. With sixteen full-page and numerous smaller Illustrations by F. T. JANE. Crown 8vo., cloth, 3s. 6d.

ANIMAL SKETCHES: a Popular Book of Natural History. By Professor C. LLOYD MORGAN, F.R.S. Crown 8vo., cloth, 3s. 6d.

ROME THE MIDDLE OF THE WORLD. By ALICE GARDNER. Illustrated Cloth, 3s. 6d.

TWO SHILLINGS AND SIXPENCE.

FRIENDS OF THE OLDEN TIME. By ALICE GARDNER, Lecturer in History at Newnham College, Cambridge. Second Edition. Illustrated. Square 8vo., 2s. 6d.

TWO SHILLINGS EACH.

THE CHILDREN'S FAVOURITE SERIES. A Charming Series of Juvenile Books, each plentifully Illustrated, and written in simple language to please young readers. Price 2s. each; or, gilt edges, 2s. 6d.

- My Book of Wonders.
- My Book of Travel Stories.
- My Book of Adventures.
- My Book of the Sea.
- My Book of Fables.
- Deeds of Gold.
- My Book of Heroism.
- My Book of Perils.
- My Book of Fairy Tales.
- My Book of History Tales.
- My Story Book of Animals.
- Rhymes for You and Me.
- My Book of Inventions.

THE LOCAL SERIES.

- The Story of Lancashire.
- The Story of Yorkshire.
- The Story of the Midlands.
- The Story of London.
- The Story of Wales.
- The Story of Scotland.
- The Story of the West Country. [*In the Press.*

ONE SHILLING AND SIXPENCE EACH.

THE CHILDREN'S HOUR SERIES.
All with Full-page Illustrations.

THE PALACE ON THE MOOR. By E. DAVENPORT ADAMS. 1s. 6d.

TOBY'S PROMISE. By A. M. HOPKINSON. 1s. 6d.

MASTER MAGNUS. By Mrs. E. M. Field. 1s. 6d.

MY DOG PLATO. By M. H. CORNWALL LEGH. 1s. 6d.

AN ILLUSTRATED GEOGRAPHY. By ALEXIS FRYE and A. J. HERBERTSON Royal 4to., 7s. 6d. and 5s.

Index to Authors.

	PAGE
About	20
'Adalet'	20
Adams, E. Davenport	31
Adderley, Hon. and Rev. J.	20
Alexander, W. Gordon	15
Ames, Ernest	8
A Moral Alphabet	8
Andersen, Hans Christian	30
Arnold-Forster, H. O.	28
Arnold, Thomas	1, 15
Ashbee, C. R.	11
Bell, Canon	16, 19
Bell, Mrs. Hugh	9, 18
Bell, Napier	2
Belloc, Hilaire	9
Benson, A. C.	17
Berkeley, Hon. Grantley F.	24
Beynon, W. G. L.	22
Bottome, Margaret	22
Boyle, Very Rev. G. D.	15
Bradley, Cuthbert	27
Brown, Edward	25
Bull, H. J.	22
Bunsen, Marie von	7
Bunyan's Pilgrim's Progress	12
Burgess, John W.	28
Burkitt, F. Crawford	11
Burneside, Amelia	20
Burton, Capt. R. G.	22
Butler, A. J.	18
Chapman, Abel	22
Charleton, R. J.	20
Cherbuliez, Victor	20
Cholmondeley, Mary	7, 20
Clough, Blanche A.	15
Clouston, K. Warren	27
Clowes, W. Laird	31
Coleridge, M. E.	26
Collingwood, W. G.	18, 20
Collins, J. Churton	19
Cook, Prof. A. S.	18
Cosmopolite	24
Crane, Stephen	20
Cunningham, J. G.	25
Custance, Henry	22
Davidson, Thomas	18
Dawkins, Clinton E.	4
De Vere, Aubrey	15
Dunmore, Earl of	20
Dymond, T. S.	29
Eastern Essays	7
Edwards, R. W. K.	20
Ellacombe, H. N.	18, 26
Falkner, J. Meade	21
Fawcett, E. D.	30, 31
Fell, H. Granville	30
Fell, Rev. J.	5
Field, Mrs. E. M.	31
Fisher, J. R.	3
Fleming, Canon	18
Ford, Isabella O.	21
Freshfield, Douglas W.	22
Frye, Alexis	31
Gardner, Alice	17

	PAGE
Garnett, J. M.	18
Gaunt, Mary	21
Gleichen, Count	22
Glencairn, R. J.	7
Gordon, Sir T. E.	22
Goschen, Rt. Hon. G. J.	18
Gossip, G. H. D.	26
Graham, W.	6
Great Public Schools	27
Greene, Harvey B.	10
Grey, Earl	3
Grey, H. M.	4
Gummere, F. B.	19
Hall, Bradnock	22
Halliday, G.	29
Hare, Augustus J. C.	15
Harrison, Frederic	18
Harrison, S. Frances	21
Hartshorne, Albert	27
Herbertson, Andrew	14
Herschell, Lady	27
Hervey, M. H.	30
Hill, Leonard	14
Hoff, Dr. J. H. Van 'T.	14
Hole, Dean	15, 16
Holland, Bernard	7, 15
Holland, Hon. Lionel	28
Holland, Maud	19
Holland, Rev. F. J.	6
Holt, Ardern	26
Hopkinson, A. M.	31
Hopkinson, E. W.	28
Hudson, H. N.	18
Hutchinson, Horace G.	21
Johnston, Annie Fellows	30
Jowett, Benjamin	15
Kenny-Herbert	26
Knox, T. W.	30
Knutsford, Lady	21
Kuhns, L. Oscar	18
Ladd, G. T.	28
Lane, Rev. C. A.	17
Lang, Andrew	18
Le Fanu, W. R.	15
Legh, M. H. Cornwall	30
Lehfeldt, Dr. R. A.	14
Lighthall, W. D.	21
Local Histories	13
Lockwood, Sir Frank	27
Macdonald, Major J. R.	23
Macdonald, Sir John A.	15
Mathews, Margaret H.	30
Maud, Constance	18, 19
Maxse, L. J.	29
McNab, Frances	23
McNulty, Edward	21
Merivale, J. A.	1, 15
Milner, Sir Alfred	4
Montrésor, F. F.	21
Morgan, C. Lloyd	6
Morley, Henry	16
Mott, E. S.	16
Munroe, Kirk	30

	PAGE
Nash, Henry	30
Nimrod	25
Oman, C. W.	12, 17
Onyx	19
Oxenden, Maud	21
Paget, Charles E.	28
Pearson, Karl	28
Perry, Prof. John	28
Pigou, Very Rev. Francis	16
Pike, Warburton	23
Pilkington, E. M. S.	27
Pinsent, Ellen F.	21
Pollok, Lieut.-Colonel	23
Portal, Sir Gerald H.	23
Pritchett, R. T.	5
Quiller Couch, A. J.	8
Raleigh, Walter	19
Ransome, Cyril	17
Raymond, Evelyn	30
Reed, E. T.	27
Reid, Arnot	23
Rendel, Hon. Daphne	17
Reynolds, Rev. S. H.	19
Ricketts, E. Bengough	27
Roberts, Morley	7
Rochefort, Henri	16
Rodd, Sir Rennel	19
Roebuck, Rt. Hon. J. A.	16
Schelling, Prof. F. E.	19
Scrope, William	25
Shaw, C. Weeks	28
Shorland, F. W.	26
Simpson, Mrs. M. C.	16
Slatin Pasha, Sir Rudolf	23
Smith, A. Donaldson	23
Smith, H. H.	26
Smith, Thomas	24
Spinner, Alice	21
Stevenson, R. L.	16
Stone, S. J.	23
Streamer, Colonel D.	9
Symes, E. S.	12
Tatham, H. F. W.	17
Taylor, Isaac	28
Thompson, Col. R. F. Meysey	23
Thornton, Col. T.	24
Tollemache, Hon. L. A.	16
Toynbee, Arnold	16
Twining, Louisa	16
Various Quills	19
Warkworth, Lord	23
Webb, E. J.	13
White, C. N.	26
Whitman, C. O.	29
Williams, N. Wynne	21
Wilson, Ernest	29
Wingate, Sir F. R.	23
Wyllie, W. L.	13
Young, Charles A.	29

www.ingramcontent.com/pod-product-compliance
Lightning Source LLC
Chambersburg PA
CBHW022109290426
44112CB00008B/610